A Bardic Tale
of the
Ancient Lineages
of the
Reagan Family

The Ancestry of
Elzie Reagan Christian

As Told by

James Frank Hatcher III

ex·libris

DEDICATION

This book is dedicated to my Cousin

ELZIE REAGAN CHRISTIAN

and secondarily to her descendants,

who are in the direct lineage of

TIMOTHY REAGAN
2ND REGIMENT
MARYLAND CONTINENTAL LINE
REVOLUTIONARY WAR

May you always honor and remember
your ancestors, and teach your children
and grand-children to do the same.

Each one of us only occupies one line
in our long geneaological list. We must strive
to make that single line entry one of importance,
worthy of admittance into a noble line of ancestors.

CONTENTS

Foreward 1

Timothy Reagan and the Irish Immigrants 3

1 Quarks & Stuff, the Scientific Lineage 19

2 Lineages from Charlemagne 23

3 The Anglo-Saxon Lineage 28

4 The Burgundian Lineage 39

5 The Byzantine Lineage 45

6 The Carolingian Lineage 48

7 The Celtic-Gallic Lineage 57

8 The Egyptian-Roman Lineage 63

9 The Egyptian-Trojan Lineage 69

10 The Elven Kings of Alfheim Lineage 75

11 The Germanic-Teutonic Lineage 79

12 The Germanic-Vandal Lineage 85

13 The Goths-Visigoths-Langobards Lineage 90

14 The Greco-Roman Lineage 100

15 The Greco-Roman-Irish Lineage 111

16 The Heruli-Obotrite Lineage 118

17 The Indo-European/Hindu Lineage 127

18 The Irish Kings Lineage 133

19   The Jewish Lineage 152

20   The Jute-Saxon Lineage 159

21   The Kings of Arcadia and Pelasgian Lineage 164

22   The Kings of Argos Lineage 168

23   The Kings of Thessaly-Ithaca-Latium-Alba Longa-Rome
      Lineage 173

24   The Lombardian Lineage 184

25   The Macedonian Kings Lineage 189

26   The Merovingian Lineage 194

27   The Mesopotamian Lineage 201

28   The Minoan-Cretan-Mycenaen Lineage 208

29   The Norse-Danish Lineage 212

30   The Norse-Saxon Lineage 218

31   The Ostragoth Lineage 224

32   The Phoenician (Tyrian-Carthagenian) Lineage 230

33   The Phrygian (Lydian) Lineage 235

34   The Polish-Slavic Lineage 239

35   The Scottish Kings Lineage 242

36   The Trojan-Cimmerian-Sicambrian Lineage 253

37   The Trojan-Norse-Frankish Lineage 260

38   The William the Conqueror Lineage 266

Additional Family Records 278

Family Births Registry 279

Family Marriages Registry 289

Family Deaths Registry 299

Military Service Registry 309

Other Important Dates Registry 315

Notes 327

Here begins the telling of
the story of the ancestors of
my cousin and her children ...

FOREWARD

This book is dedicated to my cousin, Elzie Reagan Christian, and her descendants. It is a telling of the story of our Ancestors. It is the story of a descendant from many noble and historical figures and civilizations. Many sources were consulted, from the oral histories of the Celts, to the walls and monuments of Egypt, the sagas of the Norse, the records of the British Crown, and many others. Most of the older lineages we can only speculate and can regard as missing some generations. We simply just can't go back and verify anything in person, and in many cases, the history is oral or written incompletely. What we do know is that the important people in history preserved their names, deeds, and accomplishments as best as they could, and we in the modern age hold these lineages acceptable, until proven otherwise.

Through these lineages, we find the connection to Charlemagne, King of the Franks, William the Conqueror, and connections to the many ancient personages, civilizations, and lineages of history.

Sometimes the dates don't make sense but I've left the impossible reconstruction intact because scholars don't know whether it is the date or the name that is wrong and both might be "almost'" right.

I've included pedigrees which were probably fabricated in the Middle Ages, in part because there's no proof that they're wrong; in part because such ancient fabrications seem interesting on their own account. Similarly, I don't comment when historical lineages drift into mythical ancestors: one may not be sure precisely where fact turns to fiction. In addition to errors introduced accidentally, or copied unknowingly from other sources, there are some spelling deviations introduced deliberately.

Of the many prefixes used to mean "son of" in Celtic Britain (ab, ap, map, mac, Mac, Mc), generally, ap and Mac are used: they are all the same. No space is placed after Mac, nor after Fitz. Similarly only the spellings "verch, fil, ingen and NIC" are used for Celtic "daughter of." I do not reproduce non-English alphabetic symbols like Ñ (Spanish), Á, Í (Celtic), Æ (Old English), Ü, ß (German), ð, Þ (Viking), Ç, Â, È (French). Many works introduce fictitious surnames like "PLANTAGENET" or "of EGYPT" to catalog ancient families, and I include many such "surnames." While this may make the book seem more "amateurish," it makes distinguishing many people with similar names a little easier. The lineages herein begin with the oldest ancestor and continue to the youngest ancestor.

The book reads like the history of the western world, but on a personal basis. I am honored to be with and among such company.

Good Reading,
Chip

Your Cousin,
Author,
Bard of the British Druid Order,
& Skáld of Volslend

TIMOTHY REAGAN & THE IRISH IMMIGRANTS

NOTE: This article had been submitted to the editor for SMOKY MOUNTAIN HISTORICAL SOCIETY'S JOURNAL/NEWSLETTER for inclusion in their quarterly publication. It had appeared in the Summer 2013 issue. So, it is official declaration on the ancestry of Timothy Ragan/Reagan, Revolutionary War Soldier.

The colonial ancestors of Timothy Ragan/Reagan who served in the Revolutionary War from the province of Maryland, and lived in Pittsylvania County, Virginia and Caswell County, North Carolina before the migration to Sevier County, Tennessee in 1795 are Timothy Ragan, Sr. (grandfather) who married Mary Lary; and Timothy Ragan, Jr. (father) who married Rachael Nelson. I have had researched these Ragan/Reagan and allied families in Maryland and surrounding areas for contemporary sources for twenty years since my last publication, THE BOOK OF RAGAN/REAGAN in 1993. All these data come from the research files of this writer. It is my desire to share these exciting findings on the line Ragan/Reagan family history!

TIMOTHY RAGAN, SR. AND MARY LARY

Grandparents of Timothy Ragan/Reagan, Revolutionary War soldier.

The real proof for the naming of Timothy and Mary came from Holy Bible. You can find it in New Testament.Timothy and Mary are the given names that does appear in the contemporary sources today.

Having reached at legal age (21 years), Timothy Ragan, Sr. was one of three witnesses to the will of Richard Moss which was written on Thursday, 15 Jul 1700 in Anne Arundel County, Maryland. He was living in the area of Magothy River there.

He was married 24 Nov 1703 in Westminister Parish, Anne Arundel County, Maryland to Mary Lary. Mary was born circa 1686 probably in Ireland or Anne Arundel County, Maryland. No data had been attempted on her parents.

Timothy Ragan, Sr. bought from Christopher Miller on 14 Nov 1705, one hundred (100) acres of land known as "Souldiers Fortune" which was surveyed for Richard Snowdon, Jr. on 08 Dec 1701, in Anne Arundel County, Maryland. This land was located on "North Branch of Patuxant River in a place called ye fork."

The 1706 tax roll of Baltimore County, Maryland showed Timothy Ragan, Sr. and his family as living in area of "the Upper Part of North Side of Patapsco Hundred."

Then Timothy Ragan, Sr. was listed on 1707 rent rolls for Anne Arundel and Baltimore Counties, Maryland. He was charged four Shillings for one hundred acres of land known as "Souldiers Fortune." This land was located on "the North Branch of Patuxent River near Ivey Hill."

He was the one of three witnesses to the will of Nicholas Dorsey which was written on 15 Sep 1717 in St. Paul's Parish, Baltimore County, Maryland.

There is a clause written in Caleb Dorsey's deed on 24 Mar 1721 to John Beale. It mentioned "50 acres part thereof whereon Timothy Ragan now lives." This deed showed that Timothy Ragan, Sr. and his family was still living in Anne Arundel County, Maryland.

There is a Bill of Sale document between Timothy Ragan, Sr. of Baltimore County, Maryland and Daniel Hearne of Prince George's

County, Maryland for two (2) heifers on 10 Nov 1723. Then Daniel Hearne of Anne Arundel County, Maryland later executed the same Bill of Sale on 10 Jan 1728 for two (2) heifers back to John Ragan and Timothy Ragan, Jr. that he purchased from Timothy Ragan, Sr. previously. On the same document, these two Bill of Sale have had been approved by Provincial Court and were recorded in Archives of Maryland, Volume 697, page 310-311. This Bill of Sale document provided the crucial evidence to prove the relationships between Timothy Ragan, Sr. and his two sons, John Ragan and Timothy Ragan, Jr. Also, here we find real signatory mark for him on this Bill of Sale. It is unique signature mark, "V".

We find that there is a clause written again in Caleb Dorsey's deed on 26 Mar 1732 to John Beale. It stated "50 acres part there of whereon Timothy Ragan now lives." It showed again that he and his family still lives there in Anne Arundel County, Maryland.

On 06 Jan 1739/40, there have had been a capital crime, "breaking and entering," by Negro slave Abraham, property of Henry Dorsey against Mary Ragan, wife of Timothy Ragan in Anne Arundel County, Maryland. This Negro slave, Abraham, was convicted by the County Court of Anne Arundel County, Maryland in Mar 1739/1740. The death warrant was issued on 20 Mar 1739/40 for Negro slave, Abraham; and was hanged on Wednesday, 26 Mar 1740 at the court house in Annapolis, Anne Arundel County, Maryland. This is very unusual crime that have had been committed against her in our Ragan/Reagan family history.

From 14 Mar 1744 deed from Basil Dorsey, son & heir of Caleb Dorsey, late, in Anne Arundel County, Maryland, it stated that he "expressed his intentions to give to Timothy Regan where Mary Regan, mother of Timothy then lived." Timothy Ragan who purchased 'Chew Vineyard,' fifty (50) acress of land in Elk Ridge community in Anne Arundel County, Maryland was Timothy Ragan, Jr.

Timothy Ragan, Sr. must have died before 14 Mar 1744 in Elk Ridge community, Westminister Parish, Anne Arundel County, Maryland. It is the belief of this writer that he was buried in unmarked grave beside his wife in the environs of Elk Ridge, Westminister Parish, Anne Arundel County, Maryland.

Mary Lary Ragan, wife of Timothy Ragan, Sr. remained a widow until her death circa Jan 1764. She left a last will and testament which was written on Sunday, 10 Dec 1752 and was probated on Monday, 23 Jan 1764 in Anne Arundel County, Maryland.

A verbatim transcript follows:

'IN THE NAME OF GOD AMEN. I, Mary Ragon of Anne [Arundell] County in the province of Maryland being weak in Body but of Sound Memory blessed to God, do this 10th Day of December in the year of Our Lord God oneThousand Seven Hundred and Fifty Two make and publish this my last will and Testaments in a manner following that is to say
'Item I give my son John Ragon One Shilling.
'Item I give my son Timothy Ragon One Shilling.
'Item I give my son Rezin Ragaon One Shilling.
'Item I give my son Cornelius Ragon One Shilling.
'Item I give my Daugther Eleanor Ragon all my pewters and all my Irons Poths and bed and Furnitures that I lye and one cow and calf.
'Item I give all the remainders of my Estates after my Just Deb is paid to my Son Cornelius Ragon and my Daughter Eleanor Ragon to be Equally Divided.
'And Lastly I make Constitute and Ordain my Son Cornelius Ragon and my Daughter Eleanor Ragon to be my Whole and Sole Executors and Exec. of this my last Will and Testament.
'In Witness Whereof, I the said Mary Ragan have to this my last Will and Testament Set my hand and Seal first above written.

'Signed, Sealed and) Her
Published in the) Mary Ragon [S E A L]
presence of us who) Mark
was present at the)
Signing and Sealing)
thereof.)
'Brice TB Worthington
'Caleb Dorsey, Jun."

There were no records of inventories and settlements of her estate at that time as stated by Maryland State Archives.

Mary Lary Ragan, widow of Timothy Ragan, Sr. must have had died before 23 Jan 1764 in Elk Ridge community, Westminister Parish, Anne Arundel County, Maryland. It is the belief of this writer that she was buried in unmarked grave beside her husband in the environs of Elk Ridge, Westminister Parish, Anne Arundel County, Maryland.

FAMILY OF TIMOTHY RAGAN, SR. AND MARY LARY:

[All born in Anne Arundel County, Maryland]

1. CATHERINE RAGAN
    b ca. 1704 d bef 10 Dec 1752 Anne Arundel Co, MD?
    m ?

2. ELEANOR RAGAN
    b ca. 1706 d aft 23 Jan 1764 Anne Arundel County,MD
    Unmarried.

3. JOHN RAGAN
    b ca. 1708 d bef 04 Aug 1767 Frederick County,VA
    m 21 Jan 1733, Baltimore County, MD to Mary Morrice

4. INFANT RAGAN
    b ca. 1710 d ca. 1710/1711 Anne Arundel County,MD
    Died young.

5. MARY RAGAN
    b ca. 1712 d bef 10 Dec 1752 Anne Arundel Co, MD?
    m ?

6. TIMOTHY RAGAN, JR.
    b ca. 1714 d bef 1790 Baltimore County, MD
    m ca. 1738, Anne Arunel County, Maryland to Rachael Nelson

7. DANIEL RAGAN
    b 04 Dec 1717 d bef 10 Mar 1760 Frederick County,MD
    m 25 Dec 1732, Baltimore County, Maryland to Sarah Lewis

8. REZIN RAGAN
    b ca. 1720 d bet. 1791/1797 Fayette County,PA
    m ca. 1740, Cecil County, Maryland to Anne Beaumont

9.   INFANT RAGAN
        b ca. 1723 d ca. 1723/1724 Anne Arundel County,MD
        Died young.

10.   CORNELIUS RAGAN
        b ca. 1726 d aft. 23 Jan 1764 Anne Arundel County,MD?
        m ca. 1744, Anne Arundel County, Maryland to Anne Ayton

TIMOTHY RAGAN, JR. AND RACHAEL NELSON

Parents of Timothy Ragan/Reagan, Revolutionary War soldier

The real proof for the naming of Timothy and Rachel came from Holy Bible. You can find it in Old and New Testament.Timothy and Rachel are the given name that does appear in the contemporary sources today.

On the relationship between Timothy Ragan, Sr. and Timothy Ragan, Jr., it is necessary to repeat one particular source here again. After searching the Provincial Court Land Records in the Archives of Maryland, it is found that there is first offical document, Bill of Sale, to prove the relationship between Timothy Ragan, Sr. and his sons, John Ragan and Timothy Ragan, Jr. There is a Bill of Sale document between Timothy Ragan, Sr. of Baltimore County, Maryland and Daniel Herne of Prince George's County, Maryland for two (2) heifers on 10 Nov 1723. Then Daniel Herne of Anne Arundel County, Maryland later executed the same Bill of Sale for two (2) heifers back to John Regan and Timothy Regan,Jr. that he purchased from Timothy Ragan, Sr. on 10 Jan 1728. On the same document, these two Bill of Sale have had been approved by Provincial Court and were recorded in Archives of Maryland, Volume 697, page 310-311. This Bill of Sale provided the crucial evidence to prove the relationships between Timothy Ragan, Sr. and his two sons, John Ragan and Timothy Ragan, Jr.

Based on this writer's family, genealogical and historical research, Timothy Ragan, Jr. was married circa 1738 in Westminister Parish, Anne Arundel County, Maryland to Rachael Nelson, daughter of Robert and Eleanor Hanks Nelson; and granddaughter of Peter Hanks and Mary Beez in Anne Arundel County, Maryland. Rachel was born circa 1720 in Elk Ridge community, Anne Arundel County, Maryland.

Timothy Ragan, Jr. and his brother Rezin Ragan witnessed the deed between John Talbott and Edward Talbot, both of Anne Arundel County, Maryland on 23 Feb 1741/42. It was recorded on 27 Feb 1741/42 in Anne Arundel County, Maryland.

From 14 Mar 1744 deed from Basil Dorsey, son & heir of Caleb Dorsey, late, in Anne Arundel County, Maryland to Timothy Ragan, Jr., it stated that he was listed as a planter at this time. From same deed, Basil Dorsey carry out his father's wishes that he "expressed his intentions to give to Timothy Regan to be laid out Commodinus to the plantation where Mary Regan, mother of Timothy then lived now." He sold fifty (50)acres of land known as "Chew's Vineyard" for five Shillings to Timothy Ragan, Jr.

Timothy Ragan, Jr. was paying two (2) Shillings as annual rent to Lord Baltimore from 1744 (date he bought the land) to 1765 (date he sold the land) on 50 acres of "Chew's Vineyard" according to Rent Rolls 1733-1768 for Anne Arundel County, Maryland. These rent rolls are still in custody of Maryland State Archives at Annapolis, Maryland.

Then he appeared on the petition from "Inhabitants of the Upper Part of Anne Arundel County and Adjacent Places" to the Governor Samuel Ogle and the Upper and Lower Houses of Assembly about 1748. This petition is to expedite the formation of Elk Ridge Landing as a town. An Act for this purpose was passed in 1732, but the commissioners made no move to put it into execution because of natural advantages.

Timothy Ragan, Jr. was mentioned as "my son" in Mary Ragan's Last Will of Testament which was written on 10 Dec 1752 and was probated on 23 Jan 1764 in Anne Arundel County, Maryland.

There is one contemporary source which was found in County Clerk's office in Frederick County courthouse at Winchester, **Frederick County, Virginia. It is as follows:**

"List of Frederick County, Virginia Clerk Fees Belonging to

James Wood, Anno Dom.1757

"Tobacco Payments
"REAGAN, Rach.--------------------------------140 lbs"

NOTE: This appears to have been Rachael Nelson Ragan/Reagan, wife of Timothy Ragan/Reagan,Jr. This is pivotal clue to why Timothy Ragan/Reagan,Jr. and his wife Rachael Nelson had settled in Frederick County, Virginia from 1756 to 1760. Later, the children of Timothy Ragan/Reagan,Jr. and Rachael Nelson had settled in then Augusta County, Virginia, and now Rockingham County, Virginia from 1760 to 1790.

From 28 Oct 1765 deed, it showed that he was of "Anne Arundell County and province of Maryland Carpenter." At this time, his occupation have been changed from planter (farmer) to carpenter. He was selling 50 acres of land known as "Chew's Vineyard" in Anne Arundel County, Maryland for 50 Pounds to Eli Dorsey,Junior of Anne Arundel County, Maryland. Here we find a signatory mark for him on this deed. It is another unique signature mark ... "TR."

Timothy Ragan, Jr. was living in St. Paul's Parish, Baltimore County, Maryland before 1768. Then he signed the petition "for and against the removal of the County Seat of Baltimore County from Joppa to Baltimore Town, 1768" at the church in St. Paul's Parish, Baltimore County, Maryland. It appears that he may have favored the removal of county seat from Joppa to Baltimore Town.

He was listed as "Timothey Ragan" on "A List of Taxables in Back River Upper Hundred" in 1773. This "Back River Upper Hundred" was part of St. Paul's Parish in Baltimore County, Maryland.

As we gleaned from "Shenandoah Valley Pioneers and Their Descendants" by T. K. Cartmell, it appears that, on 10 Sep 1773, the County Court of Frederick County, Virginia "ordered that Daniel Morgan carry Timothy Ragan, a felon who broke the jail at Anne Arundel County, Maryland, and deliver him to the Sheriff of said county, and bring in his account of expenses, at laying of the County levy." In October of that year, Daniel Morgan was paid 6 Pounds 28 Shillings for that service. Wonder what did he commit there in order to be classified as felon!!!

As enacted by the Maryland General Assembly in 1777, all persons holding any office of profit or trust, including attorneys at law, and all voters were required to take the oath no later than March 1, 1778. Timothy Ragan, who resided in St. Paul's Parish, Baltimore County, Maryland, took "Oath of Fidelity" to the State of Maryland. It is this writer's belief that he was Revolutionary War patriot by taking the oath of allegiance in 1778.

The Maryland General Assembly have passed the law for "assessments levied in order to raise funds to support Maryland's Revolutionaty war effort" in 1782/1783. It showed that he was living in the area of Middle River Upper, and Back River Upper Hundred of Baltimore County, Maryland. He was listed as head of household and was classified "pauper" with three (3) white inhabitants in his household.

It has been noted by this writer that Timothy Ragan, Jr. and his wife Rachael Nelson were not listed in 1790 Federal Census of Baltimore County, Maryland.

Based on this writer's genealogical research, Timothy Ragan and his wife Rachael Nelson must have died before 1790 in Baltimore County, Maryland. It is not known about the location of their burial place.

My Personal Note

My 94 years old father, Bruce Walter Reagan (direct descendant from Richard Ragan, eldest son of Timothy and Elizabeth Trigg Ragan), told me that he have had heard these family stories from his grandfather, Charles C. Reagan when he was a boy in Gatlinburg, Sevier County, Tennessee. From family stories in my father's family, he mentioned that Timothy Ragan (Revolutionary War soldier) had four brothers and two sisters who came to East Tennessee from Virginia at the close of Revolutionary War. He also remembered that there was another brother who went to Kentucky from Virginia in early days too. At same time, another family story in my father's family mentioned Jeremiah Ragan of Washington County, TN as brother of Timothy Ragan (Revolutionary War soldier).

From these family stories, I was able to find contemporary sources that it proved Jeremiah Ragan who lived and died in Washington County, TN; Darby Daniel Ragan who lived and diedin Greene County, TN; Jonathan Ragan who lived and died in Wilkes County/Oglethorpe County, GA; and Robert Ragan who lived and died in Mercer County, KY; and Mary Ragan, wife of Isaiah Harrison who lived and died in Greene County, TN as brothers and sister.Only one sister had not been found yet.In addition to all of them, I found Richard Ragan who stayed in Rockingham County, Virginia as another brother too. And this Richard Ragan of Rockingham County, Virginia was the progenitor of the Ragan/Reagan families in Dupont commuity, Sevier County, Tennessee. Again, I was glad to find contemporary sources to prove our family stories from Sevier County, Tennessee.

FAMILY OF TIMOTHY RAGAN, JR. AND RACHAEL NELSON:

[All born in Anne Arundel County, Maryland.]

1. JEREMIAH RAGAN
    b ca. 1740, d ca. 1833 Washington County, TN
    m 01 Oct 1765, Augusta County, Virginia to Abigail Harrison

2. RICHARD BAZEL RAGAN
    b ca. 1742, d 16 May 1827 Rockingham County, VA
    m ca. 1765, Augusta County, Virginia to Cecilia Creppy

3. JONATHAN RAGAN
    b ca. 1744, d bef. 06 Sep 1813 Oglethorpe County, GA
    m ca. 1760, ?Augusta County, Virginia? to Anne ?____?

4. DARBY DANIEL RAGAN
    b ca. 1747, d aft. 1812 ?Greene County, TN?
    m ca. 1765, Frederick County, Virginia to Elizabeth ?Wright?

5. TIMOTHY RAGAN,III
    b ca. 1750, d bef. 1830 Sevier County, TN
    m ca. 1776, Prince George's County, Maryland to Elizabeth Trigg

6.   Son ? or Dau ? RAGAN
         b ca. 1753, d bef. 1790
         m ?

7.   Son ? or Dau ? RAGAN
         b ca. 1756, d bef. 1790
         m ?

8.   ROBERT [NELSON] RAGAN
         b 19 Jun 1758, d ca. Mar 1800 Mercer County, KY
         m 27 Jan 1786, Caroline County, Virginia to Sarah Samuel

9.   MARY RAGAN
         b ca. 1762, d ca. 1798 Greene County, TN
         m ca. 1782, Rockingham County, Virginia to Isaiah Harrison

Sources for Timothy Ragan, Sr. and Mary Lary: [In chronological order]

- Wright, F. Edward, ANNE ARUNDEL COUNTY CHURCH RECORDS OF THE 17TH AND 18TH CENTURIES, Family Line Publications, Westimister, Maryland, pages 66, 81, 82,129.
- Cotten, Jane Baldwin, Editor, THE MARYLAND CALENDAR OF WILLS, Wills from 1685 to 1702, Volume II, Genealogical Pubishing Company, Baltimore, Maryland, page 206.
- Dodd, Rosemary B., and Patricia M. Bausell, editors, ABSTRACTS OF LAND RECORDS-ANNE ARUNDEl COUNTY, MARYLAND, VOLUME II (Book WT1 and WT2), The Anne Arundel Genealogical Society, Pasadena, Maryland, page148.
- Maryland State Archive, LAND OFFICE (RENT ROLLS) 1, Annapolis, Maryland, page 57a.
- Maryland Historical Society, MARYLAND RENT ROLLS: ANNE ARUNDEL AND BALTIMORE COUNTIES, Baltimore, Maryland, page 134.
- _____, BALTIMORE COUNTY TAXABLES - 1706, Baltimore, Maryland, page 62.
- Cotten, Jane Baldwin, Editor, THE MARYLAND CALENDAR OF WILLS, Wills from 1713 to 1720, Volume IV, Genealogical Pubishing Company, Baltimore, Maryland, page 130.
- Newman, Harry Wright, ANNE ARUNDEL GENTRY, Volume 1, Annapolis, Maryland, page 87.

- Maryland State Archive, ARCHIVES OF MARYLAND, Provincial Court Land Records, 1724-1731, Volume 697, Annapolis, Maryland, pages 310-311.
- Dodd, Rosemary B., and Michael E. Flood, editors, ABSTRACTS OF LAND RECORDS-ANNE ARUNDEl COUNTY, MARYLAND, VOLUME V (Book RD1, Book TI 1, Book 1HT1 1, and Book RD2), The Anne Arundel Genealogical Society, Pasadena, Maryland, pages 95-96-97.
- Maryland State Archive, ARCHIVES OF MARYLAND ONLINE, "Capital Crimes: Hanged, Pardoned, and Reprieved - All Classes by Name 1726-1775", Annapolis, Maryland.
- Dodd, Rosemary B., and Michael E. Flood, editors, ABSTRACTS OF LAND RECORDS-ANNE ARUNDEl COUNTY, MARYLAND, VOLUME VII (Book RB 2, Book RD3), The Anne Arundel Genealogical Society, Pasadena, Maryland, page14.
- Cotten, Jane Baldwin, Editor, THE MARYLAND CALENDAR OF WILLS, Wills from 1764 to 1767, Volume XIII, Genealogical Pubishing Company, Baltimore, Maryland, page 12.
- Maryland State Archive, Prerogative Court (Will) 31 - Will of Mary Ragon, Anne Arundel County, Annapolis, Maryland, pages 67-68.

Sources for Timothy Ragan, Jr. and Rachel Nelson: [In chronological order]

- Maryland State Archive, ARCHIVES OF MARYLAND, Provincial Court Land Records, 1724-1731, Volume 697, Annapolis, Maryland, pages 310-311.
- Dodd, Rosemary B., and Michael E. Flood, editors, ABSTRACTS OF LAND RECORDS-ANNE ARUNDEl COUNTY, MARYLAND, VOLUME VI (Book RD2 3, Book RB3 1), The Anne Arundel Genealogical Society, Pasadena, Maryland, page103.
- Maryland State Archive, LAND OFFICE (RENT ROLLS) 2, Annapolis, Maryland, pages 395a-395b.
- Maryland State Archive, CALENDAR OF MARYLAND STATE PAPERS, No. 1 The Black Books, Annapolis, Maryland, pages 85-86.
- Maryland State Archive, Prerogative Court (Will) 31 - Will of Mary Ragon, Anne Arundel County, Annapolis, Maryland, pages 67-68.
- Cotten, Jane Baldwin, Editor, THE MARYLAND CALENDAR OF

WILLS, Wills from 1767 to 1772, Volume XIV, Genealogical Pubishing Company, Baltimore, Maryland, page 12.

- Maryland State Archive, ANNE ARUNDEL COUNTY, MARYLAND DEED BOOK BB-3, Part 2, Ragan, Timothy to Eli Dorsey, Jun. "Chews Vineyard" (microfilm by interlibrary loan), Annapolis, Maryland, page 559.
- Maryland State Archive, LAND OFFICE, ANNE ARUNDEL COUNTY RENT ROLLS 14, AA, i of tracts, folio 122-173 (1733-1768), Waldo (Woofs) Books, Annapolis, Maryland, page 35.
- Maryland State Archive, PROCEEDINGS AND ACTS OF THE GENERAL ASSEMBLY OF MARYLAND, 1766-1768, Volume LXI, pages 520-523, 535.
- Cartmell, T. K., SHENANDOAH VALLEY PIONEERS AND THEIR DESCENDANTS - A History of Frederick County, Virginia, Genealogical Publishing Company, Baltimore County, Maryland, page 270.
- Peden,Jr., Henry C., INHABITANTS OF BALTIMORE COUNTY 1763-1774, Family Line Publications, Westminster, Maryland, page 53
- Carothers, Bettie Stirling, Compiler, SIGNERS OF THE OATH OF FIDELITY TO MARYLAND DURING THE REVOLUTION, Volume II, Chesterfield, Missouri, page 19.
- Maryland State Archive, MARYLAND INDEXES: Assessment of 1783-Index to Property Owners,1782-1783 for Baltimore County (MSA S 1437) Online, Annapolis, Maryland.
- Barnes, Robert W., and Bettie Stirling Carothers, Compilers, 1783 TAX LIST OF BALTIMORE COUNTY, MARYLAND, Family Line Publications, Westminster, Maryland, pages 52-53.

FAMILY OF TIMOTHY REAGAN AND ELIZABETH TRIGG

Timothy Reagan, grandson of Timothy Ragan - Colonial Ancestor was probably born in the Elk Ridge community. His parents have not been identified, but research on this continues.

In his youth, he was probably taught to read and write by his mother, and was taught the art of farming and blacksmithing by his father. So this was one of his lifetime occupations. He was also a carpenter and as most men did in those days, he could do almost any chore needed in daily life.

An early church census verifies their birth years. The census was taken in St. John and Prince George Parishes, Prince George County, Maryland on 31 31 August 1776 and listed; Timothy Ragan, age 26, and Elizabeth Ragan, age 16. No children were listed.

Traditions say that Timothy had four brothers who all served in the Revolutionary War and afterward moved to Tennessee. Other Reagans found in that early period include: Jeremiah in Washington County, Daniel in Greene County, Charles in Blount County, and James in Sevier County and a James in Knox County. These men were all of an age to have been Timothy's brothers but no definite connection to any of them has been made.

Timothy Reagan served in the Revolution with the Continental Troops of Maryland. He was seriously wounded at the Battle of Brandywine and again later in the war. Muster roll records found in the National Archives, Washington, D.C. show that he served as private with Captain John Eccleston, in the 2nd Regiment of Maryland Troops, commanded by Colonel Thomas Price. The records also show that he was left at a hospital in Chester, Pennsylvania, on 12 September 1777, the day after the Battle of Brandywine. He was reported as still being in the hospital six months later. No records of a pension or bounty land grants were found.

Timothy's name is found on the 1783 tax lists of Pittsylvania County, Virginia with five people in his family at that time. He does not appear on the tax lists for 1785.

His name is found in Caswell County, North Carolina, in the January and April counts of 1786. There were then seven persons in his family: a male age 21-60, 3 males under 21 or over 60, and 3 females.

Two grants of land, located in Caswell County, North Carolina, were recorded for Timothy Reagan. The first was issued in 1791 to Timothy Regan for 200 acres "on the waters of Fish Pond." Disposal of this land was recorded in Caswell County, North Carolina Deed Book 'H', pages 110/11. The deed says

"THIS INDENTURE made the thirteenth day of October and in the year of our Lord one thousand seven hundred and ninety two Between Timothy Regan of the County of Caswell, North

Carolina of the one part and Solomon Clark of the said County and State of the other part..."
The second grant, dated 3 December 1795, was issued to Timothy Ragan and John Grant for 157 acres of land "on waters of Wolf Island." Records of disposal of this land have not been located yet but it is believed that Timothy moved to East Tennessee very soon after this date of 1795.

No mention of his name has been found in early records of the counties of Washington, Sullivan, Hawkins, Greene, or Jefferson. He is said to have joined a group of pioneers who pushed farther into the Indians' lands and built the settlement around the Shield's Fort, later Lawson's Fort, in Sevier County Tennessee. The late Joe A. Sharp, County Historian, believed this fort was located on Middle Creek. The date was probably a little later than the settlement of Sevierville.

The State of Tennessee began issuing land grants in 1806 and the earliest found for Timothy Reagan was surveyed in 1807. According to the State Archivist, both land grants still in existence for Timothy were for purchased land, not bounty land. The first grant was surveyed 26 February 1807 and was granted 22 May 1810:

"... a certain tract or parcel of land containing fifty acres and one hundred and sixteen poles lying in the County of Sevier in the District South of French Broad and Holston on the waters of Middle Creek there being due and chargeable on said land the sum of fifty dollars and seventy-three cents with interest thereon..."

This tract joined the lands of Jennett (Shields) Tipton, widow of Joshua Tipton and the land of John Marshall. The second grant was entered 13 May 1824 and granted on 6 August 1824. This land joined a corner of Nancy Robinson's land:

"... or parcel of land containing twenty-five acres, lying in the County aforesaid. Beginning at a white oak on a line of said Reagan's old survey..."

Since this tract joined the old survey it is believed that this is where Timothy lived until his death, or until he went to live with his son,

Richard, who had settled in White Oak Flats now Gatlinburg.

His great grandson, John H. Reagan, described Timothy as a tall, fine looking man, strong and having great vitality even in his older years. He was loved and respected by people and was fun-loving and witty. Being an Irishman, he enjoyed a practical joke now and then. A story handed down through the years tells that although he had built the stocks for the jail in Sevierville, he pretended that he did not know how they operated and persuaded the sheriff to sit in them to demonstrate for him. When the sheriff did he promptly locked them and enjoyed the fun at the sheriff's expense. (Wonder what happened when the sheriff did get out!)

We don't know the exact date of Timothy or Elizabeth's death. That he was living in 1824 is indicated by the entry of the land record above. Neither of them appear on the 1830 census of Sevier County so it is assumed their deaths occurred before that date.

Family traditions say that Timothy Reagan was buried in an unmarked grave at White Oak Flats Cemetery, Gatlinburg, Tennessee near where the first person buried, in the lower left hand corner of the old part of the cemetery, looking up the Graveyard hill from the gate.

Timothy and Elizabeth Reagan had a large family, some say ten sons and one daughter. The North Carolina census indicates there were three females in the family in 1786 so there may have been more daughters in the family. Most of these children moved from Sevier County farther to the West and South. The oldest son, Richard, remained and was one of the first settlers of White Oak Flats, now Gatlinburg, Tennessee.

References:

- "Smoky Mountain Clans", Donald B. Reagan, 1978, p 1-3.
- "The Book of Ragan/Reagan", Donald B. Reagan, 1993, p 396.

1

QUARKS & STUFF: THE SCIENTIFIC LINEAGE

Creation of the Universe to Adam the First Man Lineage

1. Purpose + Determination   Magic
2. |Purpose |Serendipity
3. ||Divine Teleology   + ||Schrodinger Teleology
4. Impulse of Creation + Void
5. Conception + Boundaries and Conditions
6. Chaos + Randomness/Chance
7. Potentiality + Symmetry Breaking
8. Instantiation + Gravitational Singularity (Time Zero)
9. Big Bang Era / Planck Epoch (0 - 10^-43 sec)
10. Grand Unification Epoch
11. Inflationary Epoch (10^-36 sec - 10^-32 sec)
12. Subatomic Era / Electroweak Epoch + Baryogenesis
13. Quark Epoch
14. Hadron Epoch
15. Lepton Epoch
16. Photon Epoch
17. Primordial Age / Subatomic Era / Nucleosynthesis Epoch
18. Radiation Era / Matter Domination Epoch

19.   Radiation Era / Recombination Epoch
20.   Stelliferous Age / Reionization Epoch
21.   Protogalaxies, first stars (13.3 Billion BC)
22.   Quasars, Spherical Galaxies (11 Billion BC)
23.   Spiral Galaxies (9 Billion BC)
24.   Our Galactic Cluster
25.   Milky Way GALAXY
26.   (NN), a Population III star
27.   Remnants of a supernova
28.   (NN), a Population II star
29.   Remnants of a supernova
30.   Sol, a Population I star
31.   Condensing solar system
32.   Earth before collision (4567 M BC) + Pre-collision Theia
33.   Earth Collides with Theia (4533 M BC)
34.   Earth of Cryptic Era (Hadean Eon)
35.   Earth of Basin Groups Era (Hadean Eon)
36.   Earth of Nectarian Era (Hadean Eon)
37.   Earth of Lower Imbrian Era (Hadean Eon)
38.   Earth of Eoarchean Era (Archean Eon)
39.   Non-reproducing Precursor Organism + Montmorillonite-
           based Vesicles
40.   Earliest life (Based on AEG -based nucleic acid chains)
41.   Earlier life (Based on RNA) (3850+ M BC)
42.   Earlier Life (Based on RNA and Protein) (3800+ M BC)
43.   Last Universal Ancestor of Present Life
44.   Proto-Bacteria (3700 M BC)
45.   Glycobacteria
46.   Eurybacteria
47.   Superphylum Endobacteria
48.   Phylum Actinobacteria
49.   Class Actinobacteridae
50.   (NN), a thermophilic Bacterium + (NN), a Cell Nucleus
51.   (NN), a Nucleated Cell + Pre-Mitochondrion Bacteria
52.   Domain of Eukaryotes (2100 M BC)
53.   Superempire Unikonta
54.   Empire of Opisthokonts (Fungi & Animals)
55.   Empire of Opisthokonts (Animals)
56.   Superkingdom Holozoa
57.   Kingdom of Animals
58.   Subkingdom of Metazoa (Multicellular Animals)

59.   Superbranch Eumetazoa
60.   Superphylum Planulozoa
61.   Clade of Bilateria and Placozoa
62.   Branch Bilateria
63.   Infrakingdom (Grade) of Coelomates (570 M BC)
64.   Superphylum Deuterostomia (Chordates, Echinoderms, & kin)
65.   Phylum Chordata (540 M BC - ?)
66.   Clade Craniata
67.   Subphylum Vertebrata (510 M BC - ?)
68.   Infraphylum Gnathostomata (Jawed Vertebrates)
69.   Microphylum Teleostomi (Bony fishes & Spiny sharks)
70.   Superclass Osteichthyes (Bony fishes)
71.   Class Sarcopterygii (Lobe-finned Fishes)
72.   Clade of Rhipidistia
73.   Subclass Tetrapodamorpha
74.   Infraphylum Tetrapoda
75.   Clade Reptiliomorpha
76.   Microphylum Amniota (Mammals, Reptiles, etc.)
77.   Superclass Synapsida
78.   Epiclass of Therapsids
79.   Suborder Cynodontia
80.   Infraorder Eucynodontia
81.   Superfamily Chiniquodontoidea
82.   Class Mammalia (180? M BC - ?)
83.   Subclass Theriiformes (Therial Mammals) (140? M BC - ?)
84.   Clade Holotheria
85.   Infraclass Eutheria (Placental Mammals)
86.   Subcohort Exafroplacentalia
87.   Superlegion Boreoeutheria (mammals from Laurasia Supercontinent)
88.   Legion of Euarchontoglires
89.   Superorder Euarchonta
90.   Order of Primates (60 M BC - ?)
91.   Suborder Haplorrhini (55 M BC - ?)
92.   Infraorder Simiiformes (Simians)
93.   Parvorder Catarrhini (Apes & Old World Monkeys)
94.   Superfamily Hominoidea (Apes) (21 M BC - ?)
95.   Family Hominidae (Great Apes) (16 M BC - ?)
96.   Subfamily Homininae (9 M BC - ?)
97.   Tribe Hominini (Hominids & Chimpanzee) (7 M BC)

98.   Proto-Chimpanzee (6.8 M BC - ?) + Subtribe Hominina (7 M BC - ?)
99.   prob. Orrorin tugenensis (6.3 M BC - ?)
100.   Ardipithecus kadabba
101.   Ardepithecus ramidus
102.   Australopithecus anamensis
103.   Australopithecus afarensis
104.   Australopithecus africanus
105.   Australopithecus sediba
106.   Genus Homo (H. habilis)
107.   Homo ergaster (2.4 M BC - 1.5 M BC)
108.   Homo antecessor (1.1 M BC - 0.8 M BC)
109.   Homo heidelbergensis (0.8 M BC - 0.2 M BC)
110.   Homo sapiens idaltu (200,000 BC - ?)
111.   Homo sapiens sapiens (120,000 BC - ?)
112.   (poss. Homo sapiens sapiens + Extraterrestrial Intervention) (ca 120,000 - 60,000 BC)
113.   Modern Man in Southern Asia (ca 60,000 BC - ?)
114.   Modern Man in Northern Asia (ca 45,000 BC - ?)
115.   Man of the Aurignacian toolkit (35,000 BC - ?)
116.   Man of the European Aurignacian
117.   Man of the European Aurignacian
118.   Man of the Gravettian toolkit
119.   Man of the Epi-Gravettian toolkit
120.   Man of the Solutrean toolkit
121.   Man of the Magdalenian toolkit
122.   Man of the Magelmose toolkit
123.   (NN) ... (NN) (many missing generations)
124.   Man of pre-Neolithic Age (9400 BC - ?)
125.   Man of the Fertile-Crescent Neolithic Age
126.   Man of the Mediterranian Neolithic Age
127.   Man of the Danubian Neolithic Age (5400 BC - ?)
128.   Man of the Chalcolithic (Aeneolithic) Age
129.   Man of the advanced Pastoral Era (4000 BC - ?)
130.   Man of late Copper Age (3500 BC - ?)
131.   Man of the Bronze Age
132.   (poss. Adam, the First Man + Extraterrestrial Intervention)
133.   Adam, the First Man + Eve, the First Woman

2

LINEAGES FROM CHARLEMAGNE

LINEAGE I

1. Charlemagne, Carolus 'Magnus', Rex Francorum & Imperator
    Romanorum + Hildegard of Vinzgouw
2. "Pépin" Carloman, King of Italy + Mistress of Pepin
3. Bernard, King of Lombardy + Cunigundis (Cunegonde)
    (Princess) de VERMANDOIS
4. Pépin II, lord of Péronne + Rothaide de Bobbio
5. Héribert I, count of Vermandois + Bertha of Morvois
6. Héribert II, count of Vermandois + Liegarde Hildebrante of
    France
7. Count Robert de Vermandois, comte de Meaux et de Troyes +
    Adélaïde-Wera de Bourgogne, Chalon et Troyes
8. Arnulf de Ganelon + Gisia de Ganelon
9. Mathilde Hildeburg, de Condé-sur-Noireau + Guillaume I,
    'Talvas' de Belleme, seigneur d'Alençon
10. Guillaume II "Talvas" Comte de Bellême, seigneur d'Alençon
    + Haberga "Hildeburge" de Beaumont
11. Mabile, dame de Bellême et d'Alençon + Roger Ii de
    Montgomery, 1st Earl of Shrewsbury

12.   Aimeria Emma de Montgomery + Warine "The Sherriff" de
          Metz
13.   Sir Guy Warin "The Bold" de Metz + Baroness Melette (Maud)
          Maud Peverell, Heiress of Whittington
14.   Fulk FitzWarin, Lord of Whittington and Alderbury + Eva
          Whittington and FitzWarin (of Whittington & Alveston)
15.   Warin FitzWarin FitzWarin
16.   Warin de Burwardslegh, Lord of Estelegh
17.   Alicia de Burwardslegh + Sir Walter Bromley
18.   Geoffrey Galffridus Bromley + Philippa Bagot
19.   Richard Bromley + Elizabeth Knockton
20.   Ranulph Bromley + Agnes de Baddington
21.   John de Bromley + Joan de Baddington
22.   Cecily Margaret Bromhall + Robert de Worsley, Lord of
          Booths
23.   William de Worsley + Ellen de Huton
24.   Robert Worsley + Isabel de Trafford
25.   Robert de Worsley + Katherine Clark
26.   Otewell Worsley, Sir + Rose verch Edward
27.   Joyce Worsley + Richard Lee II
28.   Richard Lee III + Eleanor Burgoine
29.   Geoffrey Lee, MP + Agnes Conyers
30.   Reginald Lee + Dorothy Thurland
31.   Gervase Lee of Nottinghamshire
32.   Thomas Lee, of Ashfield + Margaret Mary Oscroft
33.   Elizabeth Lee + Thomas Hanks
34.   Robert Hanks + Margaret NLN
35.   Peter Hanks I + Mary Bressie
36.   Elinor Hanks + Robert Nelson
37.   Rachael Nelson + Timothy Ragan
38.   Timothy Reagan + Elizabeth Trigg
39.   Richard Bazel Reagan + Cecelia Creppy
40.   Richard Reagan + Phoebe Samples
41.   Reuben Perry Reagan + Elizabeth Cagle
42.   George Reagan + Emaline Garner
43.   Marshall Reagan + Emma Rogers
44.   Elzie Reagan + Delmar Raines
       ------- Gina Davis
              ------- Jackson Davis
       ------- Patricia Stuart
              ------- Bobby Caldwell

         ------- Jennifer Caldwell
    ------- Mike Raines
         ------- Leah Raines
         ------- Kendra Raines
         ------- Joshua Raines
         ------- Michael Raines
  ------- Frank Raines
         ------- Franklin Cody Raines
         ------- Kip Allen Raines
  ------- Richard Raines
         ------- Tyler Lee
         ------- Devin Lee
         ------- Emma Lundy

LINEAGE II (THRU WILLIAM THE CONQUEROR)

1. CHARLEMAGNE, Carolus 'Magnus', Rex Francorum & Imperator Romanorum + Hildegard of Vinzgouw
2. "Pépin" Carloman, King of Italy + Mistress of Pepin
3. Bernard, King of Lombardy + Cunigundis (Cunegonde) (Princess) de VERMANDOIS
4. Pépin II, lord of Péronne + Rothaide de Bobbio
5. Pepin (I; Count) de SENLIS de VALOIS
6. (Miss) de SENLIS de VALOIS (845? - ?) + Berenger (Count) de RENNES (? - 931)
7. Poppa (Poppaeia) de VALOIS (872? - ?) + Rollo (Hrolf Rollon Rou Robert) `the Dane' RAGNVALDSSON
8. Guillaume (2nd Duke) of NORMANDY + Sprota de BRETAGNE (concubine)
9. Richard I `the Fearless' (Count) of NORMANDY + Gunnora (Gonnor) de CREPON
10. Richard II `the Good' of NORMANDY (963? - 1027) + Judith (Princess) of BRITTANY
11. Robert II (Duke) of NORMANDY + Herleve (Salburpyr) de FALAISE (1003? - 1050?)
12. WILLIAM the CONQUEROR (Duke) of NORMANDY + Matilda (Maud) FLEMING (1032 - 1083 Caan)
13. Henry I BEAUCLERC (King) of ENGLAND + Matilda (Edith Eagdith) `Atheling' STEWART of SCOTLAND
14. Matilda (Maud Augusta) the EMPRESS + Geoffrey V `the Fair' (`Plantagenet')

15. Henry II (King) of ENGLAND + Eleanor (Duchess/Princess) of
        AQUITAINE
16. John `Lackland' (King) of ENGLAND + Isabella (d'
        ANGOULEME) TAILLEFER
17. Eleanor (Alianor) of ENGLAND (1215? - 1275) + Simon V de
        MONTFORT (1208 - 4/8/1265)
18. Eleanor de MONTFORT (1252 - 1282) + Llywellyn (II) ap
        GRUFFYDD (? - 1282)
19. Catherine verch LLYWELLYN + Philip ap IFOR
20. Eleanor (of ISCOED; GOCH) verch PHILIP + Thomas ap
        LLEWELLYN
21. Lowri verch GRUFFUDD FYCHAN + Robert (Sir; of Emral)
        PULESTON (1358? - 1399?)
22. Angharad PULESTON + Edward TREVOR ap DAFFYD (? -
        1448?)
23. Otewell Worsley, Sir + Rose (TREVOR) verch EDWART
24. Joyce Worsley + Richard Lee II
25. Richard Lee III + Eleanor Burgoine
26. Geoffrey Lee, MP + Agnes Conyers
27. Reginald Lee + Dorothy Thurland
28. Gervase Lee of Nottinghamshire
29. Thomas Lee, of Ashfield + Margaret Mary Oscroft
30. Elizabeth Lee + Thomas Hanks
31. Robert Hanks + Margaret NLN
32. Peter Hanks I + Mary Bressie
33. Elinor Hanks + Robert Nelson
34. Rachael Nelson + Timothy Ragan
35. Timothy Reagan + Elizabeth Trigg
36. Richard Bazel Reagan + Cecelia Creppy
37. Richard Reagan + Phoebe Samples
38. Reuben Perry Reagan + Elizabeth Cagle
39. George Reagan + Emaline Garner
40. Marshall Reagan + Emma Rogers
41. Elzie Reagan + Delmar Raines
        ------- Gina Davis
                ------- Jackson Davis
        ------- Patricia Stuart
                ------- Bobby Caldwell
                ------- Jennifer Caldwell
        ------- Mike Raines
                ------- Leah Raines

------- Kendra Raines
------- Joshua Raines
------- Michael Raines
------- Frank Raines
------- Franklin Cody Raines
------- Kip Allen Raines
------- Richard Raines
------- Tyler Lee
------- Devin Lee
------- Emma Lundy

3

THE ANGLO-SAXON LINEAGE

The Angles Branch to Creoda of the Gewissae

1. Sesostris + Nefret
2. Amenemhat I Sehetepibre (Founder) of 12th Dynasty +
      Nefrutotenen
3. Sesotris I Kheperkare (PHARAOH) of EGYPT (? - 1928? BC) +
      Nefrusheri (Princess) of EGYPT
4. Amenemhat (Ammenemes) II Nubkaure (PHARAOH) of
      EGYPT + Keminnub (Queen) of EGYPT
5. Sesotris II Khakheperre (PHARAOH) of EGYPT + Nofret of
      EGYPT
6. Sesotris III Khakaure of EGYPT + Sebekshedty-Neferu
      (Queen) of EGYPT
7. Amenemhat III Nemare (PHARAOH) of EGYPT + Sebeknefru
      (Queen) of EGYPT
8. Amenemhat (Ammenemes) IV (PHARAOH) of EGYPT
9. Wegaf (PHARAOH) of 13th Dynasty + daughter of
      Amenemhet IV
10. Ameny Intef (Inyotef) IV (PHARAOH) of EGYPT
11. Hor (PHARAOH) of EGYPT (? - 1760? BC)

12.   Sobekhotep II (PHARAOH) of EGYPT (? - 1750? BC)
13.   Khendjer (PHARAOH) of EGYPT (? - 1747? BC)
14.   Sobekhotep III (PHARAOH) of EGYPT (? - 1745? BC)
15.   Neferhotep I (PHARAOH) of EGYPT
16.   Sobekhotep IV Khaneferre (PHARAOH) of 13th Dynasty +
       Tjan
17.   Sebekhotep (Princess) of THEBES + Senebhanef, son of
       Renressonb
18.   Mentuhotep (Queen) of EGYPT + Sekhemre-Sementawi
       Djehuti (PHARAOH) of EGYPT
19.   Sekhemre-Se'ankhtawi Neferhotep (PHARAOH) of EGYPT
20.   Sobekemsaf Sekhemre-Shedtawi (PHARAOH) of EGYPT +
       Nubkhas (Queen) of EGYPT
21.   Inyotef VII (PHARAOH) at THEBES + Sobkemsaf
       (Sebekamzaf) of EGYPT (1635? BC - ?)
22.   Sekenenre Tao I (PHARAOH) at THEBES + Tetisheri of
       THEBES
23.   Sekenenre Tao II (King) of THEBES + Ahhotep (Ahotop) I
       (Queen) of EGYPT
24.   Ahmose I (1st PHARAOH) of 18th Dynasty + Nefretiri
       (Queen) of EGYPT
25.   Amenhotep I Djeserkare (PHARAOH) of EGYPT + Senisonb
       (Seneseneb) of EGYPT
26.   Thutmose I (PHARAOH) of EGYPT (? - 1481? BC) + Amhose
       (Aahmes II) (Queen) of EGYPT
27.   Hatshepsut (Queen & PHARAOH) of EGYPT (? - 1482 BC) +
       Thutmose (Tuthmosis) II (PHARAOH) of EGYPT
28.   Meryetre Hatshepsut of EGYPT + Thutmose III `the Great' of
       EGYPT (Moses of the Bible)
29.   Akheperure Amenhotep II THUTMOSID (PHARAOH) of
       EGYPT + Tio (Tiye Tiaa)
30.   Menkheprure' Thutmose IV (PHARAOH) of EGYPT +
       Mutemwiya, daughter of Artatama (I; King) of MITANNI
31.   Nebma'atre' Amenhotep III (PHARAOH) of EGYPT + Tiye-
       Nefertari (Tiy) of EGYPT (1382 BC - 1344 BC)
32.   Akhenaton (Iknaton) (10th PHARAOH) of 18th Dynasty
       EGYPT + Nefertiti (Chief Queen) of EGYPT
33.   Meritaten (Royal Daughter) of EGYPT + Judah (Judas Juda)
       ibn JACOB, son of Jacob ibn ISAAC (King of GOSHEN)
34.   Zerah (Zehrah Zarah Zare) ibn JUDAH + Electra the PLEIADE
35.   Dardanus (Dara) (King) of ACADIA + Batea of TEUCRI

36.   Erichthonius (King) of ACADIA (? - 1386? BC) + Astyoche of
        ACADIA
37.   Trois of ACADIA + Callirhoe (TEUCRI)
38.   Ilus (Ilyus) (King) of TROY (? - 1282? BC) + Eurydice
        (Eurydike) of TROY
39.   Priam Podarces (High King) of TROY (? - 1183? BC) + Hecuba
        (Hecabe) of PHRYGIA
40.   Troana Iluim of TROY + Memnon (Munon) of TROY (? - 1183?
        BC)
41.   Thor (Tror) (King) of THRACE + Sibil (Sif)
42.   Einridi LORIDESSON
43.   Vingethor (Vingethior) EINRIDISSON
44.   Moda (Mode) VINGENERSSON
45.   Maji (Magi) MODASSON
46.   Seskef (Sceaf Scaef)
47.   Bedwig (Bedvig; of SCEAF)
48.   Hwala (Hvala Hawala Guala)
49.   Hathra (Athra)
50.   Itermon (Itormann)
51.   Heremod (King) in DENMARK
52.   Sceldwa (King) in DENMARK
53.   Beaw (Gram) (King) in DENMARK
54.   Taetwa (Tatwa Tecti)
55.   Jat (Geatwa Geata Geat Gaut Geot Gauti)
56.   Godwulf (Gudolfr)
57.   Flocwald (of Asgard)
58.   Finn (the TROJAN ?) (Asgard 130? - ?)
59.   Frithuwulf (the TROJAN ?)
60.   Frealaf (Friallaf Froethelaf)
61.   Frithuwald (Bor) (190? - ?) + Beltsea (Beltsa) of ASGARD
62.   Woden (Wodan Odin) of ASGARD + Frigg (Frigida) of
        ASALAND
63.   Baeldaeg of the AESIR (243? - ?) + Nanna (GEWARSDATTER)
        of SCANDINAVIA (247? - ?), daughter of Gewar (King) of
        NORWAY (220? - ?)
64.   Brond (Brand Brandr) of SCANDINAVIA (271? - ?)
65.   Bernic of the ANGLES
66.   Beorns (Beorn) of the ANGLES
67.   Weybrand of the ANGLES
68.   Ingebrand of the ANGLES
69.   Aloc (Alek) of the ANGLES

70.   Angenwit (Angenwyt) of the ANGLES
71.   Ethelbert (Edibrith) of the ANGLES
72.   Oessa of the ANGLES (1st King of BERNICIA)
73.   Gorpe + Cerdic (Cedric) of the GEWISSAE (ANCIENT
          SAXONY)
74.   Creoda of the GEWISSAE (493? - 534?)

The Saxon Branch to Creoda of the Gewissae

1.   Sesostris + Nefret
2.   Amenemhat I Sehetepibre (Founder) of 12th Dynasty +
          Nefrutotenen
3.   Sesotris I Kheperkare (PHARAOH) of EGYPT (? - 1928? BC) +
          Nefrusheri (Princess) of EGYPT
4.   Amenemhat (Ammenemes) II Nubkaure (PHARAOH) of
          EGYPT + Keminnub (Queen) of EGYPT
5.   Sesotris II Khakheperre (PHARAOH) of EGYPT + Nofret of
          EGYPT
6.   Sesotris III Khakaure of EGYPT + Sebekshedty-Neferu
          (Queen) of EGYPT
7.   Amenemhat III Nemare (PHARAOH) of EGYPT + Sebeknefru
          (Queen) of EGYPT
8.   Amenemhat (Ammenemes) IV (PHARAOH) of EGYPT
9.   Wegaf (PHARAOH) of 13th Dynasty + daughter of
          Amenemhet IV
10.   Ameny Intef (Inyotef) IV (PHARAOH) of EGYPT
11.   Hor (PHARAOH) of EGYPT (? - 1760? BC)
12.   Sobekhotep II (PHARAOH) of EGYPT (? - 1750? BC)
13.   Khendjer (PHARAOH) of EGYPT (? - 1747? BC)
14.   Sobekhotep III (PHARAOH) of EGYPT (? - 1745? BC)
15.   Neferhotep I (PHARAOH) of EGYPT
16.   Sobekhotep IV Khaneferre (PHARAOH) of 13th Dynasty +
          Tjan
17.   Sebekhotep (Princess) of THEBES + Senebhanef, son of
          Renressonb
18.   Mentuhotep (Queen) of EGYPT + Sekhemre-Sementawi
          Djehuti (PHARAOH) of EGYPT
19.   Sekhemre-Se'ankhtawi Neferhotep (PHARAOH) of EGYPT
20.   Sobekemsaf Sekhemre-Shedtawi (PHARAOH) of EGYPT +
          Nubkhas (Queen) of EGYPT

21.   Inyotef VII (PHARAOH) at THEBES + Sobkemsaf
        (Sebekamzaf) of EGYPT (1635? BC - ?)
22.   Sekenenre Tao I (PHARAOH) at THEBES + Tetisheri of
        THEBES
23.   Sekenenre Tao II (King) of THEBES + Ahhotep (Ahotop) I
        (Queen) of EGYPT
24.   Ahmose I (1st PHARAOH) of 18th Dynasty + Nefretiri
        (Queen) of EGYPT
25.   Amenhotep I Djeserkare (PHARAOH) of EGYPT + Senisonb
        (Seneseneb) of EGYPT
26.   Thutmose I (PHARAOH) of EGYPT (? - 1481? BC) + Amhose
        (Aahmes II) (Queen) of EGYPT
27.   Hatshepsut (Queen & PHARAOH) of EGYPT (? - 1482 BC) +
        Thutmose (Tuthmosis) II (PHARAOH) of EGYPT
28.   Meryetre Hatshepsut of EGYPT + Thutmose III `the Great' of
        EGYPT (Moses of the Bible)
29.   Akheperure Amenhotep II THUTMOSID (PHARAOH) of
        EGYPT + Tio (Tiye Tiaa)
30.   Menkheprure' Thutmose IV (PHARAOH) of EGYPT +
        Mutemwiya, daughter of Artatama (I; King) of MITANNI
31.   Nebma'atre' Amenhotep III (PHARAOH) of EGYPT + Tiye-
        Nefertari (Tiy) of EGYPT (1382 BC - 1344 BC)
32.   Akhenaton (Iknaton) (10th PHARAOH) of 18th Dynasty
        EGYPT + Nefertiti (Chief Queen) of EGYPT
33.   Meritaten (Royal Daughter) of EGYPT + Judah (Judas Juda)
        ibn JACOB, son of Jacob ibn ISAAC (King of GOSHEN)
34.   Zerah (Zehrah Zarah Zare) ibn JUDAH + Electra the PLEIADE
35.   Dardanus (Dara) (King) of ACADIA + Batea of TEUCRI
36.   Erichthonius (King) of ACADIA (? - 1386? BC) + Astyoche of
        ACADIA
37.   Trois of ACADIA + Callirhoe (TEUCRI)
38.   Ilus (Ilyus) (King) of TROY (? - 1282? BC) + Eurydice
        (Eurydike) of TROY
39.   Priam Podarces (High King) of TROY (? - 1183? BC) + Hecuba
        (Hecabe) of PHRYGIA
40.   Troana Iluim of TROY + Memnon (Munon) of TROY (? - 1183?
        BC)
41.   Thor (Tror) (King) of THRACE + Sibil (Sif)
42.   Einridi LORIDESSON
43.   Vingethor (Vingethior) EINRIDISSON
44.   Moda (Mode) VINGENERSSON

45.   Maji (Magi) MODASSON
46.   Seskef (Sceaf Scaef)
47.   Bedwig (Bedvig; of SCEAF)
48.   Hwala (Hvala Hawala Guala)
49.   Hathra (Athra)
50.   Itermon (Itormann)
51.   Heremod (King) in DENMARK
52.   Sceldwa (King) in DENMARK
53.   Beaw (Gram) (King) in DENMARK
54.   Taetwa (Tatwa Tecti)
55.   Jat (Geatwa Geata Geat Gaut Geot Gauti)
56.   Godwulf (Gudolfr)
57.   Flocwald (of Asgard)
58.   Finn (the TROJAN ?) (Asgard 130? - ?)
59.   Frithuwulf (the TROJAN ?)
60.   Frealaf (Friallaf Froethelaf) (160? - ?)
61.   Frithuwald (Bor) (190? - ?)
62.   Woden (Wodan, Odin) of ASGARD + Frigg (Frigida) of
         ASALAND
63.   Baeldaeg of the AESIR (243? - ?) + Nanna (GEWARSDATTER)
         of SCANDINAVIA (247? - ?), daughter of Gewar (King) of
         NORWAY (220? - ?)
64.   Brond (Brand, Brandr) of SCANDINAVIA
65.   Frithugar DEIRA of ANCIENT SAXONY
66.   Freawine (Freovin) of ANCIENT SAXONY
67.   Wig (Uvigg, Wigga) of ANCIENT SAXONY
68.   Gewis (Gewisch) of ANCIENT SAXONY
69.   Esla (Esle) of ANCIENT SAXONY (411? - ?)
70.   Elesa (Elistus) of ANCIENT SAXONY
71.   Cerdic (Cedric) of the GEWISSAE (ANCIENT SAXONY)
72.   Creoda of the GEWISSAE (493? - 534?)

Merge into Anglo-Saxon Branch with Creoda of the Gewissae

Norse-Danish Line from Creoda of the Gewissae

LINEAGE I

72.   Creoda of the GEWISSAE (493? - 534?)

73.   Cynric (Centric) (King) of WESSEX (525? - 581?)
74.   Moalde `Digri' (KINRIKSDOTTER ?) + Halfdan HAROLDSSON
        (Jutland 590? - ?)
75.   Ivar `Wide Fathom' HALFDANSSON of SCANE (612? - 647?) +
        Gauthild (Gothilda) ALFSDOTTER
76.   Audur IVARSDOTTIR (Queen) of HOLMGARD + Radbart
        (King) of GARDGARIGE (Russia)
77.   Randver RADBARDSSON of LETHRA (? - 770?) + Signy of
        ESSEX
78.   Sigurd Ring (King of DENMARK) RANVERSSON
79.   Halfdan SIGURDSSON (750+ - ?)
80.   Ragnar `LoTHbrock' of Uppsala HALFDANSSON + Asberga
        (Aslaug) SIGURDSDOTTIR
81.   Ingvar (Yngvar) RAGNARSSON (802? - 873)
a.   Gommeri (Gormeric Gorm) YNGVARSSON
82.   Roger de MONTE GOMERII (873? - ?) + (Miss) de HIEMOIS
83.   Guillaume de MONTE GOMERII (930? - ?) + Elizabeth de
        TRIPON (Normandy 930? - ?)
84.   Hugh (Hugues) de MONTGOMERY (955? - 1034?) + Josceline
        (? - 1067+)
85.   Roger (I; `the Great') de MONTGOMERY + Emma (? - 1067+)
86.   Gilbert de MONTGOMERY (? - 1064)
87.   Aimera MONTGOMERY + Warine I MEEZE (Metz ? - 1115)
88.   William FitzWARIN (? - 1172+)
89.   Warin de Burwardslegh, Lord of Estelegh
90.   Alicia de Burwardslegh + Sir Walter Bromley
91.   Geoffrey Galffridus Bromley + Philippa Bagot
92.   Richard Bromley + Elizabeth Knockton
93.   Ranulph Bromley + Agnes de Baddington
94.   John de Bromley + Joan de Baddington
95.   Cecily Margaret Bromhall + Robert de Worsley, Lord of
        Booths
96.   William de Worsley + Ellen de Huton
97.   Robert Worsley + Isabel de Trafford
98.   Robert de Worsley + Katherine Clark
99.   Otewell Worsley, Sir + Rose verch Edward
100.   Joyce Worsley + Richard Lee II
101.   Richard Lee III + Eleanor Burgoine
102.   Geoffrey Lee, MP + Agnes Conyers
103.   Reginald Lee + Dorothy Thurland
104.   Gervase Lee of Nottinghamshire

105.   Thomas Lee, of Ashfield + Margaret Mary Oscroft
106.   Elizabeth Lee + Thomas Hanks
107.   Robert Hanks + Margaret NLN
108.   Peter Hanks I + Mary Bressie
109.   Elinor Hanks + Robert Nelson
110.   Rachael Nelson + Timothy Ragan
111.   Timothy Reagan + Elizabeth Trigg
112.   Richard Bazel Reagan + Cecelia Creppy
113.   Richard Reagan + Phoebe Samples
114.   Reuben Perry Reagan + Elizabeth Cagle
115.   George Reagan + Emaline Garner
116.   Marshall Reagan + Emma Rogers
117.   Elzie Reagan + Delmar Raines
        ------- Gina Davis
            ------- Jackson Davis
        ------- Patricia Stuart
            ------- Bobby Caldwell
            ------- Jennifer Caldwell
        ------- Mike Raines
            ------- Leah Raines
            ------- Kendra Raines
            ------- Joshua Raines
            ------- Michael Raines
        ------- Frank Raines
            ------- Franklin Cody Raines
            ------- Kip Allen Raines
        ------- Richard Raines
            ------- Tyler Lee
            ------- Devin Lee
            ------- Emma Lundy

Kingdom of Wessex Lineage from Creoda of the Gewissae

LINEAGE I

72.   Creoda of the GEWISSAE (493? - 534?)
73.   Cynric (Centric) (King) of WESSEX
74.   Ceawlin (King) of WESSEX (547? - 593)
75.   Cuthwine (Cutha) (Prince; Under-ruler) of WESSEX
76.   Cuthwulf (Cutha) (Under-ruler) of WESSEX

77.   Ceolwold (Ceolwald) (Under-ruler) of WESSEX
78.   Cenred (Kenred) (Under-ruler) of SOMERSET
79.   Ingild (Inigisilo) of WESSEX (680? - 718?) + Nothgyth(?) of
       SUSSEX
80.   Eoppa (INGILDING) of WESSEX +====> [255 „p,&]
81.   Eaba (Eafa Esa) of WESSEX (732? - ?)
82.   Ealhmund (EAFFING) of KENT (758? - 786?) + Alburga(?)
       AETHELBRYHTING of KENT (? - 803?)
83.   Egbert III `the Great' (1st King) of ENGLAND + Redburh
       (Redburga) (788? - ?)
84.   Ethelwulf (2nd King) of ENGLAND (806? - 858) + Osburga
       OSLACING of ISLE OF WIGHT (810? - 876+)
85.   Alfred "the Great" KING OF WESSEX b: 0848 d: 26 OCT 0899
       + Ealhswith OF THE GAINI of Mercia b: 0852 d: 05 DEC
       0905
86.   Edward "the Elder" of Wessex KING OF ENGLAND b: 0871 d:
       AUG 0924 + Ædgifu OF KENT b: 0896 d: 25 AUG 0968
87.   Edmund I "the Magnificent" KING OF ENGLAND b: 0920 d: 26
       MAY 0946 + Ælfgifu OF WESSEX b: 0922 d: 0944
88.   Edgar "the Peaceful" KING OF ENGLAND b: 0943 d: 08 JUL
       0975 + Ælfthryth OF DEVON b: 0945 d: 1000
89.   Æthelred II "the Unready" KING OF ENGLAND b: 0968 d: 23
       APR 1016 + Alfflaed (Elfreda Aelfgifu) GUNNARSDOTTIR
       of NORTHUMBRIA b: ABT 0963 d: 1002
90.   Edmund II `Ironside' of WESSEX (994? - 30/11/1016) +
       Ealdgyth (Algitha) MORCARSON of NORTHUMBRIA
91.   Edward `the OutLaw' of ENGLAND (1016? - 1057?) + Agatha
       (RURIKID) (? - 1066+)
92.   Margaret (Queen; Saint) of SCOTLAND + Malcolm III
       MacCRINAN (CANMORE)(19th King) of SCOTS
93.   Matilda (Edith Eagdith) `Atheling' STEWART of SCOTLAND +
       Henry I BEAUCLERC (King) of ENGLAND
94.   Matilda (Maud Augusta) the EMPRESS + Geoffrey V `the Fair'
       (`Plantagenet')
95.   Henry II (King) of ENGLAND + Eleanor (Duchess/Princess) of
       AQUITAINE
96.   John `Lackland' (King) of ENGLAND + Isabella (d'
       ANGOULEME) TAILLEFER
97.   Eleanor (Alianor) of ENGLAND (1215? - 1275) + Simon V de
       MONTFORT (1208 - 4/8/1265)
98.   Eleanor de MONTFORT (1252 - 1282) + Llywellyn (II) ap

GRUFFYDD (? - 1282)
99.	Catherine verch LLYWELLYN + Philip ap IFOR
100.	Eleanor (of ISCOED; GOCH) verch PHILIP + Thomas ap LLEWELLYN
101.	Lowri verch GRUFFUDD FYCHAN + Robert (Sir; of Emral) PULESTON (1358? - 1399?)
102.	Angharad PULESTON + Edward TREVOR ap DAFFYD (? - 1448?)
103.	Otewell Worsley, Sir + Rose (TREVOR) verch EDWART
104.	Joyce Worsley + Richard Lee II
105.	Richard Lee III + Eleanor Burgoine
106.	Geoffrey Lee, MP + Agnes Conyers
107.	Reginald Lee + Dorothy Thurland
108.	Gervase Lee of Nottinghamshire
109.	Thomas Lee, of Ashfield + Margaret Mary Oscroft
110.	Elizabeth Lee + Thomas Hanks
111.	Robert Hanks + Margaret NLN
112.	Peter Hanks I + Mary Bressie
113.	Elinor Hanks + Robert Nelson
114.	Rachael Nelson + Timothy Ragan
115.	Timothy Reagan + Elizabeth Trigg
116.	Richard Bazel Reagan + Cecelia Creppy
117.	Richard Reagan + Phoebe Samples
118.	Reuben Perry Reagan + Elizabeth Cagle
119.	George Reagan + Emaline Garner
120.	Marshall Reagan + Emma Rogers
121.	Elzie Reagan + Delmar Raines
	------- Gina Davis
		------- Jackson Davis
	------- Patricia Stuart
		------- Bobby Caldwell
		------- Jennifer Caldwell
	------- Mike Raines
		------- Leah Raines
		------- Kendra Raines
		------- Joshua Raines
		------- Michael Raines
	------- Frank Raines
		------- Franklin Cody Raines
		------- Kip Allen Raines
	------- Richard Raines

JAMES FRANK HATCHER III

------- Tyler Lee
------- Devin Lee
------- Emma Lundy

4

THE BURGUNDIAN LINEAGE

1. Sesostris + Nefret
2. Amenemhat I Sehetepibre (Founder) of 12th Dynasty + Nefrutotenen
3. Sesotris I Kheperkare (PHARAOH) of EGYPT (? - 1928? BC) + Nefrusheri (Princess) of EGYPT
4. Amenemhat (Ammenemes) II Nubkaure (PHARAOH) of EGYPT + Keminnub (Queen) of EGYPT
5. Sesotris II Khakheperre (PHARAOH) of EGYPT + Nofret of EGYPT
6. Sesotris III Khakaure of EGYPT + Sebekshedty-Neferu (Queen) of EGYPT
7. Amenemhat III Nemare (PHARAOH) of EGYPT + Sebeknefru (Queen) of EGYPT
8. Amenemhat (Ammenemes) IV (PHARAOH) of EGYPT
9. Wegaf (PHARAOH) of 13th Dynasty + daughter of Amenemhet IV
10. Ameny Intef (Inyotef) IV (PHARAOH) of EGYPT
11. Hor (PHARAOH) of EGYPT (? - 1760? BC)
12. Sobekhotep II (PHARAOH) of EGYPT (? - 1750? BC)
13. Khendjer (PHARAOH) of EGYPT (? - 1747? BC)

14. Sobekhotep III (PHARAOH) of EGYPT (? - 1745? BC)
15. Neferhotep I (PHARAOH) of EGYPT
16. Sobekhotep IV Khaneferre (PHARAOH) of 13th Dynasty + Tjan
17. Sebekhotep (Princess) of THEBES + Senebhanef, son of Renressonb
18. Mentuhotep (Queen) of EGYPT + Sekhemre-Sementawi Djehuti (PHARAOH) of EGYPT
19. Sekhemre-Se'ankhtawi Neferhotep (PHARAOH) of EGYPT
20. Sobekemsaf Sekhemre-Shedtawi (PHARAOH) of EGYPT + Nubkhas (Queen) of EGYPT
21. Inyotef VII (PHARAOH) at THEBES + Sobkemsaf (Sebekamzaf) of EGYPT (1635? BC - ?)
22. Sekenenre Tao I (PHARAOH) at THEBES + Tetisheri of THEBES
23. Sekenenre Tao II (King) of THEBES + Ahhotep (Ahotop) I (Queen) of EGYPT
24. Ahmose I (1st PHARAOH) of 18th Dynasty + Nefretiri (Queen) of EGYPT
25. Amenhotep I Djeserkare (PHARAOH) of EGYPT + Senisonb (Seneseneb) of EGYPT
26. Thutmose I (PHARAOH) of EGYPT (? - 1481? BC) + Amhose (Aahmes II) (Queen) of EGYPT
27. Hatshepsut (Queen & PHARAOH) of EGYPT (? - 1482 BC) + Thutmose (Tuthmosis) II (PHARAOH) of EGYPT
28. Meryetre Hatshepsut of EGYPT + Thutmose III `the Great' of EGYPT (Moses of the Bible)
29. Akheperure Amenhotep II THUTMOSID (PHARAOH) of EGYPT + Tio (Tiye Tiaa)
30. Menkheprure' Thutmose IV (PHARAOH) of EGYPT + Mutemwiya, daughter of Artatama (I; King) of MITANNI
31. Nebma'atre' Amenhotep III (PHARAOH) of EGYPT + Tiye-Nefertari (Tiy) of EGYPT (1382 BC - 1344 BC)
32. Akhenaton (Iknaton) (10th PHARAOH) of the 18th Dynasty EGYPT + Nefertiti (Chief Queen) of EGYPT
33. Meritaten (Royal Daughter) of EGYPT + Judah (Judas Juda) ibn JACOB, son of Jacob ibn ISAAC (King of GOSHEN)
34. Zerah (Zehrah Zarah Zare) ibn JUDAH + Electra the PLEIADE
35. Dardanus (Dara) (King) of ACADIA + Batea of TEUCRI
36. Erichthonius (King) of ACADIA (? - 1386? BC) + Astyoche of ACADIA

37.   Trois of ACADIA + Callirhoe (TEUCRI)
38.   Ilus (Ilyus) (King) of TROY (? - 1282? BC) + Eurydice
            (Eurydike) of TROY
39.   Priam Podarces (High King) of TROY (? - 1183? BC) + Hecuba
            (Hecabe) of PHRYGIA
40.   Troana Iluim of TROY + Memnon (Munon) of TROY (? - 1183?
            BC)
41.   Thor (Tror) (King) of THRACE + Sibil (Sif)
42.   Einridi LORIDESSON
43.   Vingethor (Vingethior) EINRIDISSON
44.   Moda (Mode) VINGENERSSON
45.   Maji (Magi) MODASSON
46.   Seskef (Sceaf Scaef)
47.   Bedwig (Bedvig; of SCEAF)
48.   Hwala (Hvala Hawala Guala)
49.   Berik (King) of the GOTHS (160? BC - ?) + Drott
50.   (NN) ... (NN)
51.   Giuki (King) of the GOTHS
52.   Guntharich (Gaderik) I (Over-king) of the GOTHS
53.   Filimer (Prince) of Baltic GOTHS
54.   Knivida (Prince) of West GOTHS (? - 249?)
55.   Ovida der BURGUNDER (? - 273+ (or 249+))
56.   Hilderic (King) of the BURGUNDIANS (? - 300+)
57.   Guntharich III (King) of the BURGUNDIANS
58.   Guntharich III of the BURGUNDIANS
59.   Gundomar (King) of the BURGUNDIANS + Hrotildis
60.   Gibihar (King) of the BURGUNDS (353? - 413?) +
            Childeramna de FRANCIE
61.   Gundicaire (Gundicus) (King) of BURGUNDY + Hrothildis von
            WESTGOTEN (414? - ?)
62.   Gunderic (King) of BURGUNDY (413? - 473+)
63.   Gundobad (Gundobald) (King) of the BURGUNDIANS +
            Swanhilde von XANTEN
64.   Sigismund (King) of the BURGUNDIANS + Theodogotho
65.   Wacho (9th King) of the LOMBARDS (490? - 539?) +
            Ostragotha (Austrigusa) of the GEPIDAE (504? - ?)
66.   Waldrada (Princess) of the LOMBARDS (528? - 571?) +
            Garibald I (AGILOFINGES ?) of BAVARIA
67.   Theudelinde of BAVARIA + Agilolf of the LOMBARDS
68.   (Miss) of TURIN + Rotbert I (King) of LONGOBARDS
69.   Gundwald (Duke) of ASTI (? - 613?) + Harinanda, daughter of

Rotbert I (King) of LONGOBARDS + Gundwald (Duke) of
ASTI (? - 613?)
70. Aripert I (Viscount) of LOMBARDY (? - 661?)
71. Berthari (21st King) of the LANGOBARDS
72. Kunibert (25th King) of the LANGOBARDS (? - 702?)
73. Liutpert (26th King) of the LANGOBARDS (? - 712?)
74. Theoderada (of the LOMBARDS) + Ansbrand (28th King) of
the LANGOBARDS (655? - 712?)
75. Sigiprand of the LOMBARDS
76. Ansbrand of LOMBARDS
77. Ansia of LOMBARDS (? - 774?) + Desiderio (last King) of
LOMBARDS (? - 774+)
78. Gerberga of LOMBARDY (? - 774) + Carloman II (Archduke)
of AUSTRASIA (747? - 771)
79. Kunigunde (Auberge) of AUSTRASIA + Adelgis (Count) of
PARMA (of SPOLETO-PARMA) (? - 836?)
80. Cunegonde (Princess) de VERMANDOIS + Bernard
(Bernhard; I) (King) of ITALY (Lombardy)
81. Pépin II, lord of Péronne + Rothaide de Bobbio
82. Pepin (I; Count) de SENLIS de VALOIS
83. (Miss) de SENLIS de VALOIS (845? - ?) + Berenger (Count) de
RENNES (? - 931)
84. Poppa (Poppaeia) de VALOIS (872? - ?) + Rollo (Hrolf Rollon
Rou Robert) `the Dane' RAGNVALDSSON
85. Guillaume (2nd Duke) of NORMANDY + Sprota de
BRETAGNE (concubine)
86. Richard I `the Fearless' (Count) of NORMANDY + Gunnora
(Gonnor) de CREPON
87. Richard II `the Good' of NORMANDY (963? - 1027) + Judith
(Princess) of BRITTANY
88. Robert II (Duke) of NORMANDY + Herleve (Salburpyr) de
FALAISE (1003? - 1050?)
89. WILLIAM the CONQUEROR (Duke) of NORMANDY + Matilda
(Maud) FLEMING (1032 - 1083 Caan)
90. Henry I BEAUCLERC (King) of ENGLAND + Matilda (Edith
Eagdith) `Atheling' STEWART of SCOTLAND
91. Matilda (Maud Augusta) the EMPRESS + Geoffrey V `the Fair'
(`Plantagenet')
92. Henry II (King) of ENGLAND + Eleanor (Duchess/Princess) of
AQUITAINE
93. John `Lackland' (King) of ENGLAND + Isabella (d'

ANGOULEME) TAILLEFER

94.   Eleanor (Alianor) of ENGLAND (1215? - 1275) + Simon V de MONTFORT (1208 - 4/8/1265)
95.   Eleanor de MONTFORT (1252 - 1282) + Llywellyn (II) ap GRUFFYDD (? - 1282)
96.   Catherine verch LLYWELLYN + Philip ap IFOR
97.   Eleanor (of ISCOED; GOCH) verch PHILIP + Thomas ap LLEWELLYN
98.   Lowri verch GRUFFUDD FYCHAN + Robert (Sir; of Emral) PULESTON (1358? - 1399?)
99.   Angharad PULESTON + Edward TREVOR ap DAFFYD (? - 1448?)
100. Otewell Worsley, Sir + Rose (TREVOR) verch EDWART
101. Joyce Worsley + Richard Lee II
102. Richard Lee III + Eleanor Burgoine
103. Geoffrey Lee, MP + Agnes Conyers
104. Reginald Lee + Dorothy Thurland
105. Gervase Lee of Nottinghamshire
106. Thomas Lee, of Ashfield + Margaret Mary Oscroft
107. Elizabeth Lee + Thomas Hanks
108. Robert Hanks + Margaret NLN
109. Peter Hanks I + Mary Bressie
110. Elinor Hanks + Robert Nelson
111. Rachael Nelson + Timothy Ragan
112. Timothy Reagan + Elizabeth Trigg
113. Richard Bazel Reagan + Cecelia Creppy
114. Richard Reagan + Phoebe Samples
115. Reuben Perry Reagan + Elizabeth Cagle
116. George Reagan + Emaline Garner
117. Marshall Reagan + Emma Rogers
118. Elzie Reagan + Delmar Raines
        ------- Gina Davis
              ------- Jackson Davis
        ------- Patricia Stuart
              ------- Bobby Caldwell
              ------- Jennifer Caldwell
        ------- Mike Raines
              ------- Leah Raines
              ------- Kendra Raines
              ------- Joshua Raines
              ------- Michael Raines

------- Frank Raines
      ------- Franklin Cody Raines
      ------- Kip Allen Raines
------- Richard Raines
      ------- Tyler Lee
      ------- Devin Lee
      ------- Emma Lundy

5

THE BYZANTINE (EASTERN ROMAN) LINEAGE

1. Mummu the Creator GOD + Nammu, Goddess of the Sea
2. Apsu, Ocean of Sweet Water + Tiamat, Ocean of Salt Water
3. Lahmu, The Primordial God + Lahamu, the Primordial GODDESS
4. Anshar, the Primordial God + Kishar, the Primordial GODDESS
5. Anu, GOD of the Sky + Ki Urash, GODDESS of the Earth
6. Enlil, GOD of Wind
7. El Shaddai, Supreme GOD of CANAAN + Atiratu, Semitic GODDESS of Fertility
8. Elohim, GOD of Israel
9. Adam, the First Man + Eve, the First Woman
10. Seth + Azura, his sister
11. Enosh (Henos Enos) ADANYA (3769 BC - 2864 BC) + Noham ADANYA, Daughter of Seth and Lilleth the Demoness
12. Cainan (Keinan) + Mualeleth ADANYA
13. Mahalalel ben KENAN + Dinah
14. Jared ben MAHALALEL (ADANYA) + Baraka ADANYA
15. Enoch (Henoch) ben JARED (3382 BC - 3017 BC) + Ednah ADANYA

16. Methusaleh (Mathusale) ben ENOCH + Ednah bint AZRAIL (ADANYA)
17. Laamech ibn METHUSALEH (3130? BC - 2353 BC) + Betenos (Ashmua) ADANYA
18. Noah (Noe) ibn LAMEK (2948? BC - 1998 BC) + Emzara (Coba)
19. Shem (Sceaf Sam Sem) ibn NOAH + Sedeqetelebab
20. Arphaxad (King) of ARRAPACHTIS + Arphaxad (King) of ARRAPACHTIS
21. Cainain the SEMITE + Melka (bint MADAI) of MEDES
22. Shelah (ben CAINAN) of CHALDEA + Mu'ak (Muak) ben KESED
23. Eber ibn NOAH (2454? BC - 277? BC - 1813? BC) + Azurad bint NEBROD
24. Pelag ben EBER (Shinar 2243? BC - 2004? BC) + Lomna bint SINA'AR
25. Heraclim + Shela
26. Abram + NN of UR
27. Edna bat 'ABRAM + Terah (Thare Terih) (King) of AGADE
28. Abraham (Avraham Ibrahim) of GENESIS + Hagar (Haggai) 'the Egyptian' Ishmael (Isma'il) ibn ABRAHAM + Ra'la (al-SAYYIDA) bint MUDAD
29. (NN) ... (NN) (many missing generations)
30. Aretas I (King) of NABATAEA (? - 145? BC)
31. Malichus of NABATAEA (? - 110? BC)
32. Aretas II of the ARABS (? - 96? BC)
33. Obodas I of the ARABS
34. Aretas III of the ARABS (? - 62? BC)
35. Cypros (I; the NABATAEAN)
36. Herod I (King) of JUDAEA (JUDEA) (73? BC - 4 BC) + Mariamne (HASMONEUS) of JUDAEA (? - 29 BC)
37. Aristobulus (Aristobulos I; IV) of JUDAEA (? - 7 BC)
38. Mariamne (IV) Arria
39. Mariamne Caecina Arria + Gaius Calpernius Piso (? - 65?)
40. Arrius Antoninus Calpernius PISO (37? - 119?) + Boionia Procilla Servilia
41. Pompeia Plotina Domitia Lucilla + Trajan (EMPEROR) of ROME (? - 117)
42. Domitia Lucilla Trajanus + Annius Verus
43. Marcus Aurelius Antonius (EMPEROR) of ROME + Annia Galeria FAUSTINA

44.   Marcus Annius Severus + Silvana
45.   Fabia Orestilla + Gordian I (Marcellus) (EMPEROR) of ROME
        (157 - 238)
46.   Maecia Faustina GORDIANA (? - 241?) + Junius Licinius
        BALBUS (? - 238+)
47.   Antonia Gordiana
48.   Flavius Eutropious of the GORDIANI (220? - ?) + Claudia
        Crispina
49.   Flavius Valerius Constantius I `Chlorus' of ROME + Helena
        (Augusta) (Saint) of the CROSS
50.   Constantine `the Great' (EMPEROR) of ROME + Flavia
        Maxima Fausta (? - 326?)
51.   Constantine `the Great' of ROME + Flavia Maxima Fausta (? -
        326?)
52.   Flavia Constantia Augusta (320? - 354?) + Flavius Claudius
        CONSTANTIUS Gallus
53.   Anastasia
54.   Gallus
55.   Anastasia (Arriana) CONSTANTINA + Pompeius of
        DYRRHACHIUM
56.   Flavius PAULUS (Consul) (? - 496+) + Magna Sabiniani
57.   Flavius PROBUS (Consul) (? - 502+) + daughter of Flavius
        Sabinianus
58.   Flavius Anastasius PAULUS PROBUS Sabinianus POMPEIUS +
        Theodora(?), daughter of Theodora
59.   Paulus of ARABISSO + Joanna of ARABISSA
60.   Maurice (EMPEROR) of the EAST (539? - 27/11/602)
61.   Julius of BYZANTIUM
62.   Georgia
63.   Juliana FLAVIA + Athanagild (II; King) of the VISIGOTHS
64.   Ardabast (Count/King) of the VISIGOTHS + Goda of the
        BURGUNDIANS
65.   Ervik (King) of the VISIGOTHS (? - 687) + Liubigotona
        (Liuvigotona) of the VISIGOTHS
66.   Aupais (of SPAIN)
67.   Charles Martel "The Hammer", Mayor of the Palace +
        Rotrude, Duchess of Austrasia
68.   Pépin III, King of the Franks + Bertha Broadfoot of Laon
69.   Charlemagne, Carolus 'Magnus', Rex Francorum & Imperator
        Romanorum + Hildegard of Vinzgouw

6

THE CAROLINGIAN LINEAGE

LINEAGE I (From Charlemagne)

1. CHARLEMAGNE, Carolus 'Magnus', Rex Francorum &
        Imperator Romanorum + Hildegard of Vinzgouw
2. "Pépin" Carloman, King of Italy + Mistress of Pepin
3. Bernard, King of Lombardy + Cunigundis (Cunegonde)
        (Princess) de VERMANDOIS
4. Pépin II, lord of Péronne + Rothaide de Bobbio
5. Pepin (I; Count) de SENLIS de VALOIS
6. (Miss) de SENLIS de VALOIS (845? - ?) + Berenger (Count) de
        RENNES (? - 931)
7. Poppa (Poppaeia) de VALOIS (872? - ?) + Rollo (Hrolf Rollon
        Rou Robert) `the Dane' RAGNVALDSSON
8. Guillaume (2nd Duke) of NORMANDY + Sprota de
        BRETAGNE (concubine)
9. Richard I `the Fearless' (Count) of NORMANDY + Gunnora
        (Gonnor) de CREPON
10. Richard II `the Good' of NORMANDY (963? - 1027) + Judith
        (Princess) of BRITTANY
11. Robert II (Duke) of NORMANDY + Herleve (Salburpyr) de

FALAISE (1003? - 1050?)
12. WILLIAM the CONQUEROR (Duke) of NORMANDY + Matilda (Maud) FLEMING (1032 - 1083 Caan)
13. Henry I BEAUCLERC (King) of ENGLAND + Matilda (Edith Eagdith) `Atheling' STEWART of SCOTLAND
14. Matilda (Maud Augusta) the EMPRESS + Geoffrey V `the Fair' (`Plantagenet')
15. Henry II (King) of ENGLAND + Eleanor (Duchess/Princess) of AQUITAINE
16. John `Lackland' (King) of ENGLAND + Isabella (d' ANGOULEME) TAILLEFER
17. Eleanor (Alianor) of ENGLAND (1215? - 1275) + Simon V de MONTFORT (1208 - 4/8/1265)
18. Eleanor de MONTFORT (1252 - 1282) + Llywellyn (II) ap GRUFFYDD (? - 1282)
19. Catherine verch LLYWELLYN + Philip ap IFOR
20. Eleanor (of ISCOED; GOCH) verch PHILIP + Thomas ap LLEWELLYN
21. Lowri verch GRUFFUDD FYCHAN + Robert (Sir; of Emral) PULESTON (1358? - 1399?)
22. Angharad PULESTON + Edward TREVOR ap DAFFYD (? - 1448?)
23. Otewell Worsley, Sir + Rose (TREVOR) verch EDWART
24. Joyce Worsley + Richard Lee II
25. Richard Lee III + Eleanor Burgoine
26. Geoffrey Lee, MP + Agnes Conyers
27. Reginald Lee + Dorothy Thurland
28. Gervase Lee of Nottinghamshire
29. Thomas Lee, of Ashfield + Margaret Mary Oscroft
30. Elizabeth Lee + Thomas Hanks
31. Robert Hanks + Margaret NLN
32. Peter Hanks I + Mary Bressie
33. Elinor Hanks + Robert Nelson
34. Rachael Nelson + Timothy Ragan
35. Timothy Reagan + Elizabeth Trigg
36. Richard Bazel Reagan + Cecelia Creppy
37. Richard Reagan + Phoebe Samples
38. Reuben Perry Reagan + Elizabeth Cagle
39. George Reagan + Emaline Garner
40. Marshall Reagan + Emma Rogers
41. Elzie Reagan + Delmar Raines

------- Gina Davis
    ------- Jackson Davis
------- Patricia Stuart
    ------- Bobby Caldwell
    ------- Jennifer Caldwell
------- Mike Raines
    ------- Leah Raines
    ------- Kendra Raines
    ------- Joshua Raines
    ------- Michael Raines
------- Frank Raines
    ------- Franklin Cody Raines
    ------- Kip Allen Raines
------- Richard Raines
    ------- Tyler Lee
    ------- Devin Lee
    ------- Emma Lundy

LINEAGE II

(Complete)

1. Mummu the Creator GOD + Nammu, Goddess of the Sea
2. Apsu, Ocean of Sweet Water + Tiamat, Ocean of Salt Water
3. Lahmu, The Primordial God + Lahamu, the Primordial GODDESS
4. Anshar, the Primordial God + Kishar, the Primordial GODDESS
5. Anu, GOD of the Sky + Ki Urash, GODDESS of the Earth
6. Enlil, GOD of Wind
7. El Shaddai, Supreme GOD of CANAAN + Atiratu, Semitic GODDESS of Fertility
8. Elohim, GOD of Israel
9. Adam, the First Man + Eve, the First Woman
10. Seth + Azura, his sister
11. Enosh (Henos Enos) ADANYA (3769 BC - 2864 BC) + Noham ADANYA, Daughter of Seth and Lilleth the Demoness
12. Cainan (Keinan) + Mualeleth ADANYA
13. Mahalalel ben KENAN + Dinah
14. Jared ben MAHALALEL (ADANYA) + Baraka ADANYA
15. Enoch (Henoch) ben JARED (3382 BC - 3017 BC) + Ednah

ADANYA

16. Methusaleh (Mathusale) ben ENOCH + Ednah bint AZRAIL (ADANYA)

17. Laamech ibn METHUSALEH (3130? BC - 2353 BC) + Betenos (Ashmua) ADANYA

18. Noah (Noe) ibn LAMEK (2948? BC - 1998 BC) + Emzara (Coba)

19. Shem (Sceaf Sam Sem) ibn NOAH + Sedeqetelebab

20. Arphaxad (King) of ARRAPACHTIS + Arphaxad (King) of ARRAPACHTIS

21. Cainain the SEMITE + Melka (bint MADAI) of MEDES

22. Shelah (ben CAINAN) of CHALDEA + Mu'ak (Muak) ben KESED

23. Eber ibn NOAH (2454? BC - 277? BC - 1813? BC) + Azurad bint NEBROD

24. Pelag ben EBER (Shinar 2243? BC - 2004? BC) + Lomna bint SINA'AR

25. Heraclim + Shela

26. Abram + NN of UR

27. Edna bat 'ABRAM + Terah (Thare Terih) (King) of AGADE

28. Abraham (Avraham Ibrahim) of GENESIS + Sarai (Sarah) (Princess) bint HARAN

29. Isaac ibn ABRAHAM (1922 BC - 1742 BC) + Rebekah (Rebecca) bint BETHEUL

30. Jacob ibn ISAAC (King of GOSHEN) + Leah (Lia) bint LABAN

31. Judah (Judas Juda) ibn JACOB + Tamar of KADESH (? - 1665? BC)

32. Perez (Phares) + Barayah (bas JACOB?)

33. Hezron ibn PHARES (Prince of JUDAH) + Ephratha bint MACHIR

34. Caleb ben HEZRON + Ephratha bint MACHIR

35. Hur (Jephunneh) ben CALEB + Miriam (the PROPHETESS) bat AMRAM

36. Salma ben HUR

37. Beth-Lehem

38. NNs of BETHLEHEM (some missing generations)

39. Ibzan of BETHLEHEM

40. (NN; 'Edal?; Abrias?) ben IBZAN

41. Abala (Habalith) + Jesse ben OBED (Bethlehem 1078? BC - ?)

42. David (1st King) of JUDAH & ISRAEL + Bathsheba (Bathshua) bat AMMIEL

43.   Solomon ben DAVID (2nd King) of ISRAEL (? - 930 BC) +
         Nicaule (Nicauli Tashere) of EGYPT
44.   Basemath bat SOLOMON + Ahimaaz the NAPHALITE
45.   Ana bat AHIMAAZ + Abia (Abijah) (4th King) of JUDAH
46.   Asa (Asaph) (5th King) of JUDEA + Azubah (Queen) of JUDEA
47.   Jehoshapat (6th King) of JUDAH + daughter of Omri
48.   Jehoram (Joram) (7th King) of JUDAH + Athalia of ISRAEL
         (9th Queen) of JUDAH
49.   Ozias (Ahaziah Ochozias) (8th King) of JUDAH + Zibiah of
         BEERSHEBA
50.   Josiah (I; 10th King) of JUDAH (871 BC - 796 BC) + Jehoaddin
         of JERUSALEM
51.   Amaziah (Amasias) (11th King) of JUDAH + Jecoliah of
         JERUSALEM
52.   Uzziah (Azariah) (12th King) of JUDAH + Jerusha of ISRAEL
53.   Joatham (Jotham) (13th King) of JUDAH + Ahio (Princess) bat
         AZRIKAM
54.   Achaz (Ahaz) (14th King) of JUDAH + Abijah bat ZECHARIAH
         (Heiress) of ISRAEL
55.   Ezechias (Hezekiah) (15th King) of JUDAH + Hephzibah bat
         ISAIAH
56.   Manasses ha-DAVID (Manasseh) (16th King) of JUDAH +
         Meshullemeth bat HARUZ of JOTBAH
57.   Amon ha-DAVID (17th King) of JUDAH + Jedidah bat ADAIAH
         of BOZKATH
58.   Josias (Josiah) ha-DAVID (18th King) of JUDAH + Zebidah
         (Zebudah; bat PEDAIAH) of RUMAH
59.   Johanan (Crown Prince) of JUDAH
60.   Tamar (Heiress) of the DAVIDIC Dynasty + Neri (Neriah) ha-
         DAVID
61.   Salathial (Shealtiel) ha-DAVID + poss. Hadast (Hetbath)
62.   Zorobabel ha-DAVID (Heir) of the DAVIDIC Dynasty +
         Rhodah (Princess) of PERSIA (? - 571? BC)
63.   Resa (Reza Rhesa) ha-DAVID
64.   Joanna (Joanan Yohannai Jehohanen) ben RESA
65.   Judah (Juda Joda Judas) ben JOANNA
66.   Joseph (Josech) ben JUDAH
67.   Semel ben JOSEPH
68.   Mattathias (Mathathias) ben SEMEL + daughter of Simon ha-
         KOHEN
69.   Maath ben MATTATHIAS ha-DAVID

70. Nagga ben MAATH
71. Esli ben NAGGA
72. Naum ben ESLI of JUDAH
73. Amos ben NAUM
74. Mattathias (Mathathias Mattathiah) ben AMOS
75. Joseph (Jose) ben MATTATHIAS
76. Janna (Janne Jannai Johanan) ben JOSEPH
77. Melchi (Melki) ben JANNA
78. Levi ben MELCHI
79. Matthat (Mathat) ben LEVI of ARIMATHEA + daughter of
     Eleazar
80. Joseph ben MATTHAT (Saint) of ARIMATHEA + Alyuba
81. Anna (Enygeus) of ARIMATHEA + Mandubratius ap LUD of
     BRITAIN
82. Boadicea (Queen) of ICENIANS (22? - 62?) + Prasutagus
     (King) of ICENIA (? - 61?)
83. Julia (Victoria) verch PRASUTAGUS of the ICENI + Meric
     (Marius Meurig Cyllin) of BRITONS (65? - 125?)
84. Coel I (Cole Coilus) (Old King Cole) King of BRITONS +
     Ystradwl (Stradwawl) of SILURIA
85. Lleurig (Lucius) MAWR (King) of EWYAS + Gladys (Gwladys)
     verch EURGEN of SILURIA
86. Gladys `the Younger' of BRITAIN (190? - ?) + Cadvan of
     CAMBRIA
87. Strada `the Fair' of COMBRIA + Coilus II (Coel Cole) of
     GLOUCESTER (by 232 - 305?)
88. Helena (Augusta) (Saint) of the CROSS + Flavius Valerius
     Constantius I of Rome
89. Constantine `the Great' of ROME + Flavia Maxima Fausta (? -
     326?)
90. Flavia Constantia Augusta (320? - 354?) + Flavius Claudius
     CONSTANTIUS Gallus
91. Anastasia
92. Gallus
93. Anastasia (Arriana) CONSTANTINA + Pompeius of
     DYRRHACHIUM
94. Flavius PAULUS (Consul) (? - 496+) + Magna Sabiniani
95. Flavius PROBUS (Consul) (? - 502+) + daughter of Flavius
     Sabinianus
96. Flavius Anastasius PAULUS PROBUS Sabinianus POMPEIUS +
     Theodora(?), daughter of Theodora

97.   Paulus of ARABISSO + Joanna of ARABISSA
98.   Maurice (EMPEROR) of the EAST (539? - 27/11/602)
99.   Julius of BYZANTIUM
100.   Georgia
101.   Juliana FLAVIA + Athanagild (II; King) of the VISIGOTHS
102.   Ardabast (Count/King) of the VISIGOTHS + Goda of the
           BURGUNDIANS
103.   Ervik (King) of the VISIGOTHS (? - 687) + Liubigotona
           (Liuvigotona) of the VISIGOTHS
104.   Aupais (of SPAIN)
105.   Charles Martel "The Hammer", Mayor of the Palace +
           Rotrude, Duchess of Austrasia
106.   Pépin III, King of the Franks + Bertha Broadfoot of Laon
107.   CHARLEMAGNE, Carolus 'Magnus', Rex Francorum &
           Imperator Romanorum + Hildegard of Vinzgouw
108.   "Pépin" Carloman, King of Italy + Mistress of Pepin
109.   Bernard, King of Lombardy + Cunigundis (Cunegonde)
           (Princess) de VERMANDOIS
110.   Pépin II, lord of Péronne + Rothaide de Bobbio
111.   Pepin (I; Count) de SENLIS de VALOIS
112.   (Miss) de SENLIS de VALOIS (845? - ?) + Berenger (Count) de
           RENNES (? - 931)
113.   Poppa (Poppaeia) de VALOIS (872? - ?) + Rollo (Hrolf Rollon
           Rou Robert) `the Dane' RAGNVALDSSON
114.   Guillaume (2nd Duke) of NORMANDY + Sprota de
           BRETAGNE (concubine)
115.   Richard I `the Fearless' (Count) of NORMANDY + Gunnora
           (Gonnor) de CREPON
116.   Richard II `the Good' of NORMANDY (963? - 1027) + Judith
           (Princess) of BRITTANY
117.   Robert II (Duke) of NORMANDY + Herleve (Salburpyr) de
           FALAISE (1003? - 1050?)
118.   WILLIAM the CONQUEROR (Duke) of NORMANDY + Matilda
           (Maud) FLEMING (1032 - 1083 Caan)
119.   Henry I BEAUCLERC (King) of ENGLAND + Matilda (Edith
           Eagdith) `Atheling' STEWART of SCOTLAND
120.   Matilda (Maud Augusta) the EMPRESS + Geoffrey V `the Fair'
           (`Plantagenet')
121.   Henry II (King) of ENGLAND + Eleanor (Duchess/Princess) of
           AQUITAINE
122.   John `Lackland' (King) of ENGLAND + Isabella (d'

ANGOULEME) TAILLEFER
123. Eleanor (Alianor) of ENGLAND (1215? - 1275) + Simon V de
     MONTFORT (1208 - 4/8/1265)
124. Eleanor de MONTFORT (1252 - 1282) + Llywellyn (II) ap
     GRUFFYDD (? - 1282)
125. Catherine verch LLYWELLYN + Philip ap IFOR
126. Eleanor (of ISCOED; GOCH) verch PHILIP + Thomas ap
     LLEWELLYN
127. Lowri verch GRUFFUDD FYCHAN + Robert (Sir; of Emral)
     PULESTON (1358? - 1399?)
128. Angharad PULESTON + Edward TREVOR ap DAFFYD (? -
     1448?)
129. Otewell Worsley, Sir + Rose (TREVOR) verch EDWART
130. Joyce Worsley + Richard Lee II
131. Richard Lee III + Eleanor Burgoine
132. Geoffrey Lee, MP + Agnes Conyers
133. Reginald Lee + Dorothy Thurland
134. Gervase Lee of Nottinghamshire
135. Thomas Lee, of Ashfield + Margaret Mary Oscroft
136. Elizabeth Lee + Thomas Hanks
137. Robert Hanks + Margaret NLN
138. Peter Hanks I + Mary Bressie
139. Elinor Hanks + Robert Nelson
140. Rachael Nelson + Timothy Ragan
141. Timothy Reagan + Elizabeth Trigg
142. Richard Bazel Reagan + Cecelia Creppy
143. Richard Reagan + Phoebe Samples
144. Reuben Perry Reagan + Elizabeth Cagle
145. George Reagan + Emaline Garner
146. Marshall Reagan + Emma Rogers
147. Elzie Reagan + Delmar Raines
     ------- Gina Davis
        ------- Jackson Davis
     ------- Patricia Stuart
        ------- Bobby Caldwell
        ------- Jennifer Caldwell
     ------- Mike Raines
        ------- Leah Raines
        ------- Kendra Raines
        ------- Joshua Raines
        ------- Michael Raines

------- Frank Raines
     ------- Franklin Cody Raines
     ------- Kip Allen Raines
------- Richard Raines
     ------- Tyler Lee
     ------- Devin Lee
     ------- Emma Lundy

7

THE CELTIC-GALLIC LINEAGE

1. Mummu the Creator GOD + Nammu, Goddess of the Sea
2. Apsu, Ocean of Sweet Water + Tiamat, Ocean of Salt Water
3. Lahmu, The Primordial God + Lahamu, the Primordial GODDESS
4. Anshar, the Primordial God + Kishar, the Primordial GODDESS
5. Anu, GOD of the Sky + Ki Urash, GODDESS of the Earth
6. Enlil, GOD of Wind
7. El Shaddai, Supreme GOD of CANAAN + Atiratu, Semitic GODDESS of Fertility
8. Elohim, GOD of Israel
9. Adam, the First Man + Eve, the First Woman
10. Seth + Azura, his sister
11. Enosh (Henos Enos) ADANYA (3769 BC - 2864 BC) + Noham ADANYA, Daughter of Seth and Lilleth the Demoness
12. Cainan (Keinan) + Mualeleth ADANYA
13. Mahalalel ben KENAN + Dinah
14. Jared ben MAHALALEL (ADANYA) + Baraka ADANYA
15. Enoch (Henoch) ben JARED (3382 BC - 3017 BC) + Ednah ADANYA

16.   Methusaleh (Mathusale) ben ENOCH + Ednah bint AZRAIL
          (ADANYA)
17.   Laamech ibn METHUSALEH (3130? BC - 2353 BC) + Betenos
          (Ashmua) ADANYA
18.   Noah (Noe) ibn LAMEK (2948? BC - 1998 BC) + Emzara
          (Coba)
19.   Japhet (Iaphet) ibn NOAH
20.   Samothes (1st King) of CELTICA
21.   Magus (King) of BRITONS
22.   Sarronius (King) of BRITONS
23.   Druis (King) of BRITONS
24.   Bardus (King) of SAMOTHEA (BRITONS)
25.   Longhus (King) of CELTS
26.   Vardus II (King) of CELTS
27.   Lucus (King) of CELTS
28.   (NN) ... (NN) (Kings) of CELTS
29.   Narbos CELTAE (of CELTS)
30.   Galatea Keltine (Queen) of CELTS
31.   Albiorix `Galates' (King) of CELTS
32.   Arbonus (King) of CELTS
33.   Lugdus of GAUL
34.   Beligios of GAUL
35.   Jasius of GAUL
36.   Janigenas of GAUL
37.   Allobrox (King) of CELTS
38.   Romus of GAUL
39.   Paris of GAUL
40.   Lemannus of GAUL
41.   Olbius of GAUL
42.   Galates II (King of GAULS)
43.   (NN) ... (NN) (some missing generations)
44.   Ambigatus `the Great' (King) in GAUL
45.   (NN) ... (NN) in GAUL (few missing generations)
46.   Galates III (King) in GAUL
47.   Namnes (King) in GAUL
48.   (NN) ... (NN) in GAUL (few missing generations)
49.   Akichorix `the Great' (King) in GAUL (? - 300+ BC)
50.   Brennus (Prince) in GAUL
51.   Eporedorix (King) in GAUL
52.   Concolitanus (King) in GAUL (? - 225? BC)
53.   Aritasgix (King) in GAUL + Chiomara

54. Luxovinus (King) in GAUL + Brixia (Princess) of BRITONS
55. Moritasgus (King) in GAUL
56. Bituitus (King) in GAUL (? - 122+ BC)
57. Congentiatus (King) in GAUL
58. Divitaticus (King) of GAUL (? - 58 BC)
59. Celtillos (100? BC - ?) + daughter of Fonteius (Governor) of
        GAUL (? - 76+ BC)
60. Vercingetorix (King) of ARVERNI + Cassandra
61. Verica Cassandra
62. Cymbeline (King) of BRITONS
63. Aviragus (King) of the BRITONS
64. Meric (Marius Meurig Cyllin) of BRITONS (65? - 125?) + Julia
        (Victoria) verch PRASUTAGUS of the ICENI
65. Coel I (Cole Coilus) (Old King Cole) King of BRITONS +
        Ystradwl (Stradwawl) of SILURIA
66. Lleurig (Lucius) MAWR (King) of EWYAS + Gladys (Gwladys)
        verch EURGEN of SILURIA
67. Gladys `the Younger' of BRITAIN (190? - ?) + Cadvan of
        CAMBRIA
68. Strada `the Fair' of COMBRIA + Coilus II (Coel Cole) of
        GLOUCESTER (by 232 - 305?)
69. Helena (Augusta) (Saint) of the CROSS + Flavius Valerius
        Constantius I of Rome
70. Constantine `the Great' of ROME + Flavia Maxima Fausta (? -
        326?)
71. Flavia Constantia Augusta (320? - 354?) + Flavius Claudius
        CONSTANTIUS Gallus
72. Anastasia
73. Gallus
74. Anastasia (Arriana) CONSTANTINA + Pompeius of
        DYRRHACHIUM
75. Flavius PAULUS (Consul) (? - 496+) + Magna Sabiniani
76. Flavius PROBUS (Consul) (? - 502+) + daughter of Flavius
        Sabinianus
77. Flavius Anastasius PAULUS PROBUS Sabinianus POMPEIUS +
        Theodora(?), daughter of Theodora
78. Paulus of ARABISSO + Joanna of ARABISSA
79. Maurice (EMPEROR) of the EAST (539? - 27/11/602)
80. Julius of BYZANTIUM
81. Georgia
82. Juliana FLAVIA + Athanagild (II; King) of the VISIGOTHS

83.   Ardabast (Count/King) of the VISIGOTHS + Goda of the
           BURGUNDIANS
84.   Ervik (King) of the VISIGOTHS (? - 687) + Liubigotona
           (Liuvigotona) of the VISIGOTHS
85.   Aupais (of SPAIN)
86.   Charles Martel "The Hammer", Mayor of the Palace +
           Rotrude, Duchess of Austrasia
87.   Pépin III, King of the Franks + Bertha Broadfoot of Laon
88.   CHARLEMAGNE, Carolus 'Magnus', Rex Francorum &
           Imperator Romanorum + Hildegard of Vinzgouw
89.   "Pépin" Carloman, King of Italy + Mistress of Pepin
90.   Bernard, King of Lombardy + Cunigundis (Cunegonde)
           (Princess) de VERMANDOIS
91.   Pépin II, lord of Péronne + Rothaide de Bobbio
92.   Pepin (I; Count) de SENLIS de VALOIS
93.   (Miss) de SENLIS de VALOIS (845? - ?) + Berenger (Count) de
           RENNES (? - 931)
94.   Poppa (Poppaeia) de VALOIS (872? - ?) + Rollo (Hrolf Rollon
           Rou Robert) `the Dane' RAGNVALDSSON
95.   Guillaume (2nd Duke) of NORMANDY + Sprota de
           BRETAGNE (concubine)
96.   Richard I `the Fearless' (Count) of NORMANDY + Gunnora
           (Gonnor) de CREPON
97.   Richard II `the Good' of NORMANDY (963? - 1027) + Judith
           (Princess) of BRITTANY
98.   Robert II (Duke) of NORMANDY + Herleve (Salburpyr) de
           FALAISE (1003? - 1050?)
99.   WILLIAM the CONQUEROR (Duke) of NORMANDY + Matilda
           (Maud) FLEMING (1032 - 1083 Caan)
100.   Henry I BEAUCLERC (King) of ENGLAND + Matilda (Edith
           Eagdith) `Atheling' STEWART of SCOTLAND
101.   Matilda (Maud Augusta) the EMPRESS + Geoffrey V `the Fair'
           (`Plantagenet')
102.   Henry II (King) of ENGLAND + Eleanor (Duchess/Princess) of
           AQUITAINE
103.   John `Lackland' (King) of ENGLAND + Isabella (d'
           ANGOULEME) TAILLEFER
104.   Eleanor (Alianor) of ENGLAND (1215? - 1275) + Simon V de
           MONTFORT (1208 - 4/8/1265)
105.   Eleanor de MONTFORT (1252 - 1282) + Llywellyn (II) ap
           GRUFFYDD (? - 1282)

106. Catherine verch LLYWELLYN + Philip ap IFOR
107. Eleanor (of ISCOED; GOCH) verch PHILIP + Thomas ap
        LLEWELLYN
108. Lowri verch GRUFFUDD FYCHAN + Robert (Sir; of Emral)
        PULESTON (1358? - 1399?)
109. Angharad PULESTON + Edward TREVOR ap DAFFYD (? -
        1448?)
110. Otewell Worsley, Sir + Rose (TREVOR) verch EDWART
111. Joyce Worsley + Richard Lee II
112. Richard Lee III + Eleanor Burgoine
113. Geoffrey Lee, MP + Agnes Conyers
114. Reginald Lee + Dorothy Thurland
115. Gervase Lee of Nottinghamshire
116. Thomas Lee, of Ashfield + Margaret Mary Oscroft
117. Elizabeth Lee + Thomas Hanks
118. Robert Hanks + Margaret NLN
119. Peter Hanks I + Mary Bressie
120. Elinor Hanks + Robert Nelson
121. Rachael Nelson + Timothy Ragan
122. Timothy Reagan + Elizabeth Trigg
123. Richard Bazel Reagan + Cecelia Creppy
124. Richard Reagan + Phoebe Samples
125. Reuben Perry Reagan + Elizabeth Cagle
126. George Reagan + Emaline Garner
127. Marshall Reagan + Emma Rogers
128. Elzie Reagan + Delmar Raines
        ------- Gina Davis
            ------- Jackson Davis
        ------- Patricia Stuart
            ------- Bobby Caldwell
            ------- Jennifer Caldwell
        ------- Mike Raines
            ------- Leah Raines
            ------- Kendra Raines
            ------- Joshua Raines
            ------- Michael Raines
        ------- Frank Raines
            ------- Franklin Cody Raines
            ------- Kip Allen Raines
        ------- Richard Raines
            ------- Tyler Lee

------- Devin Lee
------- Emma Lundy

62

8

THE EGYPTIAN-ROMAN LINEAGE

1. Sesostris + Nefret
2. Amenemhat I Sehetepibre (Founder) of 12th Dynasty + Nefrutotenen
3. Sesotris I Kheperkare (PHARAOH) of EGYPT (? - 1928? BC) + Nefrusheri (Princess) of EGYPT
4. Amenemhat (Ammenemes) II Nubkaure (PHARAOH) of EGYPT + Keminnub (Queen) of EGYPT
5. Sesotris II Khakheperre (PHARAOH) of EGYPT + Nofret of EGYPT
6. Sesotris III Khakaure of EGYPT + Sebekshedty-Neferu (Queen) of EGYPT
7. Amenemhat III Nemare (PHARAOH) of EGYPT + Sebeknefru (Queen) of EGYPT
8. Amenemhat (Ammenemes) IV (PHARAOH) of EGYPT
9. Wegaf (PHARAOH) of 13th Dynasty + daughter of Amenemhet IV
10. Ameny Intef (Inyotef) IV (PHARAOH) of EGYPT
11. Hor (PHARAOH) of EGYPT (? - 1760? BC)
12. Sobekhotep II (PHARAOH) of EGYPT (? - 1750? BC)
13. Khendjer (PHARAOH) of EGYPT (? - 1747? BC)

14. Sobekhotep III (PHARAOH) of EGYPT (? - 1745? BC)
15. Neferhotep I (PHARAOH) of EGYPT
16. Sobekhotep IV Khaneferre (PHARAOH) of 13th Dynasty + Tjan
17. Sebekhotep (Princess) of THEBES + Senebhanef, son of Renressonb
18. Mentuhotep (Queen) of EGYPT + Sekhemre-Sementawi Djehuti (PHARAOH) of EGYPT
19. Sekhemre-Se'ankhtawi Neferhotep (PHARAOH) of EGYPT
20. Sobekemsaf Sekhemre-Shedtawi (PHARAOH) of EGYPT + Nubkhas (Queen) of EGYPT
21. Inyotef VII (PHARAOH) at THEBES + Sobkemsaf (Sebekamzaf) of EGYPT (1635? BC - ?)
22. Sekenenre Tao I (PHARAOH) at THEBES + Tetisheri of THEBES
23. Sekenenre Tao II (King) of THEBES + Ahhotep (Ahotop) I (Queen) of EGYPT
24. Ahmose I (1st PHARAOH) of 18th Dynasty + Nefretiri (Queen) of EGYPT
25. Amenhotep I Djeserkare (PHARAOH) of EGYPT + Senisonb (Seneseneb) of EGYPT
26. Thutmose I (PHARAOH) of EGYPT (? - 1481? BC) + Amhose (Aahmes II) (Queen) of EGYPT
27. Hatshepsut (Queen & PHARAOH) of EGYPT (? - 1482 BC) + Thutmose (Tuthmosis) II (PHARAOH) of EGYPT
28. Meryetre Hatshepsut of EGYPT + Thutmose III `the Great' of EGYPT (Moses of the Bible)
29. Akheperure Amenhotep II THUTMOSID (PHARAOH) of EGYPT + Tio (Tiye Tiaa)
30. Menkheprure' Thutmose IV (PHARAOH) of EGYPT + Mutemwiya, daughter of Artatama (I; King) of MITANNI
31. Nebma'atre' Amenhotep III (PHARAOH) of EGYPT + Tiye-Nefertari (Tiy) of EGYPT (1382 BC - 1344 BC)
32. Akhenaton (Iknaton) (10th PHARAOH) of 18th Dynasty EGYPT + Nefertiti (Chief Queen) of EGYPT
33. Meritaten (Royal Daughter) of EGYPT + Judah (Judas Juda) ibn JACOB, son of Jacob ibn ISAAC (King of GOSHEN)
34. Zerah (Zehrah Zarah Zare) ibn JUDAH + Electra the PLEIADE
35. Dardanus (Dara) (King) of ACADIA + Batea of TEUCRI
36. Erichthonius (King) of ACADIA (? - 1386? BC) + Astyoche of ACADIA

37.   Trois of ACADIA + Callirhoe (TEUCRI)
38.   Assaracus (Ascaoracus) the DARDANIAN + Hieromneme
39.   Capys (Capis Capps) the DARDANIAN
40.   Anchises the DARDANIAN + Themiste of TROY
41.   Aeneas `the Dardanian' (King) of LATIUM + Lavinia of
          LATIUM
42.   Iulus ASCANIUS (founder & 1st King) of ALBA LONGA +
          Roma (wife of Iulus Ascanius)
43.   Jullus (Julus) of ROME
44.   Lucius JULIUS Iullii (Julus)
45.   Caius Julius Iullii
46.   Caius Julius Iullii
47.   Caius JULIUS Iullii
48.   Lucius Julius Iullus (Julus)
49.   Caius JULIUS Iullus
50.   Vopiscus Julius Iullus
51.   Lucius Julius Iullus
52.   Lucius JULIUS Iullus
53.   Lucius Julius Iullus
54.   Lucius Julius (Libo) Iullus + Caecilia Metellus Macedonicus
55.   Lucius Julius Caesar (? - 183+ BC)
56.   Lucius JULIUS Caesar (? - 166 BC)
57.   Sextus Julius CAESAR (? - 147 BC)
58.   Gaius JULIUS CAESAR
59.   Gaius Julias (II) CAESAR + Marcia
60.   Gaius JULIUS Caesar (Praetor) of ROME + Aurelia COTTA (? -
          54 BC)
61.   Julia I Minor (? - 51? BC) + Marcus ATIUS Balbus (? - 58 BC)
62.   Atia Maior of ROME (85? BC - 43? BC) + Gaius (IV) OCTAVIUS
          (Praetor) of ROME (? - 59? BC)
63.   Octavia `the Younger' THURINIA (69? BC - 11? BC) + Marcus
          ANTONIUS (Triumvir of ROME) (83 BC - 30 BC)
64.   Antonia Minor `the Younger' Augusta + Nero Claudius
          DRUSUS (Germanicus)
65.   Claudius I (EMPEROR) of ROME + Aemilia LEPIDA (? - 26)
66.   Genuissa (Venessa Julia) Claudia of ROME (? - 50?) +
          Aviragus (King) of the BRITONS (15? - 74? Avalon?)
67.   Meric (Marius Meurig Cyllin) of BRITONS (65? - 125?) + Julia
          (Victoria) verch PRASUTAGUS of the ICENI
68.   Coel I (Cole Coilus) (Old King Cole) King of BRITONS +
          Ystradwl (Stradwawl) of SILURIA

69. Lleurig (Lucius) MAWR (King) of EWYAS + Gladys (Gwladys) verch EURGEN of SILURIA

70. Gladys `the Younger' of BRITAIN (190? - ?) + Cadvan of CAMBRIA

71. Strada `the Fair' of COMBRIA + Coilus II (Coel Cole) of GLOUCESTER (by 232 - 305?)

72. Helena (Augusta) (Saint) of the CROSS + Flavius Valerius Constantius I of Rome

73. Constantine `the Great' of ROME + Flavia Maxima Fausta (? - 326?)

74. Flavia Constantia Augusta (320? - 354?) + Flavius Claudius CONSTANTIUS Gallus

75. Anastasia

76. Gallus

77. Anastasia (Arriana) CONSTANTINA + Pompeius of DYRRHACHIUM

78. Flavius PAULUS (Consul) (? - 496+) + Magna Sabiniani

79. Flavius PROBUS (Consul) (? - 502+) + daughter of Flavius Sabinianus

80. Flavius Anastasius PAULUS PROBUS Sabinianus POMPEIUS + Theodora(?), daughter of Theodora

81. Paulus of ARABISSO + Joanna of ARABISSA

82. Maurice (EMPEROR) of the EAST (539? - 27/11/602)

83. Julius of BYZANTIUM

84. Georgia

85. Juliana FLAVIA + Athanagild (II; King) of the VISIGOTHS

86. Ardabast (Count/King) of the VISIGOTHS + Goda of the BURGUNDIANS

87. Ervik (King) of the VISIGOTHS (? - 687) + Liubigotona (Liuvigotona) of the VISIGOTHS

88. Aupais (of SPAIN)

89. Charles Martel "The Hammer", Mayor of the Palace + Rotrude, Duchess of Austrasia

90. Pépin III, King of the Franks + Bertha Broadfoot of Laon

91. CHARLEMAGNE, Carolus 'Magnus', Rex Francorum & Imperator Romanorum + Hildegard of Vinzgouw

92. "Pépin" Carloman, King of Italy + Mistress of Pepin

93. Bernard, King of Lombardy + Cunigundis (Cunegonde) (Princess) de VERMANDOIS

94. Pépin II, lord of Péronne + Rothaide de Bobbio

95. Pepin (I; Count) de SENLIS de VALOIS

96. (Miss) de SENLIS de VALOIS (845? - ?) + Berenger (Count) de RENNES (? - 931)
97. Poppa (Poppaeia) de VALOIS (872? - ?) + Rollo (Hrolf Rollon Rou Robert) `the Dane' RAGNVALDSSON
98. Guillaume (2nd Duke) of NORMANDY + Sprota de BRETAGNE (concubine)
99. Richard I `the Fearless' (Count) of NORMANDY + Gunnora (Gonnor) de CREPON
100. Richard II `the Good' of NORMANDY (963? - 1027) + Judith (Princess) of BRITTANY
101. Robert II (Duke) of NORMANDY + Herleve (Salburpyr) de FALAISE (1003? - 1050?)
102. WILLIAM the CONQUEROR (Duke) of NORMANDY + Matilda (Maud) FLEMING (1032 - 1083 Caan)
103. Henry I BEAUCLERC (King) of ENGLAND + Matilda (Edith Eagdith) `Atheling' STEWART of SCOTLAND
104. Matilda (Maud Augusta) the EMPRESS + Geoffrey V `the Fair' (`Plantagenet')
105. Henry II (King) of ENGLAND + Eleanor (Duchess/Princess) of AQUITAINE
106. John `Lackland' (King) of ENGLAND + Isabella (d' ANGOULEME) TAILLEFER
107. Eleanor (Alianor) of ENGLAND (1215? - 1275) + Simon V de MONTFORT (1208 - 4/8/1265)
108. Eleanor de MONTFORT (1252 - 1282) + Llywellyn (II) ap GRUFFYDD (? - 1282)
109. Catherine verch LLYWELLYN + Philip ap IFOR
110. Eleanor (of ISCOED; GOCH) verch PHILIP + Thomas ap LLEWELLYN
111. Lowri verch GRUFFUDD FYCHAN + Robert (Sir; of Emral) PULESTON (1358? - 1399?)
112. Angharad PULESTON + Edward TREVOR ap DAFFYD (? - 1448?)
113. Otewell Worsley, Sir + Rose (TREVOR) verch EDWART
114. Joyce Worsley + Richard Lee II
115. Richard Lee III + Eleanor Burgoine
116. Geoffrey Lee, MP + Agnes Conyers
117. Reginald Lee + Dorothy Thurland
118. Gervase Lee of Nottinghamshire
119. Thomas Lee, of Ashfield + Margaret Mary Oscroft
120. Elizabeth Lee + Thomas Hanks

121.   Robert Hanks + Margaret NLN
122.   Peter Hanks I + Mary Bressie
123.   Elinor Hanks + Robert Nelson
124.   Rachael Nelson + Timothy Ragan
125.   Timothy Reagan + Elizabeth Trigg
126.   Richard Bazel Reagan + Cecelia Creppy
127.   Richard Reagan + Phoebe Samples
128.   Reuben Perry Reagan + Elizabeth Cagle
129.   George Reagan + Emaline Garner
130.   Marshall Reagan + Emma Rogers
131.   Elzie Reagan + Delmar Raines
       ------- Gina Davis
              ------- Jackson Davis
       ------- Patricia Stuart
              ------- Bobby Caldwell
              ------- Jennifer Caldwell
       ------- Mike Raines
              ------- Leah Raines
              ------- Kendra Raines
              ------- Joshua Raines
              ------- Michael Raines
       ------- Frank Raines
              ------- Franklin Cody Raines
              ------- Kip Allen Raines
       ------- Richard Raines
              ------- Tyler Lee
              ------- Devin Lee
              ------- Emma Lundy

9

THE EGYPTIAN-TROJAN LINEAGE

1. Ptah, Creator GOD + Sekhmet, GODDESS of Destruction
2. Ra, GOD of the Sun
3. Thoth, GOD of Wisdom + Maat, GODDESS of Universal Order
4. Shu, GOD of Wind + Tefnut, GODDESS of Moisture
5. Geb, GOD of the Earth + Nut, GODDESS of the Sky
6. Osiris, GOD of Egypt + Isis, GODDESS of EGYPT
7. Kenkenes Horus (1st PHARAOH) of EGYPT
8. (NN) ... (NN) in EGYPT (many missing generations)
9. Telegonus (PHARAOH) of EGYPT + Io (the NYMPH) of ARGOS
10. Epaphus (PHARAOH) of EGYPT + Memphis, daughter of the NILE
11. Libya (Queen) of EGYPT + Poseidon (the OLYMPIAN; GOD of the Sea)
12. Belus (King) of EGYPT + Anchinoe of EGYPT, daughter of the NILE
13. Aegyptus (King) of EGYPT + Argyphia
14. Lynceus (I; King) of ARGOS + Hypermnestra the DANAID
15. Abas (II; King) of ARGOS (& Abae) + Aglaia of ARGOS
16. Acrisius (King) of ARGOS + Eurydice of LACEDAEMON
17. Danae of ARGOS + Proetus (King) of TIRYNS (& ARGOS)

18.   Perseus of MYCENAE + Andromeda of ETHIOPIA
19.   Alcaeus of MYCENAE + Astydamia (II) of PISA
20.   Amphitryon of MYCENAE + Alcmena of MYCENAE
21.   Heracles (ALCIDES) of THEBES + Echidna
22.   Scythes (1st King) of SCYTHIA
23.   daughter of Scythes + Helenus of TROY (King of the
            SCYTHIANS)
24.   Genger of the SCYTHIANS
25.   Esdron the TROJAN
26.   Gelio the TROJAN
27.   Bosabiliano (Basabelian I) the TROJAN
28.   Plaserio (Plaserius I) the TROJAN
29.   Plesron (King of CIMMERIANS)
30.   Eliacor the TROJAN
31.   Gaberiano (Zaberian) the TROJAN
32.   Plaserius II the TROJAN
33.   Antenor I the TROJAN
34.   Priam II Trianus the TROJAN
35.   Helenus II the TROJAN
36.   Plesron II the TROJAN
37.   Basabelian (Basabiliano) II the TROJAN
38.   Alexandre the TROJAN
39.   Priam III of the CIMMERIANS
40.   Gentilanor (Prince) of the CIMMERIANS
41.   Almadius (King) of the CIMMERIANS
42.   Dilulius I (King) of the CIMMERIANS
43.   Helenus III (King) of the CIMMERIANS
44.   Plaserius (Plaserio) III (King) of the CIMMERIANS
45.   Dilulius (Diluglio) II (King) of the CIMMERIANS
46.   Marcomir (King) of the CIMMERIANS
47.   Priam IV (King) of the CIMMERIANS
48.   Helenus IV (King) of the CIMMERIANS
49.   Antenor I (II; King) of the CIMMERIANS (? - 433? BC)
50.   Marcomir I (King) of SICAMBRI (? - 412? BC)
51.   Antenor II (III; King) of SICAMBRI (? - 384? BC) + Cambra
52.   Helenus V (King) of SICAMBRI
53.   Diocles (King) of SICAMBRI
54.   Bassanus Magnus (King) of SICAMBRI
55.   Clodimir I (King) of SICAMBRI
56.   Nicanor I (King) of SICAMBRI
57.   Marcomir II (King) of SICAMBRI

58.   Clodius I (King) of SICAMBRI
59.   Antenor III (King) of SICAMBRI
60.   Clodimir II (King) of SICAMBRI (? - 123? BC)
61.   Merodachus (King) of SICAMBRI (? - 95? BC)
62.   Cassander (King) of SICAMBRI
63.   Antharius (King) of the SICAMBRI (77? BC - 36? BC)
64.   Francus (King) of the WEST FRANKS (57? BC - 5?)
65.   Clodius II (King) of the FRANKS (37? BC - 20?)
66.   Marcomir III (King) of the FRANKS (17? BC - 50?)
67.   Clodomir III (King) of the FRANKS
68.   Antenor IV (King) of the WEST FRANKS
69.   Ratherius (King) of the FRANKS
70.   Richemer I (King) of FRANKS + Ascyla of the FRANKS
71.   Odomir (Odomar) (King) of FRANKS
72.   Marcomir IV (King) of FRANKS + Althildis (Princess) of
            BRITAIN
73.   Clodimir IV (King) of FRANKS (by 125 - 166) + Hafilda
            (Princess) of the RUGIJ (? - 179?)
74.   Farabert (King) of FRANKS (by 145 - 186?)
75.   Sunno (Huano Hunno) (King) of FRANKS (165? - 213)
76.   Childeric (Hilderic) (King) of FRANKS (185? - 253?)
77.   Bartherus (King) of FRANKS (? - 272)
78.   Clodius (III) of FRANKS
79.   Walter (King) of the EAST FRANKS
80.   Dagobert I (King) of FRANKS (? - 317?)
81.   Genebald (I; 1st Duke) of the EAST FRANKS + Athildis
82.   Dagobert II (Duke) of EAST FRANKS
83.   Clodius (I; IV; Duke) of EAST FRANKS + Blesinde (Princess)
            of the SUEVI (350? - 403?)
84.   Blesinde of the FRANKS (375? - by 418) + Theodemer des
            FRANCS RIPUAIRES (374? - 15/8/414)
85.   Clovis (Chlodion) the RIPARIAN of COLOGNE + Ildegonde of
            the FRANKS
86.   Childebert (King) of COLOGNE + Amalberge of the FRANKS
87.   Sigebert (Siegbert) (I; King) of COLOGNE
88.   Cloderic `the Parricide' (King) of COLOGNE + Agilofinginne of
            the AGILOFING
89.   Munderic of VITRY-EN-PERTHOIS + Arthemia(?) of GENEVA
            (503? - 530+)
90.   Mummolin des FRANCS RIPUAIRES (505? - 558?)
91.   Baudgise II (Duke) of AQUITAINE + Oda (Saint) of SAVOY

(562? - 611+)

92.   Saint Arnoul, bishop of Metz + Saint Dode (Clotilde) of Metz

93.   Ansigisel of Metz, Mayor of the Palace of Austrasia + Saint
        Beggue of Austrasia

94.   Pépin ll "the Fat"; d'Héristal, Mayor of the Palace of Austrasia
        + Alpaïde (Alpais)

95.   Charles Martel "The Hammer", Mayor of the Palace +
        Rotrude, Duchess of Austrasia

96.   Pépin III, King of the Franks + Bertha Broadfoot of Laon

97.   CHARLEMAGNE, Carolus 'Magnus', Rex Francorum &
        Imperator Romanorum + Hildegard of Vinzgouw

98.   "Pépin" Carloman, King of Italy + Mistress of Pepin

99.   Bernard, King of Lombardy + Cunigundis (Cunegonde)
        (Princess) de VERMANDOIS

100.   Pépin II, lord of Péronne + Rothaide de Bobbio

101.   Pepin (I; Count) de SENLIS de VALOIS

102.   (Miss) de SENLIS de VALOIS (845? - ?) + Berenger (Count) de
        RENNES (? - 931)

103.   Poppa (Poppaeia) de VALOIS (872? - ?) + Rollo (Hrolf Rollon
        Rou Robert) `the Dane' RAGNVALDSSON

104.   Guillaume (2nd Duke) of NORMANDY + Sprota de
        BRETAGNE (concubine)

105.   Richard I `the Fearless' (Count) of NORMANDY + Gunnora
        (Gonnor) de CREPON

106.   Richard II `the Good' of NORMANDY (963? - 1027) + Judith
        (Princess) of BRITTANY

107.   Robert II (Duke) of NORMANDY + Herleve (Salburpyr) de
        FALAISE (1003? - 1050?)

108.   WILLIAM the CONQUEROR (Duke) of NORMANDY + Matilda
        (Maud) FLEMING (1032 - 1083 Caan)

109.   Henry I BEAUCLERC (King) of ENGLAND + Matilda (Edith
        Eagdith) `Atheling' STEWART of SCOTLAND

110.   Matilda (Maud Augusta) the EMPRESS + Geoffrey V `the Fair'
        (`Plantagenet')

111.   Henry II (King) of ENGLAND + Eleanor (Duchess/Princess) of
        AQUITAINE

112.   John `Lackland' (King) of ENGLAND + Isabella (d'
        ANGOULEME) TAILLEFER

113.   Eleanor (Alianor) of ENGLAND (1215? - 1275) + Simon V de
        MONTFORT (1208 - 4/8/1265)

114.   Eleanor de MONTFORT (1252 - 1282) + Llywellyn (II) ap

GRUFFYDD (? - 1282)
115.   Catherine verch LLYWELLYN + Philip ap IFOR
116.   Eleanor (of ISCOED; GOCH) verch PHILIP + Thomas ap
            LLEWELLYN
117.   Lowri verch GRUFFUDD FYCHAN + Robert (Sir; of Emral)
            PULESTON (1358? - 1399?)
118.   Angharad PULESTON + Edward TREVOR ap DAFFYD (? -
            1448?)
119.   Otewell Worsley, Sir + Rose (TREVOR) verch EDWART
120.   Joyce Worsley + Richard Lee II
121.   Richard Lee III + Eleanor Burgoine
122.   Geoffrey Lee, MP + Agnes Conyers
123.   Reginald Lee + Dorothy Thurland
124.   Gervase Lee of Nottinghamshire
125.   Thomas Lee, of Ashfield + Margaret Mary Oscroft
126.   Elizabeth Lee + Thomas Hanks
127.   Robert Hanks + Margaret NLN
128.   Peter Hanks I + Mary Bressie
129.   Elinor Hanks + Robert Nelson
130.   Rachael Nelson + Timothy Ragan
131.   Timothy Reagan + Elizabeth Trigg
132.   Richard Bazel Reagan + Cecelia Creppy
133.   Richard Reagan + Phoebe Samples
134.   Reuben Perry Reagan + Elizabeth Cagle
135.   George Reagan + Emaline Garner
136.   Marshall Reagan + Emma Rogers
137.   Elzie Reagan + Delmar Raines
        ------- Gina Davis
            ------- Jackson Davis
        ------- Patricia Stuart
            ------- Bobby Caldwell
            ------- Jennifer Caldwell
        ------- Mike Raines
            ------- Leah Raines
            ------- Kendra Raines
            ------- Joshua Raines
            ------- Michael Raines
        ------- Frank Raines
            ------- Franklin Cody Raines
            ------- Kip Allen Raines
        ------- Richard Raines

JAMES FRANK HATCHER III

------- Tyler Lee
------- Devin Lee
------- Emma Lundy

10

THE ELVES OF ALFHEIM LINEAGE

Finnalf's Ancestors

1.   The Fire of MUSPELHEIM + The Ice of NIFLHEIM
2.   The Clouds (PRIMORDIAL) + Alfadur, the Eternal (GOD)
3.   Jotunn (1st Vaettir) + Ymir, the Frost GIANTGinnungagap)
4.   Thymr the GIANT of the JOTUNN + Freyja of the VANIR
5.   Bergdis (mistress) + Raum `the Old' NORSSON
6.   Finnalf

Svanhild's Ancestors

1.   The Fire of MUSPELHEIM + The Ice of NIFLHEIM
2.   The Clouds (PRIMORDIAL) + Alfadur, the Eternal (GOD)
3.   Audhumbla, the First Cow + Ymir, the Frost
            GIANTGinnungagap)
4.   Borr(?), the first GOD + (NN) the first GODDESS
5.   Odin (GOD) of the NORSE + Frigga (GODDESS of the Clouds)
6.   Sigyn the GODDESS + Loki (GOD of Fire), a JOTUNN
7.   Narfi (GOD)
8.   Nitt (GODDESS of the NIGHT) + Dellingr (GOD of the Dawn)

9.   Dagr (GOD of the Day) + Sunna (GODDESS of the Sun),
            daughter of Mundilfari (GOD)
10.   Svanhild

Begin Common Descendants

1.   Finnalf + Svanhild
2.   Svan `the Red'
3.   Saefari
4.   Ulf
5.   Alfi `the Old' (King) of ALFHEIM (Alf; eponym of ALFHEIM)
6.   Alfgeir (Asgeir Alfgier) (Count) of ALFHEIM
7.   Alfhild (Alhilda) GANDOLFSDOTTIR of ALFHEIM (aka Gondol
            of SWEDEN)
8.   Gandolf ASGEIRSSON (Count) of ALFHEIM

LINEAGE I

1.   Alfarinn (King) of ALFHEIM (aka Alferin (Alfarrin) of
            ALVHEIM)
2.   Alfhild ALFARINSDOTTIR + Gudrod `the Magnificent'
            HALFDANSSON
3.   Olaf II `Geirstada-Alf' GUDRODSSON (King in VESTFOLD;
            prob. founded Dublin) + Lifa ut fra NORGE
4.   Ragnvald (of AGDER; Olavsson) OLAFSSON (aka Ragnvaldr
            Heidum Haeri; aka King Ranald `Higher-than-the-Hills' de
            VESTFOLD) + Thora (Tora) SIGURDSDOTTIR
5.   Aseda (Aserida Ascrida) RAGNVALDSDOTTIR + Eystein
            Glumra IVARSSON (Earl) of MORE
6.   Ragnvald (Earl/Jarl) of MORE (`the Wise' EYSTEINSSON; Jarl
            of ORKNEY; aka Rogerwald of HAARFARER ?; 1st Earl of
            the ORKNEYS) + Groa, (prob. concubine)
7.   Turf-Einar RAGNVALDSSON
8.   Thorfin (II) EINARSSON + Grelod (of CAITHNESS)
            DUNCANSDOTTIR
9.   Hlodvir `Lodar' THORFINSSON + Audna (KIARVALSDATTER)
            of IRELAND
10.   Hvarflad HLODVERSDATTER of ORKNEY + Malcolm II
            MacKENNETH of ALBA
11.   Doda of SCOTLAND + Fulbert `the Tanner' de FALAIS

12. Herleve (Salburpyr) de FALAISE (1003? - 1050?) + Robert II (Duke) of NORMANDY
13. WILLIAM the CONQUEROR (Duke) of NORMANDY + Matilda (Maud) FLEMING (1032 - 1083 Caan)
14. Henry I BEAUCLERC (King) of ENGLAND + Matilda (Edith Eagdith) `Atheling' STEWART of SCOTLAND
15. Matilda (Maud Augusta) the EMPRESS + Geoffrey V `the Fair' (`Plantagenet')
16. Henry II (King) of ENGLAND + Eleanor (Duchess/Princess) of AQUITAINE
17. John `Lackland' (King) of ENGLAND + Isabella (d' ANGOULEME) TAILLEFER
18. Eleanor (Alianor) of ENGLAND (1215? - 1275) + Simon V de MONTFORT (1208 - 4/8/1265)
19. Eleanor de MONTFORT (1252 - 1282) + Llywellyn (II) ap GRUFFYDD (? - 1282)
20. Catherine verch LLYWELLYN + Philip ap IFOR
21. Eleanor (of ISCOED; GOCH) verch PHILIP + Thomas ap LLEWELLYN
22. Lowri verch GRUFFUDD FYCHAN + Robert (Sir; of Emral) PULESTON (1358? - 1399?)
23. Angharad PULESTON + Edward TREVOR ap DAFFYD (? - 1448?)
24. Otewell Worsley, Sir + Rose (TREVOR) verch EDWART
25. Joyce Worsley + Richard Lee II
26. Richard Lee III + Eleanor Burgoine
27. Geoffrey Lee, MP + Agnes Conyers
28. Reginald Lee + Dorothy Thurland
29. Gervase Lee of Nottinghamshire
30. Thomas Lee, of Ashfield + Margaret Mary Oscroft
31. Elizabeth Lee + Thomas Hanks
32. Robert Hanks + Margaret NLN
33. Peter Hanks I + Mary Bressie
34. Elinor Hanks + Robert Nelson
35. Rachael Nelson + Timothy Ragan
36. Timothy Reagan + Elizabeth Trigg
37. Richard Bazel Reagan + Cecelia Creppy
38. Richard Reagan + Phoebe Samples
39. Reuben Perry Reagan + Elizabeth Cagle
40. George Reagan + Emaline Garner
41. Marshall Reagan + Emma Rogers

42.   Elzie Reagan + Delmar Raines
------- Gina Davis
        ------- Jackson Davis
------- Patricia Stuart
        ------- Bobby Caldwell
        ------- Jennifer Caldwell
------- Mike Raines
        ------- Leah Raines
        ------- Kendra Raines
        ------- Joshua Raines
        ------- Michael Raines
------- Frank Raines
        ------- Franklin Cody Raines
        ------- Kip Allen Raines
------- Richard Raines
        ------- Tyler Lee
        ------- Devin Lee
        ------- Emma Lundy

11

THE GERMANIC-TEUTONIC LINEAGE

1. Alfadur, the Eternal (GOD)
2. The Fire of MUSPELHEIM + The Ice of NIFLHEIM
3. The Clouds (PRIMORDIAL) + Eitr, Substance of Life (PRIMORDIAL)
4. Ymir, the Frost GIANT (Ginnungagap) + Hrod
5. Tyr (YMIRSSON) + Zisa
6. Tuisto (1st King) of GERMANIA (? - 1500? BC) + Mannus
7. Mannus
8. Ingio (King) of GERMANS (? - 1870+ BC)
9. Ausstaeb (King) of GERMANS
10. Ausstaeb of GERMANS +
11. Herman (King) of GERMANS
12. Mers (King) of GERMANS
13. Gampar (King) of GERMANS
14. Schwab (King) of GERMANS
15. Wandler (King) of GERMANS
16. Deuto (King) of GERMANS (? - 1553+ BC)
17. Almann (King) of GERMANS (? - 1489+ BC)
18. Baier (co-King) of GERMANS in Bavaria
19. Ingram (King) of GERMANS (? - 1377+ BC)

20.   Adalger (King) of GERMANS (? - 1328+ BC)
21.   Larein (King) of GERMANS (? - 1277+ BC)
22.   Ylsing (King) of GERMANS (? - 1224+ BC)
23.   Brenner (King) of GERMANS (? - 1186+ BC)
24.   Heccar (King) of GERMANS (? - 1155+ BC)
25.   Frank of GERMANS
26.   Wolfheim Siclinger of GERMANS
27.   Gal (co-King) of GERMANS
28.   Walther (co-King) of GERMANS
29.   (NN) ... (NN) | (several missing generations)
30.   Mader (King) of GERMANS
31.   Brenner II (King) of the SUEVIA
32.   (NN) ... (NN) | (some missing generations)
33.   Breitmar
34.   Brenner III (King) of GERMANS (? - 361+ BC)
35.   Brener IV (King) of GERMANS (by 300 BC - ?)
36.   Thessel (King) of GERMANS (? - 194 BC)
37.   Dieth I (co-King) of GERMANS
38.   Diethmar (co-King) of GERMANS
39.   Beramund (co-King) of GERMANS
40.   Teutbal (King) of the TEUTONS [eponym of the Teutons]
41.   Ariovistus (King) of GERMANIA
42.   Segonax
43.   Sigimar
44.   Arminius `the Great' (King) of GERMANS + Thysnelde
45.   Thymelko
46.   Thedda (Theddo)
47.   Saxnot (Seaxneat)
48.   Gesecg SEXNEATSSON
49.   Antsecg GESECGSSON
50.   Sweppa ANTSECGSSON
51.   Sigefugel SVVEPPING
52.   Bedca (Bedican) SIGEFVGLSING
53.   Offa BEDCING
54.   Aesewine (King) of ESSEX
55.   Sledd (King) of ESSEX + Riccula of KENT
56.   Sexbald of ESSEX + Clothilde of ALLEMANNIA
57.   Sigeberht `the Good' (King) of ESSEX
58.   (NN) ... (NN) of ESSEX | (poss. few missing generations)
59.   Sigeric (Prince) of ESSEX
60.   Sigythe + Eardwulf (co-King) of KENT

61. Oswulf of BERNICIA + Bernthryth of MERCIA
62. Eardwulf (King) of BERNICIA (? - 833+)
63. Osbert (King) of BERNICIA (? - 867+)
64. Eadwulf (Ealdwulf) (Lord) of BAMBOROUGH
65. Uhtred (Ealdorman? of Hope and Ashford)
66. Wulfrun (of TAMWORTH) + (NN), father of Wulfric
67. Wulfric + Aelfthyth of MERCIA
68. Eadgyth (Ealdgyth) of MERCIA + Morcar (High Reeve) of
        NORTHUMBRIA (965? - ?)
69. Ealdgyth (Algitha) MORCARSON of NORTHUMBRIA (? -
        1016?) + Edmund II `Ironside' of WESSEX (994? -
        30/11/1016)
70. Edward `the OutLaw' of ENGLAND + Agatha (RURIKID)
71. Margaret (Queen; Saint) of SCOTLAND + Malcolm III
        MacCRINAN (CANMORE)(19th King) of SCOTS
72. Matilda (Edith Eagdith) `Atheling' STEWART of SCOTLAND +
        Henry I BEAUCLERC (King) of ENGLAND
73. Matilda (Maud Augusta) the EMPRESS + Geoffrey V `the Fair'
        (`Plantagenet')
74. Henry II (King) of ENGLAND + Eleanor (Duchess/Princess) of
        AQUITAINE
75. John `Lackland' (King) of ENGLAND + Isabella (d'
        ANGOULEME) TAILLEFER
76. Eleanor (Alianor) of ENGLAND (1215? - 1275) + Simon V de
        MONTFORT (1208 - 4/8/1265)
77. Eleanor de MONTFORT (1252 - 1282) + Llywellyn (II) ap
        GRUFFYDD (? - 1282)
78. Catherine verch LLYWELLYN + Philip ap IFOR
79. Eleanor (of ISCOED; GOCH) verch PHILIP + Thomas ap
        LLEWELLYN
80. Lowri verch GRUFFUDD FYCHAN + Robert (Sir; of Emral)
        PULESTON (1358? - 1399?)
81. Angharad PULESTON + Edward TREVOR ap DAFFYD (? -
        1448?)
82. Otewell Worsley, Sir + Rose (TREVOR) verch EDWART
83. Joyce Worsley + Richard Lee II
84. Richard Lee III + Eleanor Burgoine
85. Geoffrey Lee, MP + Agnes Conyers
86. Reginald Lee + Dorothy Thurland
87. Gervase Lee of Nottinghamshire
88. Thomas Lee, of Ashfield + Margaret Mary Oscroft

89.   Elizabeth Lee + Thomas Hanks
90.   Robert Hanks + Margaret NLN
91.   Peter Hanks I + Mary Bressie
92.   Elinor Hanks + Robert Nelson
93.   Rachael Nelson + Timothy Ragan
94.   Timothy Reagan + Elizabeth Trigg
95.   Richard Bazel Reagan + Cecelia Creppy
96.   Richard Reagan + Phoebe Samples
97.   Reuben Perry Reagan + Elizabeth Cagle
98.   George Reagan + Emaline Garner
99.   Marshall Reagan + Emma Rogers
100.   Elzie Reagan + Delmar Raines
        ------- Gina Davis
                ------- Jackson Davis
        ------- Patricia Stuart
                ------- Bobby Caldwell
                ------- Jennifer Caldwell
        ------- Mike Raines
                ------- Leah Raines
                ------- Kendra Raines
                ------- Joshua Raines
                ------- Michael Raines
        ------- Frank Raines
                ------- Franklin Cody Raines
                ------- Kip Allen Raines
        ------- Richard Raines
                ------- Tyler Lee
                ------- Devin Lee
                ------- Emma Lundy

12

THE GERMANIC-VANDAL LINEAGE

LINEAGE I

1.   Alfadur, the Eternal (GOD)
2.   The Fire of MUSPELHEIM + The Ice of NIFLHEIM
3.   The Clouds (PRIMORDIAL) + Eitr, Substance of Life
        (PRIMORDIAL)
4.   Ymir, the Frost GIANTGinnungagap) + Hrod
5.   Tyr (YMIRSSON) + Zisa
6.   Tuisto (1st King) of GERMANIA (? - 1500? BC) + Mannus
7.   Ingio (King) of GERMANS (? - 1870+ BC)
8.   Ausstaeb (King) of GERMANS
9.   Herman (King) of GERMANS
10.   Mers (King) of GERMANS (? - 1711+ BC)
11.   Gampar (King) of GERMANS (? - 1667+ BC)
12.   Schwab (King) of GERMANS (? - 1521+ BC)
13.   Wandler (King) of GERMANS (? - 1580+ BC)
14.   (NN) ... (NN) of VANDALS | (very many missing generations)
15.   Cella (Cecilia) of the VANDALS
16.   Godigiselus (King) of the VANDALS (? - 406) + Frilla (Elisa;
        Flora)

17.   Gaiseric (King) of the VANDALS
18.   Hunneric (King) of the VANDALS (in Africa)
19.   Hoamer of the VANDALS (480? - 530?) + Gossana
20.   Goiswinth of the VANDALS (525? - 582?) + Athanagild (King)
        of the VISIGOTHS (510? - 567?), son of Clotilda
        (Chrodechilde) (530? - ?), daughter of Clovis `the Great'
        (1st King) of All FRANKS and Clothilde (Saint; Princess)
        of BURGUNDY
21.   Brunhilda of the VISIGOTHS + Sigebert I of AUSTRASIA (at
        METZ)
22.   Childebert II (King) of the FRANKS (? - 596?) + Faileube
        (Failleuba)
23.   Theudebert II (7th Archduke) of AUSTRASIA + Bilichide
        (Bellichildis) (587? - ?)
24.   Emma (Ymma) of AUSTRASIA (612? - 642?) + Eadbald
        (Adolald) AETHELBRYHTING (King) of KENT
25.   Eorcenbert EADBALDING (King) of KENT + Seaxburh
        UUFFING (Princess) of EAST ANGLIA (635? - ?), daughter
        of Anna (King) of EAST ANGLIA (? - 654) and Seaxburh
        UUFFING (Princess) of EAST ANGLIA (635? - ?)
26.   Egbert I EARCONBRYHTING (King) of KENT + Sister of
        Arwald
27.   Wihtred OISCINGA (King) of KENT + Ethelburg
28.   Eadbert VVIHTREDING (co-King) of KENT
29.   Eardwulf (co-King) of KENT + Alchfleda
30.   Oswulf of BERNICIA (? - 810+) + Bernthryth of MERCIA,
        daughter of Bernnoth (Prince) of MERCIA, son of
        Beornred (usurper King) of MERCIA (? - 757+)
31.   Eardwulf (King) of BERNICIA (? - 833+)
32.   Osbert (King) of BERNICIA (? - 867+)
33.   Eadwulf (Ealdwulf) (Lord) of BAMBOROUGH
34.   Uhtred (Ealdorman? of Hope and Ashford)
35.   Wulfrun (of TAMWORTH) + (NN), father of Wulfric
36.   Wulfric + Aelfthyth of MERCIA
37.   Eadgyth (Ealdgyth) of MERCIA + Morcar (High Reeve) of
        NORTHUMBRIA (965? - ?)
38.   Ealdgyth (Algitha) MORCARSON of NORTHUMBRIA (? -
        1016?) + Edmund II `Ironside' of WESSEX (994? -
        30/11/1016)
39.   Edward `the OutLaw' of ENGLAND + Agatha (RURIKID)
40.   Margaret (Queen; Saint) of SCOTLAND + Malcolm III

MacCRINAN (CANMORE)(19th King) of SCOTS
41. Matilda (Edith Eagdith) `Atheling' STEWART of SCOTLAND + Henry I BEAUCLERC (King) of ENGLAND
42. Matilda (Maud Augusta) the EMPRESS + Geoffrey V `the Fair' (`Plantagenet')
43. Henry II (King) of ENGLAND + Eleanor (Duchess/Princess) of AQUITAINE
44. John `Lackland' (King) of ENGLAND + Isabella (d' ANGOULEME) TAILLEFER
45. Eleanor (Alianor) of ENGLAND (1215? - 1275) + Simon V de MONTFORT (1208 - 4/8/1265)
46. Eleanor de MONTFORT (1252 - 1282) + Llywellyn (II) ap GRUFFYDD (? - 1282)
47. Catherine verch LLYWELLYN + Philip ap IFOR
48. Eleanor (of ISCOED; GOCH) verch PHILIP + Thomas ap LLEWELLYN
49. Lowri verch GRUFFUDD FYCHAN + Robert (Sir; of Emral) PULESTON (1358? - 1399?)
50. Angharad PULESTON + Edward TREVOR ap DAFFYD (? - 1448?)
51. Otewell Worsley, Sir + Rose (TREVOR) verch EDWART
52. Joyce Worsley + Richard Lee II
53. Richard Lee III + Eleanor Burgoine
54. Geoffrey Lee, MP + Agnes Conyers
55. Reginald Lee + Dorothy Thurland
56. Gervase Lee of Nottinghamshire
57. Thomas Lee, of Ashfield + Margaret Mary Oscroft
58. Elizabeth Lee + Thomas Hanks
59. Robert Hanks + Margaret NLN
60. Peter Hanks I + Mary Bressie
61. Elinor Hanks + Robert Nelson
62. Rachael Nelson + Timothy Ragan
63. Timothy Reagan + Elizabeth Trigg
64. Richard Bazel Reagan + Cecelia Creppy
65. Richard Reagan + Phoebe Samples
66. Reuben Perry Reagan + Elizabeth Cagle
67. George Reagan + Emaline Garner
68. Marshall Reagan + Emma Rogers
69. Elzie Reagan + Delmar Raines
------- Gina Davis
------- Jackson Davis

```
------- Patricia Stuart
        ------- Bobby Caldwell
        ------- Jennifer Caldwell
------- Mike Raines
        ------- Leah Raines
        ------- Kendra Raines
        ------- Joshua Raines
        ------- Michael Raines
------- Frank Raines
        ------- Franklin Cody Raines
        ------- Kip Allen Raines
------- Richard Raines
        ------- Tyler Lee
        ------- Devin Lee
        ------- Emma Lundy
```

LINEAGE II

1.   Alfadur, the Eternal (GOD)
2.   The Fire of MUSPELHEIM + The Ice of NIFLHEIM
3.   The Clouds (PRIMORDIAL) + Eitr, Substance of Life
         (PRIMORDIAL)
4.   Ymir, the Frost GIANTGinnungagap) + Hrod
5.   Tyr (YMIRSSON) + Zisa
6.   Tuisto (1st King) of GERMANIA (? - 1500? BC) + Mannus
7.   Ingio (King) of GERMANS (? - 1870+ BC)
8.   Ausstaeb (King) of GERMANS
9.   Herman (King) of GERMANS
10. Mers (King) of GERMANS (? - 1711+ BC)
11. Gampar (King) of GERMANS (? - 1667+ BC)
12. Schwab (King) of GERMANS (? - 1521+ BC)
13. Wandler (King) of GERMANS (? - 1580+ BC)
14. (NN) ... (NN) of VANDALS | (very many missing generations)
15. Cella (Cecilia) of the VANDALS
16. Godigiselus (King) of the VANDALS (? - 406) + Frilla (Elisa;
         Flora)
17. Gaiseric (King) of the VANDALS
18. Hunneric (King) of the VANDALS (in Africa)
19. Hoamer of the VANDALS (480? - 530?) + Gossana
20. Goiswinth of the VANDALS (525? - 582?) + Athanagild (King)
         of the VISIGOTHS (510? - 567?), son of Clotilda

(Chrodechilde) (530? - ?), daughter of Clovis `the Great' (1st King) of All FRANKS and Clothilde (Saint; Princess) of BURGUNDY

21. Brunhilda of the VISIGOTHS + Sigebert I of AUSTRASIA (at METZ)

22. Childebert II (King) of the FRANKS (? - 596?) + Faileube (Failleuba)

23. Theudebert II (7th Archduke) of AUSTRASIA + Bilichide (Bellichildis) (587? - ?)

24. Emma (Ymma) of AUSTRASIA (612? - 642?) + Eadbald (Adolald) AETHELBRYHTING (King) of KENT

25. Eorcenbert EADBALDING (King) of KENT + Seaxburh UUFFING (Princess) of EAST ANGLIA (635? - ?), daughter of Anna (King) of EAST ANGLIA (? - 654) and Seaxburh UUFFING (Princess) of EAST ANGLIA (635? - ?)

26. Egbert I EARCONBRYHTING (King) of KENT + Sister of Arwald

27. Wihtred OISCINGA (King) of KENT + Ethelburg

28. Eadbert VVIHTREDING (co-King) of KENT

29. Eardwulf (co-King) of KENT + Alchfleda

30. Oswulf of BERNICIA (? - 810+) + Bernthryth of MERCIA, daughter of Bernnoth (Prince) of MERCIA, son of Beornred (usurper King) of MERCIA (? - 757+)

31. Eardwulf (King) of BERNICIA (? - 833+)

32. Osbert (King) of BERNICIA (? - 867+)

33. Eadwulf (Ealdwulf) (Lord) of BAMBOROUGH

34. Oswulf (Uswulf) (Earldorman) of NORTHUMBRIA (? - 965?)

35. Waltheof I (Aldred Walroef) (Earl) of NORTHUMBRIA + Elfeda (Elufleda) (965? - ?)

36. Uchtred (Ughtred) (Earl) of NORTHUMBRIA + Elgifu (Aelfgifu Elgiva) of WESSEX

37. Gospatrick FitzUGHTRED of BAMBURGH (? - 1064?)

38. Uchtred FitzGOSPATRIC

39. Dunning (FitzUGHTRED) (? - 1092)

40. Siward FitzDUNNING (1073 - 1095)

41. Huck (Hucca) de SINGLETON

42. Uchtred de SINGLETON (? - by 1183)

43. Matilda de SINGLETON

44. Maud de PARLES + Richard de WORSLEY (? - by 1233)

45. Geoffrey de WORSLEY (? - by 1268) + Agnes de WORSLEY

46. Richard de WORSLEY (? - 1292?) + Maud de WARDLEY

47.   Henry de WORSLEY (? - 1312? (or by '04)) + Margaret
            SCHORESWORTH (? - 1363?)
48.   Robert de Worsley, Lord of Booths + Cecily Margaret
            Bromhall
49.   William de Worsley + Ellen de Huton
50.   Robert Worsley + Isabel de Trafford
51.   Robert de Worsley + Katherine Clark
52.   Otewell Worsley, Sir + Rose verch Edward
53.   Joyce Worsley + Richard Lee II
54.   Richard Lee III + Eleanor Burgoine
55.   Geoffrey Lee, MP + Agnes Conyers
56.   Reginald Lee + Dorothy Thurland
57.   Gervase Lee of Nottinghamshire
58.   Thomas Lee, of Ashfield + Margaret Mary Oscroft
59.   Elizabeth Lee + Thomas Hanks
60.   Robert Hanks + Margaret NLN
61.   Peter Hanks I + Mary Bressie
62.   Elinor Hanks + Robert Nelson
63.   Rachael Nelson + Timothy Ragan
64.   Timothy Reagan + Elizabeth Trigg
65.   Richard Bazel Reagan + Cecelia Creppy
66.   Richard Reagan + Phoebe Samples
67.   Reuben Perry Reagan + Elizabeth Cagle
68.   George Reagan + Emaline Garner
69.   Marshall Reagan + Emma Rogers
70.   Elzie Reagan + Delmar Raines
        ------- Gina Davis
                ------- Jackson Davis
        ------- Patricia Stuart
                ------- Bobby Caldwell
                ------- Jennifer Caldwell
        ------- Mike Raines
                ------- Leah Raines
                ------- Kendra Raines
                ------- Joshua Raines
                ------- Michael Raines
        ------- Frank Raines
                ------- Franklin Cody Raines
                ------- Kip Allen Raines
        ------- Richard Raines
                ------- Tyler Lee

A BARDIC TALE OF THE ANCIENT LINEAGES OF THE REAGAN FAMILY

------- Devin Lee
------- Emma Lundy

13

THE GOTHS-VISIGOTHS-LANGOBARDS LINEAGE

LINEAGE I

(Egyptian)

1.   Sesostris + Nefret
2.   Amenemhat I Sehetepibre (Founder) of 12th Dynasty +
            Nefrutotenen
3.   Sesotris I Kheperkare (PHARAOH) of EGYPT (? - 1928? BC) +
            Nefrusheri (Princess) of EGYPT
4.   Amenemhat (Ammenemes) II Nubkaure (PHARAOH) of
            EGYPT + Keminnub (Queen) of EGYPT
5.   Sesotris II Khakheperre (PHARAOH) of EGYPT + Nofret of
            EGYPT
6.   Sesotris III Khakaure of EGYPT + Sebekshedty-Neferu
            (Queen) of EGYPT
7.   Amenemhat III Nemare (PHARAOH) of EGYPT + Sebeknefru
            (Queen) of EGYPT
8.   Amenemhat (Ammenemes) IV (PHARAOH) of EGYPT
9.   Wegaf (PHARAOH) of 13th Dynasty + daughter of
            Amenemhet IV

10.	Ameny Intef (Inyotef) IV (PHARAOH) of EGYPT
11.	Hor (PHARAOH) of EGYPT (? - 1760? BC)
12.	Sobekhotep II (PHARAOH) of EGYPT (? - 1750? BC)
13.	Khendjer (PHARAOH) of EGYPT (? - 1747? BC)
14.	Sobekhotep III (PHARAOH) of EGYPT (? - 1745? BC)
15.	Neferhotep I (PHARAOH) of EGYPT
16.	Sobekhotep IV Khaneferre (PHARAOH) of 13th Dynasty + Tjan
17.	Sebekhotep (Princess) of THEBES + Senebhanef, son of Renressonb
18.	Mentuhotep (Queen) of EGYPT + Sekhemre-Sementawi Djehuti (PHARAOH) of EGYPT
19.	Sekhemre-Se'ankhtawi Neferhotep (PHARAOH) of EGYPT
20.	Sobekemsaf Sekhemre-Shedtawi (PHARAOH) of EGYPT + Nubkhas (Queen) of EGYPT
21.	Inyotef VII (PHARAOH) at THEBES + Sobkemsaf (Sebekamzaf) of EGYPT (1635? BC - ?)
22.	Sekenenre Tao I (PHARAOH) at THEBES + Tetisheri of THEBES
23.	Sekenenre Tao II (King) of THEBES + Ahhotep (Ahotop) I (Queen) of EGYPT
24.	Ahmose I (1st PHARAOH) of 18th Dynasty + Nefretiri (Queen) of EGYPT
25.	Amenhotep I Djeserkare (PHARAOH) of EGYPT + Senisonb (Seneseneb) of EGYPT
26.	Thutmose I (PHARAOH) of EGYPT (? - 1481? BC) + Amhose (Aahmes II) (Queen) of EGYPT
27.	Hatshepsut (Queen & PHARAOH) of EGYPT (? - 1482 BC) + Thutmose (Tuthmosis) II (PHARAOH) of EGYPT
28.	Meryetre Hatshepsut of EGYPT + Thutmose III `the Great' of EGYPT (Moses of the Bible)
29.	Akheperure Amenhotep II THUTMOSID (PHARAOH) of EGYPT + Tio (Tiye Tiaa)
30.	Menkheprure' Thutmose IV (PHARAOH) of EGYPT + Mutemwiya, daughter of Artatama (I; King) of MITANNI
31.	Nebma'atre' Amenhotep III (PHARAOH) of EGYPT + Tiye-Nefertari (Tiy) of EGYPT (1382 BC - 1344 BC)
32.	Akhenaton (Iknaton) (10th PHARAOH) of 18th Dynasty EGYPT + Nefertiti (Chief Queen) of EGYPT
33.	Meritaten (Royal Daughter) of EGYPT + Judah (Judas Juda) ibn JACOB, son of Jacob ibn ISAAC (King of GOSHEN)

34. Zerah (Zehrah Zarah Zare) ibn JUDAH + Electra the PLEIADE
35. Dardanus (Dara) (King) of ACADIA + Batea of TEUCRI
36. Erichthonius (King) of ACADIA (? - 1386? BC) + Astyoche of ACADIA
37. Trois of ACADIA + Callirhoe (TEUCRI)
38. Ilus (Ilyus) (King) of TROY (? - 1282? BC) + Eurydice (Eurydike) of TROY
39. Priam Podarces (High King) of TROY (? - 1183? BC) + Hecuba (Hecabe) of PHRYGIA
40. Troana Iluim of TROY + Memnon (Munon) of TROY (? - 1183? BC)
41. Thor (Tror) (King) of THRACE + Sibil (Sif)
42. Einridi LORIDESSON
43. Vingethor (Vingethior) EINRIDISSON
44. Moda (Mode) VINGENERSSON
45. Maji (Magi) MODASSON
46. Seskef (Sceaf Scaef)
47. Bedwig (Bedvig; of SCEAF)
48. Hwala (Hvala Hawala Guala)
49. Berik (King) of the GOTHS + Drott
50. (NN) ... (NN)
51. Giuki (King) of the GOTHS
52. Guntharich (Gaderik) I (Over-king) of the GOTHS
53. Filimer (Prince) of Baltic GOTHS
54. Knivida (Prince) of West GOTHS (? - 249?)
55. Ovida der BURGUNDER (? - 273+ (or 249+))
56. Hilderic (King) of the BURGUNDIANS (? - 300+)
57. Geberich WESTGOTEN (? - 349+)
58. Aoric of the VISIGOTHS
59. Rocesthes (Badengaud BALTHUS)
60. Alaric I BALTHAS + Eurica of the WEST GOTHS
61. Ataulfe (III; King) of the VISIGOTHS + Aelia Galla PLACIDIA (Empress)
62. Theodoric I BALTHAS (King) of VISIGOTHS
63. Euric (King) of WEST GOTHS (420? - 485+) + Ragnahild SISEMUNDA
64. Alaric II (King) de WISIGOTHIE (476? - 507)
65. Agila
66. Answald (Duke) of TURIN
67. Agilolf (King) of the LOMBARDS + Theudelinde of BAVARIA
68. (Miss) of TURIN + Rotbert I (King) of LONGOBARDS

69. Gundwald (Duke) of ASTI (? - 613?) + Harinanda, daughter of Rotbert I (King) of LONGOBARDS + Gundwald (Duke) of ASTI (? - 613?)
70. Aripert I (Viscount) of LOMBARDY (? - 661?)
71. Berthari (21st King) of the LANGOBARDS
72. Kunibert (25th King) of the LANGOBARDS (? - 702?)
73. Liutpert (26th King) of the LANGOBARDS (? - 712?)
74. Theoderada (of the LOMBARDS) + Ansbrand (28th King) of the LANGOBARDS (655? - 712?)
75. Sigiprand of the LOMBARDS
76. Ansbrand of LOMBARDS
77. Ansia of LOMBARDS (? - 774?) + Desiderio (last King) of LOMBARDS (? - 774+)
78. Gerberga of LOMBARDY (? - 774) + Carloman II (Archduke) of AUSTRASIA (747? - 771)
79. Kunigunde (Auberge) of AUSTRASIA + Adelgis (Count) of PARMA (of SPOLETO-PARMA) (? - 836?)
80. Cunegonde (Princess) de VERMANDOIS + Bernard (Bernhard; I) (King) of ITALY (Lombardy)
81. Pépin II, lord of Péronne + Rothaide de Bobbio
82. Pepin (I; Count) de SENLIS de VALOIS
83. (Miss) de SENLIS de VALOIS (845? - ?) + Berenger (Count) de RENNES (? - 931)
84. Poppa (Poppaeia) de VALOIS (872? - ?) + Rollo (Hrolf Rollon Rou Robert) `the Dane' RAGNVALDSSON
85. Guillaume (2nd Duke) of NORMANDY + Sprota de BRETAGNE (concubine)
86. Richard I `the Fearless' (Count) of NORMANDY + Gunnora (Gonnor) de CREPON
87. Richard II `the Good' of NORMANDY (963? - 1027) + Judith (Princess) of BRITTANY
88. Robert II (Duke) of NORMANDY + Herleve (Salburpyr) de FALAISE (1003? - 1050?)
89. WILLIAM the CONQUEROR (Duke) of NORMANDY + Matilda (Maud) FLEMING (1032 - 1083 Caan)
90. Henry I BEAUCLERC (King) of ENGLAND + Matilda (Edith Eagdith) `Atheling' STEWART of SCOTLAND
91. Matilda (Maud Augusta) the EMPRESS + Geoffrey V `the Fair' (`Plantagenet')
92. Henry II (King) of ENGLAND + Eleanor (Duchess/Princess) of AQUITAINE

93.   John `Lackland' (King) of ENGLAND + Isabella (d'
            ANGOULEME) TAILLEFER
94.   Eleanor (Alianor) of ENGLAND (1215? - 1275) + Simon V de
            MONTFORT (1208 - 4/8/1265)
95.   Eleanor de MONTFORT (1252 - 1282) + Llywellyn (II) ap
            GRUFFYDD (? - 1282)
96.   Catherine verch LLYWELLYN + Philip ap IFOR
97.   Eleanor (of ISCOED; GOCH) verch PHILIP + Thomas ap
            LLEWELLYN
98.   Lowri verch GRUFFUDD FYCHAN + Robert (Sir; of Emral)
            PULESTON (1358? - 1399?)
99.   Angharad PULESTON + Edward TREVOR ap DAFFYD (? -
            1448?)
100.   Otewell Worsley, Sir + Rose (TREVOR) verch EDWART
101.   Joyce Worsley + Richard Lee II
102.   Richard Lee III + Eleanor Burgoine
103.   Geoffrey Lee, MP + Agnes Conyers
104.   Reginald Lee + Dorothy Thurland
105.   Gervase Lee of Nottinghamshire
106.   Thomas Lee, of Ashfield + Margaret Mary Oscroft
107.   Elizabeth Lee + Thomas Hanks
108.   Robert Hanks + Margaret NLN
109.   Peter Hanks I + Mary Bressie
110.   Elinor Hanks + Robert Nelson
111.   Rachael Nelson + Timothy Ragan
112.   Timothy Reagan + Elizabeth Trigg
113.   Richard Bazel Reagan + Cecelia Creppy
114.   Richard Reagan + Phoebe Samples
115.   Reuben Perry Reagan + Elizabeth Cagle
116.   George Reagan + Emaline Garner
117.   Marshall Reagan + Emma Rogers
118.   Elzie Reagan + Delmar Raines
            ------- Gina Davis
                ------- Jackson Davis
            ------- Patricia Stuart
                ------- Bobby Caldwell
                ------- Jennifer Caldwell
            ------- Mike Raines
                ------- Leah Raines
                ------- Kendra Raines
                ------- Joshua Raines

------- Michael Raines
------- Frank Raines
    ------- Franklin Cody Raines
    ------- Kip Allen Raines
------- Richard Raines
    ------- Tyler Lee
    ------- Devin Lee
    ------- Emma Lundy

LINEAGE II

(Jewish)

1. Mummu the Creator GOD + Nammu, Goddess of the Sea
2. Apsu, Ocean of Sweet Water + Tiamat, Ocean of Salt Water
3. Lahmu, The Primordial God + Lahamu, the Primordial GODDESS
4. Anshar, the Primordial God + Kishar, the Primordial GODDESS
5. Anu, GOD of the Sky + Ki Urash, GODDESS of the Earth
6. Enlil, GOD of Wind
7. El Shaddai, Supreme GOD of CANAAN + Atiratu, Semitic GODDESS of Fertility
8. Elohim, GOD of Israel
9. Adam, the First Man + Eve, the First Woman
10. Seth + Azura, his sister
11. Enosh (Henos Enos) ADANYA (3769 BC - 2864 BC) + Noham ADANYA, Daughter of Seth and Lilleth the Demoness
12. Cainan (Keinan) + Mualeleth ADANYA
13. Mahalalel ben KENAN + Dinah
14. Jared ben MAHALALEL (ADANYA) + Baraka ADANYA
15. Enoch (Henoch) ben JARED (3382 BC - 3017 BC) + Ednah ADANYA
16. Methusaleh (Mathusale) ben ENOCH + Ednah bint AZRAIL (ADANYA)
17. Laamech ibn METHUSALEH (3130? BC - 2353 BC) + Betenos (Ashmua) ADANYA
18. Noah (Noe) ibn LAMEK (2948? BC - 1998 BC) + Emzara (Coba)Japhet (Iaphet) ibn NOAH
19. Joham ben JAPHETH
20. Jobath (Iobaath Jobhath)

21. Bath (Baath Biath Baoth)
22. Hisrau (Izrau) ibn BAATH (?)
23. Esraa (Ezra)
24. Ra (Rea)
25. Aber (Abir)
26. Ooth (Oth)
27. Ethec (Ecthet)
28. Aurthack
29. Ecthactus
30. Mair
31. Semion (Simeon)
32. Boibus (Boib)
33. Thoi (Thous)
34. Ogomuin
35. Fethuir (Fetjuir, Fetebir I) + Rehea Silvia, daughter of Numa
         Pompilius (2nd King) of ROME
36. Alanus
37. Armenon
38. Longobardus, eponym of the LANGOBARDS
39. Agilulf (Agio) (Prince) of the LANGOBARDS
40. Agilmund (1st King) of the LANGOBARDS
41. (Miss) GUDINGER + Lamicho (2nd King) of the
         LANGOBARDS, son of (NN), a whoremaster (and (NN), a
         prostitute)
42. Lethuk (3rd King) of the LANGOBARDS
43. Hildiok (4th King) of the LANGOBARDS 310? - 359?)
44. Aldeoch de LOMBARDIE + Ascyla (Ascilla)
45. Ildegond of the LOMBARDS (373? - 425+) + Marcomir I (VI;
         V; Duke) of EAST FRANKS
46. Ildegonde of the FRANKS (399? - 450?) + Clovis (Chlodion)
         the RIPARIAN of COLOGNE
47. Chlodoswintha des FRANCS RIPUAIRES (418? - 449?) +
         Merovech (I; King) of (Salic) FRANKS (415 - 458?)
48. Childeric I (King) of FRANKS (of YSSEL) + Basina Andovera
         (Saint?) of THURINGIA
49. Clovis `the Great' (1st King) of All FRANKS + Clothilde (Saint;
         Princess) of BURGUNDY
50. Chlothar I (2nd King) of All FRANKS (497? - 561) + Ildegonde
         of the FRANKS
51. Sigebert (Siegbert) (I; King) of COLOGNE
52. Cloderic `the Parricide' (King) of COLOGNE + Agilofinginne of

the AGILOFING
53. Munderic of VITRY-EN-PERTHOIS + Arthemia(?) of GENEVA
        (503? - 530+)
54. Mummolin des FRANCS RIPUAIRES (505? - 558?)
55. Baudgise II (Duke) of AQUITAINE + Oda (Saint) of SAVOY
        (562? - 611+)
56. Saint Arnoul, bishop of Metz + Saint Dode (Clotilde) of Metz
57. Ansigisel of Metz, Mayor of the Palace of Austrasia + Saint
        Beggue of Austrasia
58. Pépin ll "the Fat"; d'Héristal, Mayor of the Palace of Austrasia
        + Alpaïde (Alpais)
59. Charles Martel "The Hammer", Mayor of the Palace +
        Rotrude, Duchess of Austrasia
60. Pépin III, King of the Franks + Bertha Broadfoot of Laon
61. CHARLEMAGNE, Carolus 'Magnus', Rex Francorum &
        Imperator Romanorum + Hildegard of Vinzgouw
62. "Pépin" Carloman, King of Italy + Mistress of Pepin
63. Bernard, King of Lombardy + Cunigundis (Cunegonde)
        (Princess) de VERMANDOIS
64. Pépin II, lord of Péronne + Rothaide de Bobbio
65. Pepin (I; Count) de SENLIS de VALOIS
66. (Miss) de SENLIS de VALOIS (845? - ?) + Berenger (Count) de
        RENNES (? - 931)
67. Poppa (Poppaeia) de VALOIS (872? - ?) + Rollo (Hrolf Rollon
        Rou Robert) `the Dane' RAGNVALDSSON
68. Guillaume (2nd Duke) of NORMANDY + Sprota de
        BRETAGNE (concubine)
69. Richard I `the Fearless' (Count) of NORMANDY + Gunnora
        (Gonnor) de CREPON
70. Richard II `the Good' of NORMANDY (963? - 1027) + Judith
        (Princess) of BRITTANY
71. Robert II (Duke) of NORMANDY + Herleve (Salburpyr) de
        FALAISE (1003? - 1050?)
72. WILLIAM the CONQUEROR (Duke) of NORMANDY + Matilda
        (Maud) FLEMING (1032 - 1083 Caan)
73. Henry I BEAUCLERC (King) of ENGLAND + Matilda (Edith
        Eagdith) `Atheling' STEWART of SCOTLAND
74. Matilda (Maud Augusta) the EMPRESS + Geoffrey V `the Fair'
        (`Plantagenet')
75. Henry II (King) of ENGLAND + Eleanor (Duchess/Princess) of
        AQUITAINE

76.   John `Lackland' (King) of ENGLAND + Isabella (d'
           ANGOULEME) TAILLEFER
77.   Eleanor (Alianor) of ENGLAND (1215? - 1275) + Simon V de
           MONTFORT (1208 - 4/8/1265)
78.   Eleanor de MONTFORT (1252 - 1282) + Llywellyn (II) ap
           GRUFFYDD (? - 1282)
79.   Catherine verch LLYWELLYN + Philip ap IFOR
80.   Eleanor (of ISCOED; GOCH) verch PHILIP + Thomas ap
           LLEWELLYN
81.   Lowri verch GRUFFUDD FYCHAN + Robert (Sir; of Emral)
           PULESTON (1358? - 1399?)
82.   Angharad PULESTON + Edward TREVOR ap DAFFYD (? -
           1448?)
83.   Otewell Worsley, Sir + Rose (TREVOR) verch EDWART
84.   Joyce Worsley + Richard Lee II
85.   Richard Lee III + Eleanor Burgoine
86.   Geoffrey Lee, MP + Agnes Conyers
87.   Reginald Lee + Dorothy Thurland
88.   Gervase Lee of Nottinghamshire
89.   Thomas Lee, of Ashfield + Margaret Mary Oscroft
90.   Elizabeth Lee + Thomas Hanks
91.   Robert Hanks + Margaret NLN
92.   Peter Hanks I + Mary Bressie
93.   Elinor Hanks + Robert Nelson
94.   Rachael Nelson + Timothy Ragan
95.   Timothy Reagan + Elizabeth Trigg
96.   Richard Bazel Reagan + Cecelia Creppy
97.   Richard Reagan + Phoebe Samples
98.   Reuben Perry Reagan + Elizabeth Cagle
99.   George Reagan + Emaline Garner
100. Marshall Reagan + Emma Rogers
101. Elzie Reagan + Delmar Raines
        ------- Gina Davis
              ------- Jackson Davis
        ------- Patricia Stuart
              ------- Bobby Caldwell
              ------- Jennifer Caldwell
        ------- Mike Raines
              ------- Leah Raines
              ------- Kendra Raines
              ------- Joshua Raines

------- Michael Raines
------- Frank Raines
------- Franklin Cody Raines
------- Kip Allen Raines
------- Richard Raines
------- Tyler Lee
------- Devin Lee
------- Emma Lundy

14

THE GRECO-ROMAN LINEAGE

LINEAGE I

1.   Uranus (1st Ruler GOD of the Universe) + Gaia (Gaea) the Earth GODDESS
2.   Cronos (Kronos) the TITAN + Rhea (Rheia) the TITAN
3.   Zeus the OLYMPIAN (born in Cretan cave) + Niobe of ARGOS (ARGUS)
4.   Pelasgus (1st King) of the PELASGIANS + Deianirra of the PELASGIANS
5.   Lycaon (King) of ARCADIA + Nonacris of ARCADIA
6.   Mantineus (King) of MANTINEIA
7.   Aglaia of ARGOS + Abas (II; King) of ARGOS (& Abae)
8.   Proetus (King) of TIRYNS (& ARGOS) + Danae of ARGOS
9.   Perseus of MYCENAE + Andromeda of ETHIOPIA
10.   Alcaeus of MYCENAE + Astydamia (II) of PISA
11.   Amphitryon of MYCENAE + Alcmena of MYCENAE
12.   Heracles (ALCIDES) of THEBES + Echidna
13.   Hyllus (Chief; of THEBES) HERACLIDE + Iole of OECHALIA
14.   Cleodaeos the HERACLIDE
15.   Aristomachos (of THEBES)

16. Temenos (King) of ARGOS + Dor
17. Ceisus (King) of ARGOS
18. Maron
19. Thestrus
20. Acous
21. Aristodamidas the HERACLIDE
22. Caranus ARGEAD (1st King) of MACEDONIA + Lanlike
23. Coenus ARGEAD (2nd King) of MACEDONIA + Kleonike
24. Tyrimmas (3rd King) of MACEDONIA + Cleonice
25. Perdiccas I (4th King) of MACEDONIA (690? BC - 649 BC) +
Cleopatra of Phrygia
26. Argaeus I (King) of MACEDONIA + Prothoe
27. Argaeus I of MACEDONIA
28. Philip I (King) of MACEDONIA + Nikonoe
29. Aeropus I (King) of MACEDONIA
30. Alcetas I (King) of MACEDONIA
31. Amyntas TEMENID (I; King) of MACEDONIA
32. Alexander I (King) of MACEDONIA (? - 454 BC)
33. Arrhidaeus (Prince) of MACEDONIA
34. Amyntas III (King) of MACEDONIA (? - 370? BC) + Eurydice
of LYNCESTIS (LYNCESTAE) (? - 365 BC)
35. Philip II (King) of MACEDONIA + Olympias of the
MOLOSSIANS
36. Alexander III `the Great' of MACEDONIA
37. Percefus, Greek Governor in Britain
38. Bethides (Governor) in BRITAIN + Cercia
39. Barsine of MACEDONIA + Lucius CAECILIUS Metellus
DENTER
40. Caecilia Metellus Macedonicus + Lucius Julius (Libo) Iullus
41. Lucius Julius Caesar (? - 183+ BC)
42. Lucius JULIUS Caesar (? - 166 BC)
43. Gaius JULIUS Caesar
44. Julia CAESARIS (? - 155+ BC) + Gaius Livius Drusus (? - 147+
BC)
45. Marcus Livius (II) DRUSUS `the Elder' + Cornelia Scipionis of
ROME (? - 89? BC)
46. Marcus LIVIUS Drusus + Servilia CAEPIONIS Major (? = 35?
BC)
47. Marcus Livius Drusus CLAUDIANUS + Alfidia
48. Luvia (Livia) DRUSILLA (? - 30) + Tiberius Claudius NERO
(63? BC - 33? BC)

49. Nero Claudius DRUSUS (Germanicus) + Antonia Minor `the
      Younger' Augusta
50. Claudius I (EMPEROR) of ROME + Aemilia LEPIDA (? - 26)
51. Genuissa (Venessa Julia) Claudia of ROME (? - 50?) +
      Aviragus (King) of the BRITONS (15? - 74? Avalon?)
52. Meric (Marius Meurig Cyllin) of BRITONS (65? - 125?) + Julia
      (Victoria) verch PRASUTAGUS of the ICENI
53. Coel I (Cole Coilus) (Old King Cole) King of BRITONS +
      Ystradwl (Stradwawl) of SILURIA
54. Lleurig (Lucius) MAWR (King) of EWYAS + Gladys (Gwladys)
      verch EURGEN of SILURIA
55. Gladys `the Younger' of BRITAIN (190? - ?) + Cadvan of
      CAMBRIA
56. Strada `the Fair' of COMBRIA + Coilus II (Coel Cole) of
      GLOUCESTER (by 232 - 305?)
57. Helena (Augusta) (Saint) of the CROSS + Flavius Valerius
      Constantius I of Rome
58. Constantine `the Great' of ROME + Flavia Maxima Fausta (? -
      326?)
59. Flavia Constantia Augusta (320? - 354?) + Flavius Claudius
      CONSTANTIUS Gallus
60. Anastasia
61. Gallus
62. Anastasia (Arriana) CONSTANTINA + Pompeius of
      DYRRHACHIUM
63. Flavius PAULUS (Consul) (? - 496+) + Magna Sabiniani
64. Flavius PROBUS (Consul) (? - 502+) + daughter of Flavius
      Sabinianus
65. Flavius Anastasius PAULUS PROBUS Sabinianus POMPEIUS +
      Theodora(?), daughter of Theodora
66. Paulus of ARABISSO + Joanna of ARABISSA
67. Maurice (EMPEROR) of the EAST (539? - 27/11/602)
68. Julius of BYZANTIUM
69. Georgia
70. Juliana FLAVIA + Athanagild (II; King) of the VISIGOTHS
71. Ardabast (Count/King) of the VISIGOTHS + Goda of the
      BURGUNDIANS
72. Ervik (King) of the VISIGOTHS (? - 687) + Liubigotona
      (Liuvigotona) of the VISIGOTHS
73. Aupais (of SPAIN)
74. Charles Martel "The Hammer", Mayor of the Palace +

Rotrude, Duchess of Austrasia
75. Pépin III, King of the Franks + Bertha Broadfoot of Laon
76. CHARLEMAGNE, Carolus 'Magnus', Rex Francorum &
    Imperator Romanorum + Hildegard of Vinzgouw
77. "Pépin" Carloman, King of Italy + Mistress of Pepin
78. Bernard, King of Lombardy + Cunigundis (Cunegonde)
    (Princess) de VERMANDOIS
79. Pépin II, lord of Péronne + Rothaide de Bobbio
80. Pepin (I; Count) de SENLIS de VALOIS
81. (Miss) de SENLIS de VALOIS (845? - ?) + Berenger (Count) de
    RENNES (? - 931)
82. Poppa (Poppaeia) de VALOIS (872? - ?) + Rollo (Hrolf Rollon
    Rou Robert) `the Dane' RAGNVALDSSON
83. Guillaume (2nd Duke) of NORMANDY + Sprota de
    BRETAGNE (concubine)
84. Richard I `the Fearless' (Count) of NORMANDY + Gunnora
    (Gonnor) de CREPON
85. Richard II `the Good' of NORMANDY (963? - 1027) + Judith
    (Princess) of BRITTANY
86. Robert II (Duke) of NORMANDY + Herleve (Salburpyr) de
    FALAISE (1003? - 1050?)
87. WILLIAM the CONQUEROR (Duke) of NORMANDY + Matilda
    (Maud) FLEMING (1032 - 1083 Caan)
88. Henry I BEAUCLERC (King) of ENGLAND + Matilda (Edith
    Eagdith) `Atheling' STEWART of SCOTLAND
89. Matilda (Maud Augusta) the EMPRESS + Geoffrey V `the Fair'
    (`Plantagenet')
90. Henry II (King) of ENGLAND + Eleanor (Duchess/Princess) of
    AQUITAINE
91. John `Lackland' (King) of ENGLAND + Isabella (d'
    ANGOULEME) TAILLEFER
92. Eleanor (Alianor) of ENGLAND (1215? - 1275) + Simon V de
    MONTFORT (1208 - 4/8/1265)
93. Eleanor de MONTFORT (1252 - 1282) + Llywellyn (II) ap
    GRUFFYDD (? - 1282)
94. Catherine verch LLYWELLYN + Philip ap IFOR
95. Eleanor (of ISCOED; GOCH) verch PHILIP + Thomas ap
    LLEWELLYN
96. Lowri verch GRUFFUDD FYCHAN + Robert (Sir; of Emral)
    PULESTON (1358? - 1399?)
97. Angharad PULESTON + Edward TREVOR ap DAFFYD (? -

       1448?)

98.   Otewell Worsley, Sir + Rose (TREVOR) verch EDWART
99.   Joyce Worsley + Richard Lee II
100.   Richard Lee III + Eleanor Burgoine
101.   Geoffrey Lee, MP + Agnes Conyers
102.   Reginald Lee + Dorothy Thurland
103.   Gervase Lee of Nottinghamshire
104.   Thomas Lee, of Ashfield + Margaret Mary Oscroft
105.   Elizabeth Lee + Thomas Hanks
106.   Robert Hanks + Margaret NLN
107.   Peter Hanks I + Mary Bressie
108.   Elinor Hanks + Robert Nelson
109.   Rachael Nelson + Timothy Ragan
110.   Timothy Reagan + Elizabeth Trigg
111.   Richard Bazel Reagan + Cecelia Creppy
112.   Richard Reagan + Phoebe Samples
113.   Reuben Perry Reagan + Elizabeth Cagle
114.   George Reagan + Emaline Garner
115.   Marshall Reagan + Emma Rogers
116.   Elzie Reagan + Delmar Raines
      ------- Gina Davis
          ------- Jackson Davis
      ------- Patricia Stuart
          ------- Bobby Caldwell
          ------- Jennifer Caldwell
      ------- Mike Raines
          ------- Leah Raines
          ------- Kendra Raines
          ------- Joshua Raines
          ------- Michael Raines
      ------- Frank Raines
          ------- Franklin Cody Raines
          ------- Kip Allen Raines
      ------- Richard Raines
          ------- Tyler Lee
          ------- Devin Lee
          ------- Emma Lundy

LINEAGE II

(Julius Caesar & Caesar Augustus)

1. Chronos (Primordial GOD) + Adrasteia (Necessity; Primordial GODDESS)
2. Chaos (PRIMORDIAL)
3. Erebus (Primordial GOD) + Nyx (Nox), GODDESS of NIGHT, both children of
4. Aether (the Upper Sky; PRIMORDIAL) + Hemera (GODDESS), daughter of Chaos (PRIMORDIAL), son of Chronos (Primordial GOD)
5. Uranus (1st Ruler GOD of the Universe) + Gaia (Gaea) the Earth GODDESS
6. Iapetus (Japetus) the TITAN + Clymene the OCEANID, daughter of Oceanis and Tethys the Titans, children of Uranus (1st Ruler GOD of the Universe) and Gaia (Gaea) the Earth GODDESS
7. Epimetheus the TITAN + Pandora of PTHIA, daughter of Hephaestus, GOD of Fire
8. Pyrrha of PTHIA + Deucalion (King) of PTHIA
9. Hellen (King, eponym) of the HELLENES + Orseis the NYMPH
10. Aeolus of THESSALY
11. Xuthus (King) of THESSALY (? - ? Aegialeus) + Creusa of ATHENS, daughter of Erechtheus (King) of ATHENS (and Praxithea (II) of ATHENS)
12. Diomede of PHOCIS + Deioneus (King) of PHOCIS
13. Cephalus of CEPHALLENIA + Procris of ATHENS, daughter of Erechtheus (King) of ATHENS (and Praxithea (II) of ATHENS), son of Pandion (I; King) of ATHENS (and Zeuxippe of ATHENS), son of Zeus the OLYMPIAN (and Hera the OLYMPIAN), son of Cronos (Kronos) the TITAN (and Rhea (Rheia) the TITAN), son of Uranus (1st Ruler GOD of the Universe) (and Gaia (Gaea) the Earth GODDESS)
14. Arcisius the ARGONAUT
15. Laertes (King) of ITHACA + Anticlia of PARNASSUS, daughter of Autolycus and Anticlia of PARNASSUS
16. Odysseus (King) of ITHACA + Circe (AEAEA) the Enchantress, daughter of Hecate of the UNDERWORLD [daughter of Perses and Asteria the Titans] (and Aeetes (King) of COLCHIS [son of Aeetes (King) of COLCHIS, son of Helius (God of the Sun), son of Hyperion and Theia the Titans]
17. Telegonus AEAEUS (Founder of TUSCULUM and son of Odysseus (King) of ITHACA + Penelope of SPARTA

18.   Italus (King & eponym) of ITALY + Leucaria, daughter of
          Latinus (King) of LATIUM)
19.   Roma + Iulus ASCANIUS (1st King) of ALBA LONGA
20.   Silvius (2nd King) of ALBA LONGA + Odela
21.   Aeneas (3rd King) of ALBA LONGA
22.   Latinus Silvius (4th King) of ALBA LONGA
23.   Alba (5th King) of ALBA LONGA
24.   Capetus (6th King) of ALBA LONGA
25.   Capys (7th King) of ALBA LONGA
26.   Capetus (II; 8th King) of ALBA LONGA
27.   Tiberinus Silvius (9th King) of ALBA LONGA
28.   Agrippa (10th King) of ALBA LONGA
29.   Romulus Silvius of ALBA LONGA
30.   Allodius (11th King) of ALBA LONGA
31.   Aventinus (12th King) of ALBA LONGA
32.   Procas (13th King) of ALBA LONGA
33.   Numitor (15th King) of ALBA LONGA
34.   Rhea Silvia (Princess) of ALBA LONGA + Mars, the Roman
          God of War
35.   Romulus (1st King) of ROME (? - 5/7/716? BC) + Hersilia `the
          Raped' of SABINA
36.   Jullus (Julus) of ROME [progenitor of IULLII; eponym of
          JULIUS]
37.   Numerius Julius Iullii (Julus)
38.   Lucius JULIUS Iullii (Julus)
39.   Caius Julius Iullii
40.   Caius Julius Iullii
41.   Caius JULIUS Iullii
42.   Lucius Julius Iullus (Julus)
43.   Caius Julius Iullii
44.   Caius JULIUS Iullii
45.   Lucius Julius Iullus (Julus)
46.   Lucius Julius Iullus (Julus)
47.   Caius JULIUS Iullus
48.   Vopiscus Julius Iullus
49.   Caius JULIUS Iullii
50.   Sextus Julius Iullii
51.   Lucius Julius Iullii
52.   Caius JULIUS Iullii (? - 352+ BC)
53.   Numerius JULIUS Caesar
54.   Lucius JULIUS Caesar

55. Sextus Julius Caesar
56. Lucius Julius Libo (? - 267+ BC)
57. Lucius JULIUS Caesar
58. Sextus Julius Caesar
59. Lucius Julius Caesar (? - 183+ BC) + Caecilia Metellus Macedonicus
60. Lucius JULIUS Caesar
61. Sextus Julius CAESAR (? - 147 BC)
62. Gaius JULIUS CAESAR
63. Gaius Julias (II) CAESAR
64. Gaius JULIUS Caesar (Praetor) of ROME + Aurelia COTTA (? - 54 BC)
65. Gaius JULIUS Caesar (Dictator) of ROME [THE Julius Caesar; eponym of CAESAR (Czar, Kaiser), eponym of month July; (although Augustus was first to hold the Roman title Imperator, Julius is sometimes called 1st EMPEROR of Rome)] + Cornelia CINNA, daughter of Lucius Cornelius Cinna
66. Julia Caesonia + Gnaeus Pompeius Magnus [aka Pompey `the Great'] (Consul) of ROME
67. Atia Balba Caesonia + Gaius (IV) OCTAVIUS (Praetor) of ROME
68. Gaius Octavius Augustus (1st EMPEROR) of ROME [THE Caesar Augustus] + Scribonia
69. Julia Augusta CAESONIA (? - 15?) + Marcus VIPSANIUS Agrippa
70. Julia (Minor; IV) Vipsania (12? BC - 33?) + Lucius Aemilius PAULLUS
71. Aemilia LEPIDA (? - 26) + Claudius I (EMPEROR) of ROME [aka Tiberius Claudius Nero Germanicus; aka Tiberius Nero DRUSUS; murdered by wife]
72. Genuissa (Venessa Julia) Claudia of ROME (? - 50?) + Aviragus (King) of the BRITONS (15? - 74? Avalon?)
73. Meric (Marius Meurig Cyllin) of BRITONS (65? - 125?) + Julia (Victoria) verch PRASUTAGUS of the ICENI
74. Coel I (Cole Coilus) (Old King Cole) King of BRITONS + Ystradwl (Stradwawl) of SILURIA
75. Lleurig (Lucius) MAWR (King) of EWYAS + Gladys (Gwladys) verch EURGEN of SILURIA
76. Gladys `the Younger' of BRITAIN (190? - ?) + Cadvan of CAMBRIA

77. Strada 'the Fair' of COMBRIA + Coilus II (Coel Cole) of GLOUCESTER (by 232 - 305?)
78. Helena (Augusta) (Saint) of the CROSS + Flavius Valerius Constantius I of Rome
79. Constantine 'the Great' of ROME + Flavia Maxima Fausta (? - 326?)
80. Flavia Constantia Augusta (320? - 354?) + Flavius Claudius CONSTANTIUS Gallus
81. Anastasia
82. Gallus
83. Anastasia (Arriana) CONSTANTINA + Pompeius of DYRRHACHIUM
84. Flavius PAULUS (Consul) (? - 496+) + Magna Sabiniani
85. Flavius PROBUS (Consul) (? - 502+) + daughter of Flavius Sabinianus
86. Flavius Anastasius PAULUS PROBUS Sabinianus POMPEIUS + Theodora(?), daughter of Theodora
87. Paulus of ARABISSO + Joanna of ARABISSA
88. Maurice (EMPEROR) of the EAST (539? - 27/11/602)
89. Julius of BYZANTIUM
90. Georgia
91. Juliana FLAVIA + Athanagild (II; King) of the VISIGOTHS
92. Ardabast (Count/King) of the VISIGOTHS + Goda of the BURGUNDIANS
93. Ervik (King) of the VISIGOTHS (? - 687) + Liubigotona (Liuvigotona) of the VISIGOTHS
94. Aupais (of SPAIN)
95. Charles Martel "The Hammer", Mayor of the Palace + Rotrude, Duchess of Austrasia
96. Pépin III, King of the Franks + Bertha Broadfoot of Laon
97. CHARLEMAGNE, Carolus 'Magnus', Rex Francorum & Imperator Romanorum + Hildegard of Vinzgouw
98. "Pépin" Carloman, King of Italy + Mistress of Pepin
99. Bernard, King of Lombardy + Cunigundis (Cunegonde) (Princess) de VERMANDOIS
100. Pépin II, lord of Péronne + Rothaide de Bobbio
101. Pepin (I; Count) de SENLIS de VALOIS
102. (Miss) de SENLIS de VALOIS (845? - ?) + Berenger (Count) de RENNES (? - 931)
103. Poppa (Poppaeia) de VALOIS (872? - ?) + Rollo (Hrolf Rollon Rou Robert) 'the Dane' RAGNVALDSSON

104. Guillaume (2nd Duke) of NORMANDY + Sprota de
     BRETAGNE (concubine)
105. Richard I 'the Fearless' (Count) of NORMANDY + Gunnora
     (Gonnor) de CREPON
106. Richard II 'the Good' of NORMANDY (963? - 1027) + Judith
     (Princess) of BRITTANY
107. Robert II (Duke) of NORMANDY + Herleve (Salburpyr) de
     FALAISE (1003? - 1050?)
108. WILLIAM the CONQUEROR (Duke) of NORMANDY + Matilda
     (Maud) FLEMING (1032 - 1083 Caan)
109. Henry I BEAUCLERC (King) of ENGLAND + Matilda (Edith
     Eagdith) 'Atheling' STEWART of SCOTLAND
110. Matilda (Maud Augusta) the EMPRESS + Geoffrey V 'the Fair'
     ('Plantagenet')
111. Henry II (King) of ENGLAND + Eleanor (Duchess/Princess) of
     AQUITAINE
112. John 'Lackland' (King) of ENGLAND + Isabella (d'
     ANGOULEME) TAILLEFER
113. Eleanor (Alianor) of ENGLAND (1215? - 1275) + Simon V de
     MONTFORT (1208 - 4/8/1265)
114. Eleanor de MONTFORT (1252 - 1282) + Llywellyn (II) ap
     GRUFFYDD (? - 1282)
115. Catherine verch LLYWELLYN + Philip ap IFOR
116. Eleanor (of ISCOED; GOCH) verch PHILIP + Thomas ap
     LLEWELLYN
117. Lowri verch GRUFFUDD FYCHAN + Robert (Sir; of Emral)
     PULESTON (1358? - 1399?)
118. Angharad PULESTON + Edward TREVOR ap DAFFYD (? -
     1448?)
119. Otewell Worsley, Sir + Rose (TREVOR) verch EDWART
120. Joyce Worsley + Richard Lee II
121. Richard Lee III + Eleanor Burgoine
122. Geoffrey Lee, MP + Agnes Conyers
123. Reginald Lee + Dorothy Thurland
124. Gervase Lee of Nottinghamshire
125. Thomas Lee, of Ashfield + Margaret Mary Oscroft
126. Elizabeth Lee + Thomas Hanks
127. Robert Hanks + Margaret NLN
128. Peter Hanks I + Mary Bressie
129. Elinor Hanks + Robert Nelson
130. Rachael Nelson + Timothy Ragan

131.   Timothy Reagan + Elizabeth Trigg
132.   Richard Bazel Reagan + Cecelia Creppy
133.   Richard Reagan + Phoebe Samples
134.   Reuben Perry Reagan + Elizabeth Cagle
135.   George Reagan + Emaline Garner
136.   Marshall Reagan + Emma Rogers
137.   Elzie Reagan + Delmar Raines
        ------- Gina Davis
               ------- Jackson Davis
        ------- Patricia Stuart
               ------- Bobby Caldwell
               ------- Jennifer Caldwell
        ------- Mike Raines
               ------- Leah Raines
               ------- Kendra Raines
               ------- Joshua Raines
               ------- Michael Raines
        ------- Frank Raines
               ------- Franklin Cody Raines
               ------- Kip Allen Raines
        ------- Richard Raines
               ------- Tyler Lee
               ------- Devin Lee
               ------- Emma Lundy

15

THE GRECO-ROMAN-IRISH LINEAGE

1. Uranus (1st Ruler GOD of the Universe) + Gaia (Gaea) the Earth GODDESS
2. Cronos (Kronos) the TITAN + Rhea (Rheia) the TITAN
3. Zeus the OLYMPIAN (born in Cretan cave) + Europa of PHOENICIA
4. Minos 'the Elder' (King) of CRETE + Itone of CRETE
5. Lycastus of CRETE + Ide of CRETE
6. Minos II, King of CRETE + Pasiphae of CORINTH
7. Catreus (King) of CRETE
8. Aerope of CRETE + Atreus (King) of MYCENAE in ARGOS
9. Plisthenes (King) of MYCENAE + Cleolla of MYCENAE
10. Agamemnon (King) of MYCENAE + Clytaemnestra of SPARTA
11. Orestes (King) of ARGOS, MYCENAE & Sparta
12. (NN) ... (NN) (about five missing generations)
13. Sabinus
14. son of Sabinus
15. Demophon
16. Pomponius the SABINE + Jullia Prima of ROME
17. Numa Pompilius (2nd King) of ROME + Egeria the NYMPH or CAMENAE

18.   Rehea Silvia + Fethuir (Fetjuir, Fetebir I)
19.   Lamfind MacFETHEOIR
20.   Glunfind MacLAMFIND
21.   Foenius Farsaid (King) of SCYTHIA + Belait of LATIUM
22.   Niul (Nel) Nemnach of EGYPT + Scota of EGYPT
23.   Gaodhal (Gadelas) Glas of EGYPT
24.   Asruth (Easru Esru) of CRETE
25.   Sru (Sruth Syruth) MacESRU
26.   Eimher (Iara Eubher) Scot (Scut) of CRETE
27.   Beman (Baouman Boamain Beagamon) (King) of SCTHIA
28.   Ogaman (Ogamain Agnamon) (King) of SCTHIA
29.   Tait (Tat) MacOGAMAIN (King) of SCTHIA
30.   Agnon (Adnoin Agnomain) MacTAIT of SCTHIA
31.   Lamhfionn MacAGNON of CRETE
32.   Eimhir Gunfionn MacLAMHFIONN (King) of GOTHLAND
33.   Agnan (Agni) Fionn (King) of GETULIA
34.   Faobhar (Febri Febric) Glas (King) of GOTHIA
35.   Nenuaill (Nenal) (King) of GOTHLAND
36.   Nungatt (Nuadhat) MacNENAIL (King) of GETULIA
37.   Nungatt MacNENAIL of GETULIA
38.   Ealloid (Alldoit) MacNUADAT (King) of GOTHIA
39.   Earchada MacALLDOIT (King) of GEULIA
40.   Deaghatha (Dea; MacAIRCEDA) of SCYTHIA
41.   Brath (MacDEATHA) of SPAIN
42.   Breogan MacBRATHA of SPAIN (927? BC - 872? BC)
43.   Bile (Bille) MacNEMAIN of SPAIN (889? BC - 839? BC)
44.   Gallamh `Milesius' (King) in SPAIN (853? BC - 806? BC) +
           Scota Tephi (Princess) of EGYPT
45.   Heremon (2nd MONARCH) of IRELAND
46.   Irial (Iarel Eurialus) Faidh (Faith) MacEREMOIN
47.   Ethrial MacIAREL FAITH of IRELAND
48.   Follagh MacETHREL (Prince) of IRELAND
49.   Tighearnmhas MacFOLLACH of IRELAND (? - 692? BC)
50.   Eanbothadh MacTIGERNMAS (Prince) of IRELAND
51.   Smiorgall MacENBOTH of IRELAND
52.   Fiachu Labrainn MacSMIRGOLL + (Miss) ingen MUGAETH
53.   Aeneas Olmucaidh MacFIACHACH
54.   Maen MacAENGUSA (Prince) of IRELAND + Hvarfiad
           (Princess) of IRELAND
55.   Rothectaid Rigderg (Roitheaehtaigh) MacMOEN
56.   Deman (Dian Dein Den Drin) MacROTHECTAID

57.   Sirna Sirsaeglach `the Long Lived' MacDIAN
58.   Olioll Olchaoin (Prince) of IRELAND
59.   Giallchadh of IRELAND (? - 787? BC)
60.   Nuahhas (Nuadha) FIONN FAIL (? - 745? BC)
61.   Aedham (Aodhan) GLAS (MacNUADHAT)
62.   Simon (Siomon) BREACH (? - 903? BC)
63.   Murchad (Muireadhach; I) Balgrach MacSIMON
64.   Fiacha (Fiachaidh) TOLGRACH
65.   Duach (II) Ladhghrach (LADRACH)
66.   Duach Ladhghrach
67.   Eochy Buadech MacDUACH + Tamar Tephi ha-DAVID
68.   Augaine Mor MacECHACH + Caesir (Cessair) Cruthach
          (Princess) of FRANKS
69.   Loegaire Lorc MacAUGAINE MAIR
70.   Ailill (Oilioll) Aine MacLOEGAIRE LUIRC
71.   Labraid Loingsech Moen MacAILELLA AINE + Moriat ingen
          SCORIAT
72.   Ailill Abratchbratchaedn MacLABRAID
73.   Aengus Ollam Amlongad MacAILELLA
74.   Breasal BREAC (Bregamos) MacAENGUSA
75.   Feargus Fortamail MacBRESAIL
76.   Fedlimh `Fortriuin Fir Benn'
77.   Crimthann (I) Coscrach MacFEIDEILMID (? - 288? BC)
78.   Mug Art MacCRIMTHAINN COSCRAECH
79.   Art MacMOGA
80.   Alldoit MacAIRT
81.   Nuadu Fuildon Argatlam MacALLDOIT
82.   Nemain, Frenzied Havoc of War + Neit, GOD of War
83.   Delbaeth MacNEIT
84.   Eloth (Allod) MacELATHAN + Aine
85.   Beli MAWR (King) of BRITONS
86.   Lludd I (King) in BRITAIN
87.   Gwrwst (King) in BRITAIN
88.   Pyr (Pir) (King) in BRITAIN
89.   Dunvallo Molmutius + Tonuuenna
90.   Belinus (Beli) (King) in BRITAIN
91.   Gurguint Barbtruc (King) in BRITAIN
92.   Guithelin (King) in BRITAIN + Marcia (Regent) in BRITAIN
93.   Sisillius (II; King) in BRITAIN
94.   Danius (King) in BRITAIN + Tanguesteaia
95.   Morvidus (King) in BRITAIN

96. Elidurus (King) in BRITAIN
97. (NN) ... (NN) (several missing generations)
98. Arthafel (King) in BRITAIN
99. Eidol (King) in BRITAIN
100. Rydon (King) in BRITAIN
101. Rytherch (King) in BRITAIN
102. Sawl Benisel (King) in BRITAIN
103. Pyr (ap SAWL) (King) in BRITAIN
104. Capoir of the DRUIDS
105. Digueillus (King) of BRITONS
106. Heli I (King) of BRITONS
107. Cas `the Exile'
108. Hu the MIGHTY
109. Lugh II `the Shining One' (? - 103 BC)
110. Heli II (? - 55 BC)
111. Caswallon ap BELI (King) of the CATUVELLAUNI (? - 47 BC)
112. Andocoveros (Duke in BRITAIN)
113. Tenacius (King) of the CATUVELLAUNI (BRITONS)
114. Cymbeline (King) of BRITONS (25 BC - 17?)
115. Aviragus (King) of the BRITONS (15? - 74? Avalon?)
116. Meric (Marius Meurig Cyllin) of BRITONS (65? - 125?) + Julia
        (Victoria) verch PRASUTAGUS of the ICENI
117. Coel I (Cole Coilus) (Old King Cole) King of BRITONS +
        Ystradwl (Stradwawl) of SILURIA
118. Lleurig (Lucius) MAWR (King) of EWYAS + Gladys (Gwladys)
        verch EURGEN of SILURIA
119. Gladys `the Younger' of BRITAIN (190? - ?) + Cadvan of
        CAMBRIA
120. Strada `the Fair' of COMBRIA + Coilus II (Coel Cole) of
        GLOUCESTER (by 232 - 305?)
121. Helena (Augusta) (Saint) of the CROSS + Flavius Valerius
        Constantius I of Rome
122. Constantine `the Great' of ROME + Flavia Maxima Fausta (? -
        326?)
123. Flavia Constantia Augusta (320? - 354?) + Flavius Claudius
        CONSTANTIUS Gallus
124. Anastasia
125. Gallus
126. Anastasia (Arriana) CONSTANTINA + Pompeius of
        DYRRHACHIUM
127. Flavius PAULUS (Consul) (? - 496+) + Magna Sabiniani

128. Flavius PROBUS (Consul) (? - 502+) + daughter of Flavius
         Sabinianus
129. Flavius Anastasius PAULUS PROBUS Sabinianus POMPEIUS +
         Theodora(?), daughter of Theodora
130. Paulus of ARABISSO + Joanna of ARABISSA
131. Maurice (EMPEROR) of the EAST (539? - 27/11/602)
132. Julius of BYZANTIUM
133. Georgia
134. Juliana FLAVIA + Athanagild (II; King) of the VISIGOTHS
135. Ardabast (Count/King) of the VISIGOTHS + Goda of the
         BURGUNDIANS
136. Ervik (King) of the VISIGOTHS (? - 687) + Liubigotona
         (Liuvigotona) of the VISIGOTHS
137. Aupais (of SPAIN)
138. Charles Martel "The Hammer", Mayor of the Palace +
         Rotrude, Duchess of Austrasia
139. Pépin III, King of the Franks + Bertha Broadfoot of Laon
140. CHARLEMAGNE, Carolus 'Magnus', Rex Francorum &
         Imperator Romanorum + Hildegard of Vinzgouw
141. "Pépin" Carloman, King of Italy + Mistress of Pepin
142. Bernard, King of Lombardy + Cunigundis (Cunegonde)
         (Princess) de VERMANDOIS
143. Pépin II, lord of Péronne + Rothaide de Bobbio
144. Pepin (I; Count) de SENLIS de VALOIS
145. (Miss) de SENLIS de VALOIS (845? - ?) + Berenger (Count) de
         RENNES (? - 931)
146. Poppa (Poppaeia) de VALOIS (872? - ?) + Rollo (Hrolf Rollon
         Rou Robert) `the Dane' RAGNVALDSSON
147. Guillaume (2nd Duke) of NORMANDY + Sprota de
         BRETAGNE (concubine)
148. Richard I `the Fearless' (Count) of NORMANDY + Gunnora
         (Gonnor) de CREPON
149. Richard II `the Good' of NORMANDY (963? - 1027) + Judith
         (Princess) of BRITTANY
150. Robert II (Duke) of NORMANDY + Herleve (Salburpyr) de
         FALAISE (1003? - 1050?)
151. WILLIAM the CONQUEROR (Duke) of NORMANDY + Matilda
         (Maud) FLEMING (1032 - 1083 Caan)
152. Henry I BEAUCLERC (King) of ENGLAND + Matilda (Edith
         Eagdith) `Atheling' STEWART of SCOTLAND
153. Matilda (Maud Augusta) the EMPRESS + Geoffrey V `the Fair'

('Plantagenet')

154. Henry II (King) of ENGLAND + Eleanor (Duchess/Princess) of AQUITAINE

155. John 'Lackland' (King) of ENGLAND + Isabella (d' ANGOULEME) TAILLEFER

156. Eleanor (Alianor) of ENGLAND (1215? - 1275) + Simon V de MONTFORT (1208 - 4/8/1265)

157. Eleanor de MONTFORT (1252 - 1282) + Llywellyn (II) ap GRUFFYDD (? - 1282)

158. Catherine verch LLYWELLYN + Philip ap IFOR

159. Eleanor (of ISCOED; GOCH) verch PHILIP + Thomas ap LLEWELLYN

160. Lowri verch GRUFFUDD FYCHAN + Robert (Sir; of Emral) PULESTON (1358? - 1399?)

161. Angharad PULESTON + Edward TREVOR ap DAFFYD (? - 1448?)

162. Otewell Worsley, Sir + Rose (TREVOR) verch EDWART

163. Joyce Worsley + Richard Lee II

164. Richard Lee III + Eleanor Burgoine

165. Geoffrey Lee, MP + Agnes Conyers

166. Reginald Lee + Dorothy Thurland

167. Gervase Lee of Nottinghamshire

168. Thomas Lee, of Ashfield + Margaret Mary Oscroft

169. Elizabeth Lee + Thomas Hanks

170. Robert Hanks + Margaret NLN

171. Peter Hanks I + Mary Bressie

172. Elinor Hanks + Robert Nelson

173. Rachael Nelson + Timothy Ragan

174. Timothy Reagan + Elizabeth Trigg

175. Richard Bazel Reagan + Cecelia Creppy

176. Richard Reagan + Phoebe Samples

177. Reuben Perry Reagan + Elizabeth Cagle

178. George Reagan + Emaline Garner

179. Marshall Reagan + Emma Rogers

180. Elzie Reagan + Delmar Raines

------- Gina Davis

    ------- Jackson Davis

------- Patricia Stuart

    ------- Bobby Caldwell

    ------- Jennifer Caldwell

------- Mike Raines

------- Leah Raines
------- Kendra Raines
------- Joshua Raines
------- Michael Raines
------- Frank Raines
------- Franklin Cody Raines
------- Kip Allen Raines
------- Richard Raines
------- Tyler Lee
------- Devin Lee
------- Emma Lundy

16

THE HERULI-OBOTRITE LINEAGE

LINEAGE I

(Jewish)

1.   Mummu the Creator GOD + Nammu, Goddess of the Sea
2.   Apsu, Ocean of Sweet Water + Tiamat, Ocean of Salt Water
3.   Lahmu, The Primordial God + Lahamu, the Primordial
      GODDESS
4.   Anshar, the Primordial God + Kishar, the Primordial
      GODDESS
5.   Anu, GOD of the Sky + Ki Urash, GODDESS of the Earth
6.   Enlil, GOD of Wind
7.   El Shaddai, Supreme GOD of CANAAN + Atiratu, Semitic
      GODDESS of Fertility
8.   Elohim, GOD of Israel
9.   Adam, the First Man + Eve, the First Woman
10.   Seth + Azura, his sister
11.   Enosh (Henos Enos) ADANYA (3769 BC - 2864 BC) + Noham
      ADANYA, Daughter of Seth and Lilleth the Demoness
12.   Cainan (Keinan) + Mualeleth ADANYA

13. Mahalalel ben KENAN + Dinah
14. Jared ben MAHALALEL (ADANYA) + Baraka ADANYA
15. Enoch (Henoch) ben JARED (3382 BC - 3017 BC) + Ednah ADANYA
16. Methusaleh (Mathusale) ben ENOCH + Ednah bint AZRAIL (ADANYA)
17. Laamech ibn METHUSALEH (3130? BC - 2353 BC) + Betenos (Ashmua) ADANYA
18. Noah (Noe) ibn LAMEK (2948? BC - 1998 BC) + Emzara (Coba)
19. Shem (Sceaf Sam Sem) ibn NOAH (2454? BC - 1842 BC) + Sedeqetelebab, daughter of Eliakim ben METHUSELAH
20. Arphaxad (King) of ARRAPACHTIS + Rasueja (bint SHUSHAN)
21. Cainain the SEMITE + Melka (bint MADAI) of MEDES, daughter of Madai (Medai Madian) ben JAPHETH
22. Shelah (ben CAINAN) of CHALDEA + Mu'ak (Muak) ben KESED
23. Eber ibn SHELAH (2277? BC - 1813? BC) + 'Azurad bint NEBROD
24. Joktan ben EBER (2267 BC - ?)
25. Hoeril, eponym of the HERULI
26. (NN) ... (NN) (many missing generations)
27. Anthyrius I (Curllus; 1st King) of the HERULI + Symbulla of the GOTHS
28. Anavas (2nd King) of the HERULI + Drithva (Orethyia)
29. Alimer (3rd King) of the HERULI (? - 96? BC) + IdaRugan Island)
30. Anthyrius II (4th King) of the HERULI + Mary (Marina) of JUTLAND
31. Hutterus (5th King) of the HERULI (? - 35?) + Judith of JUTLAND
32. Visalus (I; 6th King) of the HERULI (& WENDEN) + Tibernia of NORWAY
33. Vitilaus (7th King) of the HERULI (? - 127?) + Anaria of GOTLAND
34. Alaric (I; 8th King) of the HERULI (? - 162?) + Bella of COLOGNE
35. Dietric (9th King) of the HERULI (? - 201?) + Biogonna of THURINGIA
36. Teneric (10th King) of the HERULI + Biogonna of THURINGIA

37. Alberic (11th King) of the HERULI + Diomedes
38. Wisimar (12th King) of the HERULI + Amalasunta
39. Mizislaus I (13th King) of the HERULI + Belga
40. Rodagasus (14th King) of the HERULI + Cella (Cecilia) of the
     VANDALS
41. Corsicus (15th King) of the HERULI + Flora
42. Fredebaldus (16th King) of the HERULI + Themiorma
43. Gunderich (17th King) of the HERULI + Elissa of GRANADA
44. Genserich (18th King) of the HERULI + Licinia EUDOXIA
45. Visilaus (19th King) of the HERULI + Adolla of the SAXONS
46. Alaricus (20th King) of the HERULI + Theodora of the
     BURGUNDIANS
47. Albericus (21st King) of the HERULI + Syrisca (Princess) von
     SARMATIEN
48. Johannes (22nd King) of the HERULI + Euphemia of
     NORWAY
49. Radagast (II; 23rd King) of the HERULI & Wenden +
50. Wisislaus of the OBOTRITES + Hagiza of JUTLAND
51. Vislas I (King) of the OBOTRITES + Petrussa of LOMBARDS
52. Aribert I (King) of the OBOTRITES + Bertha of the FRANKS
53. Billung I of the OBOTRITES (OBODRITES) + Hildegarde
54. Billungus (26th King) of the HERULI & WENDEN + Jutta
55. Mieceslas I of the OBOTRITES (OBODRITES) + Antonia (818?
     - ?)
56. Rodigastus (King) of the OBOTRITES (835? - ?)
57. Mitsui I (Prince) of the OBOTRITES (865? - ?) + Medea von
     SARMATIEN
58. Mieceslas II (Prince) of the OBOTRITES (? - 934?) +
     Antonia(?) von PLUFFOW
59. Mitsui (Mistui) II (Prince) of the OBOTRITES + Sophia
     MIECESLAS
60. Mieceslas III (Prince) of the OBOTRITES (919? - 999?) +
     Sophia MIECESLAS
61. Astrid (Ingegerda) (Princess) of the OBOTRITES + Olaf III (II;
     King; Skot-konig) of SWEDEN
62. Ingegarda (Ingrid) OLAFSDOTTIR (1001? - 1050) + Jaroslav
     (Yaroslav Laroslav) I WLADIMIROWWITSCH
63. Agatha (RURIKID) (? - 1066+) + Edward `the OutLaw' of
     ENGLAND (1016? - 1057?)
64. Margaret (Queen; Saint) of SCOTLAND + Malcolm III
     MacCRINAN (CANMORE)(19th King) of SCOTS

65. Matilda (Edith Eagdith) `Atheling' STEWART of SCOTLAND +
Henry I BEAUCLERC (King) of ENGLAND
66. Matilda (Maud Augusta) the EMPRESS + Geoffrey V `the Fair'
(`Plantagenet')
67. Henry II (King) of ENGLAND + Eleanor (Duchess/Princess) of
AQUITAINE
68. John `Lackland' (King) of ENGLAND + Isabella (d'
ANGOULEME) TAILLEFER
69. Eleanor (Alianor) of ENGLAND (1215? - 1275) + Simon V de
MONTFORT (1208 - 4/8/1265)
70. Eleanor de MONTFORT (1252 - 1282) + Llywellyn (II) ap
GRUFFYDD (? - 1282)
71. Catherine verch LLYWELLYN + Philip ap IFOR
72. Eleanor (of ISCOED; GOCH) verch PHILIP + Thomas ap
LLEWELLYN
73. Lowri verch GRUFFUDD FYCHAN + Robert (Sir; of Emral)
PULESTON (1358? - 1399?)
74. Angharad PULESTON + Edward TREVOR ap DAFFYD (? -
1448?)
75. Otewell Worsley, Sir + Rose (TREVOR) verch EDWART
76. Joyce Worsley + Richard Lee II
77. Richard Lee III + Eleanor Burgoine
78. Geoffrey Lee, MP + Agnes Conyers
79. Reginald Lee + Dorothy Thurland
80. Gervase Lee of Nottinghamshire
81. Thomas Lee, of Ashfield + Margaret Mary Oscroft
82. Elizabeth Lee + Thomas Hanks
83. Robert Hanks + Margaret NLN
84. Peter Hanks I + Mary Bressie
85. Elinor Hanks + Robert Nelson
86. Rachael Nelson + Timothy Ragan
87. Timothy Reagan + Elizabeth Trigg
88. Richard Bazel Reagan + Cecelia Creppy
89. Richard Reagan + Phoebe Samples
90. Reuben Perry Reagan + Elizabeth Cagle
91. George Reagan + Emaline Garner
92. Marshall Reagan + Emma Rogers
93. Elzie Reagan + Delmar Raines
------- Gina Davis
------- Jackson Davis
------- Patricia Stuart

------- Bobby Caldwell
       ------- Jennifer Caldwell
------- Mike Raines
       ------- Leah Raines
       ------- Kendra Raines
       ------- Joshua Raines
       ------- Michael Raines
------- Frank Raines
       ------- Franklin Cody Raines
       ------- Kip Allen Raines
------- Richard Raines
       ------- Tyler Lee
       ------- Devin Lee
       ------- Emma Lundy

LINEAGE II

(Babylonian-Assyrian)

1. Mummu the Creator GOD + Nammu, Goddess of the Sea
2. Apsu, Ocean of Sweet Water + Tiamat, Ocean of Salt Water
3. Lahmu, The Primordial God + Lahamu, the Primordial GODDESS
4. Anshar, the Primordial God + Kishar, the Primordial GODDESS
5. Anu, GOD of the Sky + Anatu GODDESS
6. Enki (Ea), GOD OF WISDOM + Ninhursag, Mother GODDESS
7. Alulim (1st King) of ERIDU
8. Alalgar
9. Kidunnu
10. Alimma
11. Enmenluanna
12. Dumuzi
13. Ensipazianna
14. En-men-dur-anna
15. Urbar-Tutu of SHURRUPAK
16. Ziu-sudra (last King) of BABEL
17. Mashkakatu (1st King) of KISH
18. Kullassina-Bel (King) of KISH
19. Nangislishima (King) of KISH
20. Endaranna (King) of KISH

21.   Babum (King) of KISH
22.   Puannum (King) of KISH
23.   Kalibum of KISH
24.   Qalumun (King) of KISH
25.   Zuqaqip (King) of KISH
26.   Atab (King) of KISH
27.   Mashda (King) of KISH
28.   Arwium (King) of KISH
29.   Etana `the Shepherd' (King) of KISH (? - 2831 BC)
30.   Balih (King) of KISH
31.   Emennuna (King) of KISH
32.   Melam-Kish of KISH
33.   Hia-Kish of KISH
34.   Meskiaggasher (1st King) of URUK
35.   Enmerker (2nd King) of URUK + Inanna Ishtar (Queen) of
           HEAVEN
36.   Lugalbanda (3rd King) of URUK
37.   Gilgamesh (5th King) of URUK
38.   Nimrod (King) of ASSYRIA & BABYLON + Hept Ishtar
39.   Azurad bint NEBROD + Eber ibn SHELAH (2277? BC - 1813?
           BC)Joktan ben EBER (2267 BC - ?)
40.   Hoeril, eponym of the HERULI
41.   (NN) ... (NN) (many missing generations)
42.   Anthyrius I (Curllus; 1st King) of the HERULI + Symbulla of
           the GOTHS
43.   Anavas (2nd King) of the HERULI + Drithva (Orethyia)
44.   Alimer (3rd King) of the HERULI (? - 96? BC) + IdaRugan
           Island)
45.   Anthyrius II (4th King) of the HERULI + Mary (Marina) of
           JUTLAND
46.   Hutterus (5th King) of the HERULI (? - 35?) + Judith of
           JUTLAND
47.   Visalus (I; 6th King) of the HERULI (& WENDEN) + Tibernia
           of NORWAY
48.   Vitilaus (7th King) of the HERULI (? - 127?) + Anaria of
           GOTLAND
49.   Alaric (I; 8th King) of the HERULI (? - 162?) + Bella of
           COLOGNE
50.   Dietric (9th King) of the HERULI (? - 201?) + Biogonna of
           THURINGIA
51.   Teneric (10th King) of the HERULI + Biogonna of THURINGIA

52. Alberic (11th King) of the HERULI + Diomedes
53. Wisimar (12th King) of the HERULI + Amalasunta
54. Mizislaus I (13th King) of the HERULI + Belga
55. Rodagasus (14th King) of the HERULI + Cella (Cecilia) of the
         VANDALS
56. Corsicus (15th King) of the HERULI + Flora
57. Fredebaldus (16th King) of the HERULI + Themiorma
58. Gunderich (17th King) of the HERULI + Elissa of GRANADA
59. Genserich (18th King) of the HERULI + Licinia EUDOXIA
60. Visilaus (19th King) of the HERULI + Adolla of the SAXONS
61. Alaricus (20th King) of the HERULI + Theodora of the
         BURGUNDIANS
62. Albericus (21st King) of the HERULI + Syrisca (Princess) von
         SARMATIEN
63. Johannes (22nd King) of the HERULI + Euphemia of
         NORWAY
64. Radagast (II; 23rd King) of the HERULI & Wenden +
65. Wisislaus of the OBOTRITES + Hagiza of JUTLAND
66. Vislas I (King) of the OBOTRITES + Petrussa of LOMBARDS
67. Aribert I (King) of the OBOTRITES + Bertha of the FRANKS
68. Billung I of the OBOTRITES (OBODRITES) + Hildegarde
69. Billungus (26th King) of the HERULI & WENDEN + Jutta
70. Mieceslas I of the OBOTRITES (OBODRITES) + Antonia (818?
         - ?)
71. Rodigastus (King) of the OBOTRITES (835? - ?)
72. Mitsui I (Prince) of the OBOTRITES (865? - ?) + Medea von
         SARMATIEN
73. Mieceslas II (Prince) of the OBOTRITES (? - 934?) +
         Antonia(?) von PLUFFOW
74. Mitsui (Mistui) II (Prince) of the OBOTRITES + Sophia
         MIECESLAS
75. Mieceslas III (Prince) of the OBOTRITES (919? - 999?) +
         Sophia MIECESLAS
76. Astrid (Ingegerda) (Princess) of the OBOTRITES + Olaf III (II;
         King; Skot-konig) of SWEDEN
77. Ingegarda (Ingrid) OLAFSDOTTIR (1001? - 1050) + Jaroslav
         (Yaroslav Laroslav) I WLADIMIROWWITSCH
78. Agatha (RURIKID) (? - 1066+) + Edward `the OutLaw' of
         ENGLAND (1016? - 1057?)
79. Margaret (Queen; Saint) of SCOTLAND + Malcolm III
         MacCRINAN (CANMORE)(19th King) of SCOTS

80. Matilda (Edith Eagdith) `Atheling' STEWART of SCOTLAND + Henry I BEAUCLERC (King) of ENGLAND
81. Matilda (Maud Augusta) the EMPRESS + Geoffrey V `the Fair' (`Plantagenet')
82. Henry II (King) of ENGLAND + Eleanor (Duchess/Princess) of AQUITAINE
83. John `Lackland' (King) of ENGLAND + Isabella (d' ANGOULEME) TAILLEFER
84. Eleanor (Alianor) of ENGLAND (1215? - 1275) + Simon V de MONTFORT (1208 - 4/8/1265)
85. Eleanor de MONTFORT (1252 - 1282) + Llywellyn (II) ap GRUFFYDD (? - 1282)
86. Catherine verch LLYWELLYN + Philip ap IFOR
87. Eleanor (of ISCOED; GOCH) verch PHILIP + Thomas ap LLEWELLYN
88. Lowri verch GRUFFUDD FYCHAN + Robert (Sir; of Emral) PULESTON (1358? - 1399?)
89. Angharad PULESTON + Edward TREVOR ap DAFFYD (? - 1448?)
90. Otewell Worsley, Sir + Rose (TREVOR) verch EDWART
91. Joyce Worsley + Richard Lee II
92. Richard Lee III + Eleanor Burgoine
93. Geoffrey Lee, MP + Agnes Conyers
94. Reginald Lee + Dorothy Thurland
95. Gervase Lee of Nottinghamshire
96. Thomas Lee, of Ashfield + Margaret Mary Oscroft
97. Elizabeth Lee + Thomas Hanks
98. Robert Hanks + Margaret NLN
99. Peter Hanks I + Mary Bressie
100. Elinor Hanks + Robert Nelson
101. Rachael Nelson + Timothy Ragan
102. Timothy Reagan + Elizabeth Trigg
103. Richard Bazel Reagan + Cecelia Creppy
104. Richard Reagan + Phoebe Samples
105. Reuben Perry Reagan + Elizabeth Cagle
106. George Reagan + Emaline Garner
107. Marshall Reagan + Emma Rogers
108. Elzie Reagan + Delmar Raines
------- Gina Davis
------- Jackson Davis
------- Patricia Stuart

------- Bobby Caldwell
------- Jennifer Caldwell
------- Mike Raines
------- Leah Raines
------- Kendra Raines
------- Joshua Raines
------- Michael Raines
------- Frank Raines
------- Franklin Cody Raines
------- Kip Allen Raines
------- Richard Raines
------- Tyler Lee
------- Devin Lee
------- Emma Lundy

17

THE INDO-EUROPEAN/HINDU LINEAGE

1. INDO-EUROPEAN Pantheon
2. HINDUISM Pantheon (TRIMURTI)
3. Brahma (GOD)
4. Prakrti (Maya)
5. Kusha (King)
6. Kushanaabha
7. Gaadhi (King)
8. Vishwamitra `the Sage'
9. Shakuntala (Sacontale)
10. Bharata (EMPEROR & eponym) of INDIA
11. Phoroneus of ARGOS
12. Niobe of ARGOS (ARGUS)
13. Argus (King) of ARGOS
14. Criasus of ARGOS
15. Phorbas (King) of ARGOS
16. Triopas (King) of ARGOS
17. Pelasgus (II; King) of the PELASGIANS
18. Lycaon (King) of ARCADIA
19. Ceteus of ARCADIA
20. Callisto of ARCADIA

21.   Arcas (King) of ARCADIA
22.   Hyperippe of ARCADIA
23.   Aetolus (King) of AETOLIA
24.   Pleuron (King) of PLEURON, son of Pronoe, daughter of
            Phorbas (co-King) of OLENOS, son of Lapithus (+
            Orsinome) of the LAPITHS, son of Apollo the OLYMPIAN
25.   Agenor (I; King) of PLEURON
26.   Demonike
27.   Thestius of PLEURON (of AETOLIA)
28.   Althaea of CALYDON
29.   Deianira of CALYDON
30.   Hyllus (Chief; of THEBES) HERACLIDE
31.   Cleodaeos the HERACLIDE
32.   Aristomachos (of THEBES)
33.   Temenos (King) of ARGOS
34.   Ceisus (King) of ARGOS
35.   Maron
36.   Thestrus
37.   Acous
38.   Aristodamidas the HERACLIDE
39.   Caranus ARGEAD (1st King) of MACEDONIA
40.   Coenus ARGEAD (2nd King) of MACEDONIA
41.   Tyrimmas (3rd King) of MACEDONIA
42.   Perdiccas I (4th King) of MACEDONIA
43.   Argaeus I (King) of MACEDONIA (? - 611 BC), grandson of
            Gordios (1st King) of PHRYGIA (the son of a poor farmer)
44.   Philip I (King) of MACEDONIA (? - 578 BC)
45.   Aeropus I (King) of MACEDONIA (600? BC - 558 BC)
46.   Alcetas I (King) of MACEDONIA (? - 540? BC)
47.   Amyntas TEMENID (I; King) of MACEDONIA
48.   Eurynae
49.   Arrhabaeus I of LYNCESTAE
50.   Daughter of Arrhabaeus I of LYNCESTAE
51.   Eurydice of LYNCESTIS (LYNCESTAE) (? - 365 BC), daughter
            of Eurydice of LYNCESTIS (LYNCESTAE) (? - 365 BC),
            grand-daughter of Arrabaios (King) of LYNKOS
52.   Philip II (King) of MACEDONIA (382? BC - 336 BC) +
            Olympias of the MOLOSSIANS (375 BC - 316 BC)
53.   Alexander III `the Great' (King) of MACEDONIA
54.   Percefus, Greek Governor in Britain
55.   Bethides (Governor) in BRITAIN

56. Barsine of MACEDONIA
57. Caecilia Metellus Macedonicus
58. Lucius Julius Caesar (? - 183+ BC)
59. Lucius JULIUS Caesar (? - 166 BC)
60. Sextus Julius CAESAR (? - 147 BC)
61. Sextus Julius CAESAR (? - 147+ BC)
62. Lucius Julius (II) CAESAR (Sextus) (? - 124? BC)
63. Lucius JULIUS (III) CAESAR, son of Popillia (Major)
     LAENATUM, grandson of Popillius Laenas
64. Julia Caesia Caesonia of ROME (103? BC - ?)
65. Marcus ANTONIUS (Mark Antony, Triumvir of ROME)
66. Antonia
67. Prydain ap AEDD (Duke/King) of CORNWALL
68. Dyfnarth (Cynfarch Cyfnarch) (Duke/King) of CORNWALL
69. Crydon (Krydon) the CAMBRIAN
70. Cerwydr the CAMBRIAN, descendant of Hamilcar and
     Hannibal, Kings of Carthage
71. Capoir of the DRUIDS (King) of BRITONS
72. Manogan
73. Penardim (Penardun)
74. Bran Fendigaid `the Blessed' (King) of SILURIA
75. Caradoc (King) of BRITAIN
76. Guidgen (? - 85)
77. Art `Cois'
78. Quintus (5th King) of PICTS
79. Corvus (1st King) of DUMBARTON
80. Art `Vroisc' (King) of DUMBARTON
81. Fer `Fi' (King) of DUMBARTON
82. Duibne `Mor' (King) of DUMBARTON
83. poss. Art `Og' (King) of DUMBARTON
84. Con (Confer)
85. Fer (King) of DUMBARTON
86. Cursalem (King) of DUMBARTON
87. Cluim (Clemens Clium Cluian) of ROME
88. Cinhil (Quintillian) of the DAMNONII
89. Cynlop (Cynllwyb Cynloup Cynloyp) of the DAMNONII
90. Ceredig WLEDIG (King) of STRATHCLYDE
91. Erp (Erbin Seirb) ap CERETIC (? - 480?)
92. Geraint ap ERP
93. (Miss) verch GERAINT
94. Erb MacDRUST (? - 529)

95.   Nechtan (Neiton; II; III; MAWR) MacERB (? - 621?)
96.   Beli (I; King) of STRATHCLYDE
97.   daughter of Beli
98.   Spondana ingen ENFIDAIG (Princess) of the PICTS
99.   Eochaid (III) Angbaid (Angbhadh; MacECHACH) of ARGYLL
100.   Fergus (II) MacECHACH (King) of DALRIADA
101.   Constantine (67th/101th King) of PICTS (? - 820+)
102.   Drust IX (69th/103rd King) of PICTS, sister of + Alpin
            MacEOCHAID (King) of KINTYRE (778? - 834)
103.   Kenneth I (Cinaed) MacALPIN (1st King) of SCOTS; united
            Scots & Picts in 846; aka Ciniod (mac Ailpin) II (77th
            King) of PICTS; aka Kenneth `the Hardy'; `the Raven
            Feeder'; the CONQUEROR + daughter of Donald Anicom,
            Lord of the Isles [Note: Scholars generally treat the
            stories and ancestry given for Kenneth to be partly
            fictional. Defeated Picts in battle in 841 (acquiring
            nickname `Raven Feeder'); invited Pictish royal family to
            a great banquet and massacred them; became King of
            both Scots & Picts in 846. The Scots moved their capital
            to Scone, sacred heart of the Pictish Kingdom, and sat on
            a stone throne which, in legend, had come from Spain
            with the 1st Milesian monarch and spent centuries at
            Dunstaffnage Castle in Tara. Although the Picts had ruled
            much of northern Britain for over 1000 years, within a
            century after MacAlpin's Treason Pictish culture and
            language had almost disappeared.]
104.   Constantine I `the Wine-Bountiful' of ALBA (3rd King) of
            SCOTS (836? - 877, beheaded by the Norse) + Nesta
            verch RHODRI MAWR (840? - ?)
105.   Donald II Dasachtach (6th King) of SCOTS (King of ALBA);
            aka Domnall mac Causantin; `the Madman' (abt. 862-900,
            killed in Battle against Danes) + Unknown
106.   Malcolm I MacALPIN of ALBA, 8th King of SCOTS; aka Maol
            Chaluim mac Ailpin; `the Dangerous Red' (897-954, slain
            by men of Moray) + Unknown
107.   Kenneth II MacALPIN of ALBA, 12th King of SCOTS
            (murdered by his own men) + Unknown
108.   Malcolm II MacKENNETH of ALBA, 15th King of SCOTS; aka
            Mael-Coluim, Melkolf, Malbrigdeson, `the Destroyer' +
            Aefgifu, Irish Woman of OSSORY
109.   Bethoc (Beatrix) MacKENNETH of SCOTLAND (984? - ?) +

Crinan of Dunkeld, Abthane of ATHOLL (976? - 1045)
110. Duncan I `the Gracious' MacCRINAN of SCOTLAND + Bethoc MacDUFF (1009? - 1040?)
111. Malcolm III MacCRINAN (CANMORE) (19th King) of SCOTS + Margaret (Queen; Saint) of SCOTLAND
112. Matilda (Edith Eagdith) `Atheling' STEWART of SCOTLAND + Henry I BEAUCLERC (King) of ENGLAND
113. Matilda (Maud Augusta) the EMPRESS + Geoffrey V `the Fair' (`Plantagenet')
114. Henry II (King) of ENGLAND + Eleanor (Duchess/Princess) of AQUITAINE
115. John `Lackland' (King) of ENGLAND + Isabella (d' ANGOULEME) TAILLEFER
116. Eleanor (Alianor) of ENGLAND (1215? - 1275) + Simon V de MONTFORT (1208 - 4/8/1265)
117. Eleanor de MONTFORT (1252 - 1282) + Llywellyn (II) ap GRUFFYDD (? - 1282)
118. Catherine verch LLYWELLYN + Philip ap IFOR
119. Eleanor (of ISCOED; GOCH) verch PHILIP + Thomas ap LLEWELLYN
120. Lowri verch GRUFFUDD FYCHAN + Robert (Sir; of Emral) PULESTON (1358? - 1399?)
121. Angharad PULESTON + Edward TREVOR ap DAFFYD (? - 1448?)
122. Otewell Worsley, Sir + Rose (TREVOR) verch EDWART
123. Joyce Worsley + Richard Lee II
124. Richard Lee III + Eleanor Burgoine
125. Geoffrey Lee, MP + Agnes Conyers
126. Reginald Lee + Dorothy Thurland
127. Gervase Lee of Nottinghamshire
128. Thomas Lee, of Ashfield + Margaret Mary Oscroft
129. Elizabeth Lee + Thomas Hanks
130. Robert Hanks + Margaret NLN
131. Peter Hanks I + Mary Bressie
132. Elinor Hanks + Rober Nelson
133. Rachael Nelson + Timothy Ragan
134. Timothy Reagan + Elizabeth Trigg
135. Richard Bazel Reagan + Cecelia Creppy
136. Richard Reagan + Phoebe Samples
137. Reuben Perry Reagan + Elizabeth Cagle
138. George Reagan + Emaline Garner

139.   Marshall Reagan + Emma Rogers
140.   Elzie Reagan + Delmar Raines
    ------- Gina Davis
        ------- Jackson Davis
    ------- Patricia Stuart
        ------- Bobby Caldwell
        ------- Jennifer Caldwell
    ------- Mike Raines
        ------- Leah Raines
        ------- Kendra Raines
        ------- Joshua Raines
        ------- Michael Raines
    ------- Frank Raines
        ------- Franklin Cody Raines
        ------- Kip Allen Raines
    ------- Richard Raines
        ------- Tyler Lee
        ------- Devin Lee
        ------- Emma Lundy

18

THE IRISH KINGS LINEAGE

LINEAGE I

(Jewish)

1. Mummu the Creator GOD + Nammu, Goddess of the Sea
2. Apsu, Ocean of Sweet Water + Tiamat, Ocean of Salt Water
3. Lahmu, The Primordial God + Lahamu, the Primordial GODDESS
4. Anshar, the Primordial God + Kishar, the Primordial GODDESS
5. Anu, GOD of the Sky + Ki Urash, GODDESS of the Earth
6. Enlil, GOD of Wind
7. El Shaddai, Supreme GOD of CANAAN + Atiratu, Semitic GODDESS of Fertility
8. Elohim, GOD of Israel
9. Adam, the First Man + Eve, the First Woman
10. Seth + Azura, his sister
11. Enosh (Henos Enos) ADANYA (3769 BC - 2864 BC) + Noham ADANYA, Daughter of Seth and Lilleth the Demoness

12. Cainan (Keinan) + Mualeleth ADANYA
13. Mahalalel ben KENAN + Dinah
14. Jared ben MAHALALEL (ADANYA) + Baraka ADANYA
15. Enoch (Henoch) ben JARED (3382 BC - 3017 BC) + Ednah ADANYA
16. Methusaleh (Mathusale) ben ENOCH + Ednah bint AZRAIL (ADANYA)
17. Laamech ibn METHUSALEH (3130? BC - 2353 BC) + Betenos (Ashmua) ADANYA
18. Noah (Noe) ibn LAMEK
19. Japhet (Iaphet) ibn NOAH
20. Emzara (Coba)
21. Joham ben JAPHETH
22. Jobath (Iobaath Jobhath)
23. Bath (Baath Biath Baoth)
24. Hisrau (Izrau) ibn BAATH (?)
25. Esraa (Ezra)
26. Ra (Rea)
27. Aber (Abir)
28. Ooth (Oth)
29. Ethec (Ecthet)
30. Aurthack
31. Ecthactus
32. Mair
33. Semion (Simeon)
34. Boibus (Boib)
35. Thoi (Thous)
36. Ogomuin
37. Fethuir (Fetjuir, Fetebir I)
38. Lamfind MacFETHEOIR
39. Glunfind MacLAMFIND
40. Foenius Farsaid (King) of SCYTHIA + Belait of LATIUM
41. Niul (Nel) Nemnach of EGYPT
42. Gaodhal (Gadelas) Glas of EGYPT + Scota of EGYPT, daughter of Cinqueris (PHARAOH) of EGYPT
43. Asruth (Easru Esru) of CRETE
44. Sru (Sruth Syruth) MacESRU
45. Eimher (Iara Eubher) Scot (Scut) of CRETE
46. Beman (King) of SCTHIA
47. Ogaman (Ogamain Agnamon) (King) of SCTHIA
48. Tait (Tat) MacOGAMAIN (King) of SCTHIA

49.   Agnon (Adnoin Agnomain) MacTAIT of SCTHIA
50.   Lamhfionn MacAGNON of CRETE
51.   Eimhir Gunfionn MacLAMHFIONN (King) of GOTHLAND
52.   Agnan (Agni) Fionn (King) of GETULIA
53.   Faobhar (Febri Febric) Glas (King) of GOTHIA
54.   Nenuaill (Nenal) (King) of GOTHLAND
55.   Nungatt (Nuadhat) MacNENAIL (King) of GETULIA
56.   Ealloid (Alldoit) MacNUADAT (King) of GOTHIA
57.   Earchada MacALLDOIT (King) of GEULIA
58.   Deaghatha (Dea; MacAIRCEDA) of SCYTHIA
59.   Brath (MacDEATHA) of SPAIN
60.   Breogan MacBRATHA of SPAIN
61.   Bile (Bille) MacNEMAIN of SPAIN
62.   Gallamh `Milesius' (King) in SPAIN
63.   Heremon (2nd MONARCH) of IRELAND + Tamar (TEPHI) of
           JUDAH
64.   Irial (Iarel Eurialus) Faidh (Faith) MacEREMOIN
65.   Ethrial MacIAREL FAITH of IRELAND
66.   Follagh MacETHREL of IRELAND
67.   Tighearnmhas MacFOLLACH of IRELAND + Sinusa of
           IRELAND
68.   Eanbothadh MacTIGERNMAS (Prince) of IRELAND
69.   Smiorgall MacENBOTH (Prince) of IRELAND
70.   Fiachu Labrainn (Flacha LABHRIN) MacSMIRGOLL + (Miss)
           ingen MUGAETH
71.   Aeneas (Aengus Aonghus) Olmucaidh MacFIACHACH
72.   Maen MacAENGUSA (Prince) of IRELAND + Hvarfiad
           (Princess) of IRELAND
73.   Rothectaid Rigderg (Roitheaehtaigh) MacMOEN
74.   Deman (Dian Dein Den Drin) MacROTHECTAID
75.   Sirna Sirsaeglach `the Long Lived' MacDIAN
76.   Olioll Olchaoin (Prince) of IRELAND
77.   Giallchadh of IRELAND (? - 787? BC)
78.   Nuahhas (Nuadha) FIONN FAIL
79.   Aedham (Aodhan) GLAS (MacNUADHAT)
80.   Simon (Siomon) BREACH
81.   Murchad (Muireadhach; I) Balgrach MacSIMON
82.   (NN)
83.   Fiacha (Fiachaidh) TOLGRACH
84.   Duach (II) Ladhghrach (LADRACH)
85.   Eochy Buadech MacDUACH + Tamar Tephi ha-DAVID

86.   Augaine Mor MacECHACH + Caesir (Cessair) Cruthach
          (Princess) of FRANKS
87.   Cobthach Caol BREAGH (69th MONARCH) of IRELAND
88.   Melghe (Meig) Molbthach (71st MONARCH) of IRELAND
89.   Irereo Fathach `the Wise' of IRELAND
90.   Connla (Conly Connla) Cruiaidhchealgach CAEM + Sabhdh
          ingen LUGHAIDH (Princess) of IRELAND
91.   Olioll (III) Caisfhiachlach of IRELAND
92.   Eochaidh (VIII) Ailtleathair of IRELAND
93.   Aengus (III) Tuirbheach Teamhrach of IRELAND + Lava `the
          Fierce' Luire (Lorc)
94.   Enna Aignech `the Hospitable' MacAENGUSA + Sabilla
          (Princess) of IRELAND
95.   Beotach (Beothachtach)
96.   Blatact (Blathachtach)
97.   Essamain Emna MacBLATHACHTA (Prince) of IRELAND +
          Magach (Princess) of IRELAND
98.   Roignen `the Red' Ruadh (Prince) of IRELAND
99.   Fionnlogh (Finnlaoch) (Prince) in IRELAND
100.   Fionn MacFIONNLOGH (Prince) in/of IRELAND + Benia ingen
          CRIMTHANN
101.   Eochaidh (IX) Feidlech (FEIDHLIOCH) MacFINN
102.   Breas & Nar & Lothar + Clothra (Clotherne) ingen ECHACH
103.   Lewy `of the Red Circles' of IRELAND
104.   Criffan Crimthann (Criomthann; II) `Niadh-Nar' MacLUGAID
          + Naira (Mar Tath Chabob) of the PICTS
105.   Feredac `the True' MacCRIMTHAINAN NIA NAIRE + Naira
          Mar Tath Chabob
106.   Fiache II (Fiachaidh IV) Fionnolaidh MacFEREDAIG + Eithne
          Nar of ALBA (25? - ?)
107.   Tuathal (I) TECHTMAR (TEACHTMAR; MacFIACHACH) +
          Baine ingen SCAL
108.   Felim Rachtmar `the Lawgiver' MacTUATHAL + Ughna
          OLLCHROTHACH of DENMARK
109.   Conn Ceadchathach MacFEIDEILMID (? - 157?) + Eithue
          (Eithne)
110.   Airt `the Solitary' Aoinfhear MacCONN (? - 195?) + Maedhbh
          (Meidydh Leathdearg)
111.   Cormac Ulfhada (Ulfhota; `Longbeard') MacAIRT + Eithne
          Ollamhdha
112.   Cairbre Lifiochair (Lifechar) MacCORMAIC (? - 284)

113. Fiachaidh (V) Sraibhthine (Scrabhtaine) of IRELAND + Aife of
     GALL GAEDAL
114. Muireadeach (II) Tirech MacFIACHACH + Muireann ingen
     FIACHAIDH
115. Eochaid (Eochu) Mugmedon of IRELAND + Cairenn
     Chasdubh of BRITAIN
116. Niall Noigiallach MacECHACH [Niall of the Nine Hostages; aka
     Nial Mor NAOIGHIALLACH `of the Nine Hostages'; 1st
     King (but reckoned 126th MONARCH) of IRELAND;
     conquered nine countries (incl. part of France); eponym
     & progenitor of O'NEILL; Born: ? Died: abt. 405 Boulogne,
     slain by Prince of Leinster]
117. Conall Gulban MacNEILL (? - 464?)
118. Fergus Cennfota MacCONAILL + Earca ingen LOAIRN
     (Princess) of DALRIADA
119. Feidhlimidh (Fedlim) MacFEARGUSA + Eithne (Princess) of
     LEINSTER
120. Eogan (Eoghan) MacFEIDEILMID
121. Donchad (? - 600+)
122. Cuillum (Colla)
123. Eathach Feighlioch
124. Cartain (Lord) of the ISLES
125. Eirc (Lord) of the ISLES
126. Crimthanne (Lord) of the ISLES
127. Eirc (Lord) of the ISLES
128. Fergus (Lord) of the ISLES
129. Gofraidh (Goffra) (Lord) of the ISLES
130. Maine (Lord) of the ISLES
131. Niallghus (Lord) of the ISLES
132. Suibne (Lord) of the ISLES
133. Maolbruidhe (Lord) of the ISLES
134. Solaimh (Lord) of the ISLES
135. Gilladomnan (Lord) of the ISLES
136. Duncan (Thane/Priest) of DULE
137. Duncan (I) MacDONACHADH (Abthane) of DULE (DULL)
     (920? - 965?)
138. Duncan (Thane) of ATHOLL
139. Crinan `the Thane and Lay Abbot' of Dunkeld + Bethoc
     (Beatrix) MacKENNETH of SCOTLAND (984? - ?)
140. Duncan I `the Gracious' MacCRINAN of SCOTLAND + Bethoc
     MacDUFF (1009? - 1040?), daughter of Malcolm

MacDUFF (990? - ?), son of Kenneth (III) MacDUFF (14th King) of SCOTS

141.   Malcolm III MacCRINAN (19th King) of SCOTS + Margaret (Queen; Saint) of SCOTLAND

142.   Matilda (Edith Eagdith) `Atheling' STEWART of SCOTLAND + Henry I BEAUCLERC (King) of ENGLAND

143.   Matilda (Maud Augusta) the EMPRESS + Geoffrey V `the Fair' (`Plantagenet')

144.   Henry II (King) of ENGLAND + Eleanor (Duchess/Princess) of AQUITAINE

145.   John `Lackland' (King) of ENGLAND + Isabella (d' ANGOULEME) TAILLEFER

146.   Eleanor (Alianor) of ENGLAND (1215? - 1275) + Simon V de MONTFORT (1208 - 4/8/1265)

147.   Eleanor de MONTFORT (1252 - 1282) + Llywellyn (II) ap GRUFFYDD (? - 1282)

148.   Catherine verch LLYWELLYN + Philip ap IFOR

149.   Eleanor (of ISCOED; GOCH) verch PHILIP + Thomas ap LLEWELLYN

150.   Lowri verch GRUFFUDD FYCHAN + Robert (Sir; of Emral) PULESTON (1358? - 1399?)

151.   Angharad PULESTON + Edward TREVOR ap DAFFYD (? - 1448?)

152.   Otewell Worsley, Sir + Rose (TREVOR) verch EDWART

153.   Joyce Worsley + Richard Lee II

154.   Richard Lee III + Eleanor Burgoine

155.   Geoffrey Lee, MP + Agnes Conyers

156.   Reginald Lee + Dorothy Thurland

157.   Gervase Lee of Nottinghamshire

158.   Thomas Lee, of Ashfield + Margaret Mary Oscroft

159.   Elizabeth Lee + Thomas Hanks

160.   Robert Hanks + Margaret NLN

161.   Peter Hanks I + Mary Bressie

162.   Elinor Hanks + Rober Nelson

163.   Rachael Nelson + Timothy Ragan

164.   Timothy Reagan + Elizabeth Trigg

165.   Richard Bazel Reagan + Cecelia Creppy

166.   Richard Reagan + Phoebe Samples

167.   Reuben Perry Reagan + Elizabeth Cagle

168.   George Reagan + Emaline Garner

169.   Marshall Reagan + Emma Rogers

170.   Elzie Reagan + Delmar Raines
        ------- Gina Davis
                ------- Jackson Davis
        ------- Patricia Stuart
                ------- Bobby Caldwell
                ------- Jennifer Caldwell
        ------- Mike Raines
                ------- Leah Raines
                ------- Kendra Raines
                ------- Joshua Raines
                ------- Michael Raines
        ------- Frank Raines
                ------- Franklin Cody Raines
                ------- Kip Allen Raines
        ------- Richard Raines
                ------- Tyler Lee
                ------- Devin Lee
                ------- Emma Lundy

LINEAGE II

(Babylonian-Sumerian-Assyrian-Briton)

1.   Mummu the Creator GOD + Nammu, Goddess of the Sea
2.   Apsu, Ocean of Sweet Water + Tiamat, Ocean of Salt Water
3.   Lahmu, The Primordial God + Lahamu, the Primordial
            GODDESS
4.   Anshar, the Primordial God + Kishar, the Primordial
            GODDESS
5.   Anu, GOD of the Sky + Anatu GODDESS
6.   Enki (Ea), GOD OF WISDOM + Ninhursag, Mother GODDESS
7.   Alulim (1st King) of ERIDU
8.   Alalgar
9.   Kidunnu
10.   Alimma
11.   Enmenluanna
12.   Dumuzi
13.   Ensipazianna
14.   En-men-dur-anna
15.   Urbar-Tutu of SHURRUPAK
16.   Ziu-sudra (last King) of BABEL

17. Mashkakatu (1st King) of KISH
18. Kullassina-Bel (King) of KISH
19. Nangislishima (King) of KISH
20. Endaranna (King) of KISH
21. Babum (King) of KISH
22. Puannum (King) of KISH
23. Kalibum of KISH
24. Qalumun (King) of KISH
25. Zuqaqip (King) of KISH
26. Atab (King) of KISH
27. Mashda (King) of KISH
28. Arwium (King) of KISH
29. Etana `the Shepherd' (King) of KISH (? - 2831 BC)
30. Balih (King) of KISH
31. Emennuna (King) of KISH
32. Melam-Kish of KISH
33. Hia-Kish of KISH
34. Meskiaggasher (1st King) of URUK
35. Enmerker (2nd King) of URUK + Inanna Ishtar (Queen) of
        HEAVEN
36. Lugalbanda (3rd King) of URUK
37. Gilgamesh (5th King) of URUK
38. Nimrod (King) of ASSYRIA & BABYLON + Hept Ishtar
39. Azurad bint NEBROD + Eber ibn NOAH (2454? BC - 277? BC -
        1813? BC)
40. Pelag ben EBER (Shinar 2243? BC - 2004? BC) + Lomna bint
        SINA'AR
41. Heraclim + Shela
42. Abram + (Miss) de UR
43. 'Edna bat 'ABRAM + Ierah (Thare Terih) (King?) of AGADE
44. Abraham (Avraham Ibrahim) of GENESIS + Sarai (Sarah)
        (Princess) bint HARAN
45. Isaac ibn ABRAHAM (1922 BC - 1742 BC) + Rebekah
        (Rebecca) bint BETHEUL
46. Jacob ibn ISAAC (King of GOSHEN) + Leah (Lia) bint LABAN
47. Judah (Judas Juda) ibn JACOB + Tamar of KADESH (? - 1665?
        BC)
48. Perez (Phares) + Barayah (bas JACOB?)
49. Hezron ibn PHARES (Prince of JUDAH) + Ephratha bint
        MACHIR
50. Caleb ben HEZRON + Ephratha bint MACHIR

51. Hur (Jephunneh) ben CALEB + Miriam (the PROPHETESS) bat AMRAM
52. Salma ben HUR
53. Beth-Lehem
54. NNs of BETHLEHEM (some missing generations)
55. Ibzan of BETHLEHEM
56. (NN; 'Edal?; Abrias?) ben IBZAN
57. Abala (Habalith) + Jesse ben OBED (Bethlehem 1078? BC - ?)
58. David (1st King) of JUDAH & ISRAEL + Bathsheba (Bathshua) bat AMMIEL
59. Solomon ben DAVID (2nd King) of ISRAEL (? - 930 BC) + Nicaule (Nicauli Tashere) of EGYPT
60. Basemath bat SOLOMON + Ahimaaz the NAPHALITE
61. Ana bat AHIMAAZ + Abia (Abijah) (4th King) of JUDAH
62. Asa (Asaph) (5th King) of JUDEA + Azubah (Queen) of JUDEA
63. Jehoshapat (6th King) of JUDAH + daughter of Omri
64. Jehoram (Joram) (7th King) of JUDAH + Athalia of ISRAEL (9th Queen) of JUDAH
65. Ozias (Ahaziah Ochozias) (8th King) of JUDAH + Zibiah of BEERSHEBA
66. Josiah (I; 10th King) of JUDAH (871 BC - 796 BC) + Jehoaddin of JERUSALEM
67. Amaziah (Amasias) (11th King) of JUDAH + Jecoliah of JERUSALEM
68. Uzziah (Azariah) (12th King) of JUDAH + Jerusha of ISRAEL
69. Joatham (Jotham) (13th King) of JUDAH + Ahio (Princess) bat AZRIKAM
70. Achaz (Ahaz) (14th King) of JUDAH + Abijah bat ZECHARIAH (Heiress) of ISRAEL
71. Ezechias (Hezekiah) (15th King) of JUDAH + Hephzibah bat ISAIAH
72. Manasses ha-DAVID (Manasseh) (16th King) of JUDAH + Meshullemeth bat HARUZ of JOTBAH
73. Amon ha-DAVID (17th King) of JUDAH + Jedidah bat ADAIAH of BOZKATH
74. Josias (Josiah) ha-DAVID (18th King) of JUDAH + Zebidah (Zebudah; bat PEDAIAH) of RUMAH
75. Johanan (Crown Prince) of JUDAH
76. Tamar (Heiress) of the DAVIDIC Dynasty + Neri (Neriah) ha-DAVID
77. Salathial (Shealtiel) ha-DAVID + poss. Hadast (Hetbath)

78. Zorobabel ha-DAVID (Heir) of the DAVIDIC Dynasty +
       Rhodah (Princess) of PERSIA (? - 571? BC)
79. Resa (Reza Rhesa) ha-DAVID
80. Joanna (Joanan Yohannai Jehohanen) ben RESA
81. Judah (Juda Joda Judas) ben JOANNA
82. Joseph (Josech) ben JUDAH
83. Semel ben JOSEPH
84. Mattathias (Mathathias) ben SEMEL + daughter of Simon ha-
       KOHEN
85. Maath ben MATTATHIAS ha-DAVID
86. Nagga ben MAATH
87. Esli ben NAGGA
88. Naum ben ESLI of JUDAH
89. Amos ben NAUM
90. Mattathias (Mathathias Mattathiah) ben AMOS
91. Joseph (Jose) ben MATTATHIAS
92. Janna (Janne Jannai Johanan) ben JOSEPH
93. Melchi (Melki) ben JANNA
94. Levi ben MELCHI
95. Matthat (Mathat) ben LEVI of ARIMATHEA + daughter of
       Eleazar
96. Joseph ben MATTHAT (Saint) of ARIMATHEA + Alyuba
97. Anna (Enygeus) of ARIMATHEA + Mandubratius ap LUD of
       BRITAIN
98. Boadicea (Queen) of ICENIANS (22? - 62?) + Prasutagus
       (King) of ICENIA (? - 61?)
99. Julia (Victoria) verch PRASUTAGUS of the ICENI + Meric
       (Marius Meurig Cyllin) of BRITONS (65? - 125?)
100. Coel I (Cole Coilus) (Old King Cole) King of BRITONS +
       Ystradwl (Stradwawl) of SILURIA
101. Althildis (Princess) of BRITAIN (by 105 - ?) + Marcomir IV
       (King) of FRANKS (by 105 - 149?)
102. (Miss) of the FRANKS + Gall Gaodnu of CYMRU
103. Aife (Aoife) of GALL GAEDAL + Fiachaidh (V) Sraibhthine
       (Scrabhtaine) of IRELAND
104. Muireadeach (II) Tirech MacFIACHACH + Muireann ingen
       FIACHAIDH
105. Eochaid (Eochu) Mugmedon of IRELAND + Cairenn
       Chasdubh of BRITAIN
**106. Niall Noigiallach MacECHACH [Niall of the Nine Hostages;
       aka Nial Mor NAOIGHIALLACH `of the Nine Hostages';**

1st King (but reckoned 126th MONARCH) of IRELAND; conquered nine countries (incl. part of France); eponym & progenitor of O'NEILL; Born: ? Died: abt. 405 Boulogne, slain by Prince of Leinster]

107. Conall Gulban MacNEILL (? - 464?)
108. Fergus Cennfota MacCONAILL
109. Feidhlimidh (Fedlim) MacFEARGUSA + Eithne (Princess) of LEINSTER
110. Eogan (Eoghan) MacFEIDEILMID
111. Donchad (? - 600+)
112. Cuillum (Colla)
113. Eathach Feighlioch
114. Cartain (Lord) of the ISLES
115. Eirc (Lord) of the ISLES
116. Crimthanne (Lord) of the ISLES
117. Eirc (Lord) of the ISLES
118. Fergus (Lord) of the ISLES
119. Gofraidh (Goffra) (Lord) of the ISLES
120. Maine (Lord) of the ISLES
121. Niallghus (Lord) of the ISLES
122. Suibne (Lord) of the ISLES
123. Maolbruidhe (Lord) of the ISLES
124. Solaimh (Lord) of the ISLES
125. Gilladomnan (Lord) of the ISLES
126. Duncan (Thane/Priest) of DULE
127. Duncan (I) MacDONACHADH (Abthane) of DULE (DULL) (920? - 965?)
128. Duncan (Thane) of ATHOLL
129. Crinan `the Thane and Lay Abbot' of Dunkeld + Bethoc (Beatrix) MacKENNETH of SCOTLAND (984? - ?)
130. Duncan I `the Gracious' MacCRINAN of SCOTLAND + Bethoc MacDUFF (1009? - 1040?), daughter of Malcolm MacDUFF (990? - ?), son of Kenneth (III) MacDUFF (14th King) of SCOTS
131. Malcolm III MacCRINAN (19th King) of SCOTS + Margaret (Queen; Saint) of SCOTLAND
132. Matilda (Edith Eagdith) `Atheling' STEWART of SCOTLAND + Henry I BEAUCLERC (King) of ENGLAND
133. Matilda (Maud Augusta) the EMPRESS + Geoffrey V `the Fair' (`Plantagenet')
134. Henry II (King) of ENGLAND + Eleanor (Duchess/Princess) of

AQUITAINE
135. John `Lackland' (King) of ENGLAND + Isabella (d'
ANGOULEME) TAILLEFER
136. Eleanor (Alianor) of ENGLAND (1215? - 1275) + Simon V de
MONTFORT (1208 - 4/8/1265)
137. Eleanor de MONTFORT (1252 - 1282) + Llywellyn (II) ap
GRUFFYDD (? - 1282)
138. Catherine verch LLYWELLYN + Philip ap IFOR
139. Eleanor (of ISCOED; GOCH) verch PHILIP + Thomas ap
LLEWELLYN
140. Lowri verch GRUFFUDD FYCHAN + Robert (Sir; of Emral)
PULESTON (1358? - 1399?)
141. Angharad PULESTON + Edward TREVOR ap DAFFYD (? -
1448?)
142. Otewell Worsley, Sir + Rose (TREVOR) verch EDWART
143. Joyce Worsley + Richard Lee II
144. Richard Lee III + Eleanor Burgoine
145. Geoffrey Lee, MP + Agnes Conyers
146. Reginald Lee + Dorothy Thurland
147. Gervase Lee of Nottinghamshire
148. Thomas Lee, of Ashfield + Margaret Mary Oscroft
149. Elizabeth Lee + Thomas Hanks
150. Robert Hanks + Margaret NLN
151. Peter Hanks I + Mary Bressie
152. Elinor Hanks + Rober Nelson
153. Rachael Nelson + Timothy Ragan
154. Timothy Reagan + Elizabeth Trigg
155. Richard Bazel Reagan + Cecelia Creppy
156. Richard Reagan + Phoebe Samples
157. Reuben Perry Reagan + Elizabeth Cagle
158. George Reagan + Emaline Garner
159. Marshall Reagan + Emma Rogers
160. Elzie Reagan + Delmar Raines
------- Gina Davis
------- Jackson Davis
------- Patricia Stuart
------- Bobby Caldwell
------- Jennifer Caldwell
------- Mike Raines
------- Leah Raines
------- Kendra Raines

------- Joshua Raines
------- Michael Raines
------- Frank Raines
------- Franklin Cody Raines
------- Kip Allen Raines
------- Richard Raines
------- Tyler Lee
------- Devin Lee
------- Emma Lundy

LINEAGE III

(Egyptian)

1. Sesostris + Nefret
2. Amenemhat I Sehetepibre (Founder) of 12th Dynasty + Nefrutotenen
3. Sesotris I Kheperkare (PHARAOH) of EGYPT (? - 1928? BC) + Nefrusheri (Princess) of EGYPT
4. Amenemhat (Ammenemes) II Nubkaure (PHARAOH) of EGYPT + Keminnub (Queen) of EGYPT
5. Sesotris II Khakheperre (PHARAOH) of EGYPT + Nofret of EGYPT
6. Sesotris III Khakaure of EGYPT + Sebekshedty-Neferu (Queen) of EGYPT
7. Amenemhat III Nemare (PHARAOH) of EGYPT + Sebeknefru (Queen) of EGYPT
8. Amenemhat (Ammenemes) IV (PHARAOH) of EGYPT
9. Sebeknefru (Queen) of EGYPT + (NN), consort of Queen Sebeknefru
10. Wegaf (PHARAOH) of 13th Dynasty + daughter of Amenemhet IV
11. Ameny Intef (Inyotef) IV (PHARAOH) of EGYPT
12. Hor (PHARAOH) of EGYPT (? - 1760? BC)
13. Sobekhotep II (PHARAOH) of EGYPT (? - 1750? BC)
14. Khendjer (PHARAOH) of EGYPT (? - 1747? BC)
15. Sobekhotep III (PHARAOH) of EGYPT (? - 1745? BC)
16. Neferhotep I (PHARAOH) of EGYPT
17. Sobekhotep IV Khaneferre (PHARAOH) of 13th Dynasty + Tjan
18. Sebekhotep (Princess) of THEBES + Senebhanef, son of

Renressonb
19. Mentuhotep (Queen) of EGYPT + Sekhemre-Sementawi
        Djehuti (PHARAOH) of EGYPT
20. Sekhemre-Se'ankhtawi Neferhotep (PHARAOH) of EGYPT
21. Sobekemsaf Sekhemre-Shedtawi (PHARAOH) of EGYPT +
        Nubkhas (Queen) of EGYPT
22. Inyotef VII (PHARAOH) at THEBES + Sobkemsaf
        (Sebekamzaf) of EGYPT (1635? BC - ?)
23. Sekenenre Tao I (PHARAOH) at THEBES + Tetisheri of
        THEBES
24. Sekenenre Tao II (King) of THEBES + Ahhotep (Ahotop) I
        (Queen) of EGYPT
25. Ahmose I (1st PHARAOH) of 18th Dynasty + Nefretiri
        (Queen) of EGYPT
26. Amenhotep I Djeserkare (PHARAOH) of EGYPT + Senisonb
        (Seneseneb) of EGYPT
27. Thutmose I (PHARAOH) of EGYPT (? - 1481? BC) + Amhose
        (Aahmes II) (Queen) of EGYPT
28. Hatshepsut (Queen & PHARAOH) of EGYPT (? - 1482 BC) +
        Thutmose (Tuthmosis) II (PHARAOH) of EGYPT
29. Neferure of EGYPT + Thutmose III `the Great' of EGYPT
        (Moses of the Bible)
30. Amenemhat (Crown Prince) of EGYPT + Ta-Thuia
31. Webensenu (Neby)
32. Horemheb of EGYPT (Alabastronopolis?) + Mutnodjme
33. Seti (Setymeramen) + Ankhesenpaaten II (Heiress) of EGYPT,
        daughter of Akhenaton of 18th Dynasty
34. Ramses I (PHARAOH) of EGYPT (1345? BC - 1294 BC) + Sitre
        Meryamun Twosret Setepenmut, grand-dau of Nefertiti
        (Chief Queen) of EGYPT
35. Seti I (PHARAOH) of EGYPT (1323? BC - 1279 BC) + Tuya
        (Thuya) of EGYPT
36. Ramses (Ramesses) II (PHARAOH) of EGYPT + Maetnefrure
        (Princess) of KHATTI
37. Setakht (Sethnakhte) of EGYPT + Tiye-Mereniset of EGYPT
38. Nekhtseth (Prince) of EGYPT
39. Ramses (Ramesses) III `Hikon' (PHARAOH) of EGYPT + Isis,
        daughter of Habadjilat of ASIA
40. Ramses VI (Montjuhirkopshef) (PHARAOH ?) of EGYPT
41. Ramses (Ramesses) IX (PHARAOH) of EGYPT + Baktwernel
42. Tayu-Herat + Nebseny

43.   Henttawy + Piankh (Piankhi) I of EGYPT (? - 1060? BC)
44.   Istemkheb I of THEBES + Pinudjem I (PHARAOH) of EGYPT
45.   Djedkhonsefankh of THEBES + Djedmutesankh
46.   Djedmutesankh of THEBES + Shoshenk of MA'AT, son of
       Paihut (High Priest) of MA'AT, son of Nabnasi (High
       Priest) of MA'AT, son of Mawasen (High Priest) of MA'AT,
       son of Buyuwawa (High Priest) of MA'AT
47.   Tentsepah `the Libyan' of MA'AT + Nimlot the LIBYAN
48.   Shoshank I (1st PHARAOH) of 22nd Dynasty + Kar'oma
       (Karamat I) of EGYPT
49.   Osorkon I (PHARAOH) the LIBYAN + Tashedkhonsu
50.   Takelot I (PHARAOH) the LIBYAN + Kapes (925? BC - ?)
51.   Osorkon II (PHARAOH) the LIBYAN + Djedmutesankh
52.   Nimlot of THEBES
53.   Karoma Mertmout II of THEBES + Takelot II (High Priest) of
       MA'AT (875? BC - 830? BC)
54.   Shoshenk III (High Priest) of MA'AT + Djedbastesankh (II)
55.   Pami (Pamai Pimay Pemay) (High Priest) of MA'AT +
       Karomat V
56.   Osorkon IV `C' (High Priest) of MA'AT
57.   Tefnakhte (I) Shepses Re' of EGYPT
58.   Bakenranef (Bocchoris) Wah Ka Re' (PHARAOH) of EGYPT
59.   Nekauba Irib Re' (Neokhabis Nechepso) of EGYPT + Anakhka
60.   Necho I (Nekhao Memkheperre) of EGYPT + Amenirdis (II)
61.   Psamtik (Psamtek) I of EGYPT + Mehetenweskhet of
       HELIOPOLIS
62.   Necho II (Wehemibre) (PHARAOH) of EGYPT +
       Khedebnitjerbone (Chedebnitjerbone)
63.   Scota Tephi (Princess) of EGYPT + Gallamh `Milesius' (King)
       in SPAIN
64.   Heremon (2nd MONARCH) of IRELAND + Tamar (TEPHI) of
       JUDAH
65.   Irial (Iarel Eurialus) Faidh (Faith) MacEREMOIN
66.   Ethrial MacIAREL FAITH of IRELAND (769? BC - 711? BC)
67.   Follagh MacETHREL (Prince) of IRELAND
68.   Tighearnmhas MacFOLLACH of IRELANG + Sinusa of
       IRELAND
69.   Eanbothadh MacTIGERNMAS of IRELAND
70.   Smiorgall MacENBOTH (Prince) of IRELAND
71.   Fiachu Labrainn (Flacha LABHRIN) MacSMIRGOLL + (Miss)
       ingen MUGAETH

72.   Aeneas (Aengus Aonghus) Olmucaidh MacFIACHACH
73.   Maen MacAENGUSA (Prince) of IRELAND + Hvarfiad
          (Princess) of IRELAND, DAU OF Eochaidh (IV) Mumho
          (19th MONARCH) of IRELAND
74.   Rothectaid Rigderg (Roitheaehtaigh) MacMOEN
75.   Deman (Dian Dein Den Drin) MacROTHECTAID
76.   Sirna Sirsaeglach `the Long Lived' MacDIAN
77.   Olioll Olchaoin (Prince) of IRELAND
78.   Giallchadh of IRELAND (? - 787? BC)
79.   Nuahhas (Nuadha) FIONN FAIL (? - 745? BC)
80.   Aedham (Aodhan) GLAS (MacNUADHAT)
81.   Simon (Siomon) BREACH (? - 903? BC)
82.   Murchad (Muireadhach; I) Balgrach MacSIMON
83.   Fiacha (Fiachaidh) TOLGRACH
84.   Duach (II) Ladhghrach (LADRACH)
85.   Eochy Buadech MacDUACH + Tamar Tephi ha-DAVID
86.   Augaine Mor MacECHACH + Caesir Cruthach (Princess) of
          FRANKS
87.   Loegaire Lorc MacAUGAINE MAIR
88.   Ailill (Oilioll) Aine MacLOEGAIRE LUIRC
89.   Labraid Loingsech Moen MacAILELLA AINE + Moriat ingen
          SCORIAT
90.   Ailill Abratchbratchaedn MacLABRAID
91.   Aengus Ollam Amlongad MacAILELLA (? - 480? BC)
92.   Breasal BREAC (Bregamos) MacAENGUSA
93.   Feargus Fortamail MacBRESAIL
94.   Fedlimh `Fortriuin Fir Benn'
95.   Crimthann (I) Coscrach MacFEIDEILMID (? - 288? BC)
96.   Benia ingen CRIMTHANN + Fionn MacFIONNLOGH of
          IRELAND
97.   Eochaidh (IX) Feidlech (FEIDHLIOCH) MacFINN + Cloth
          Fionn ingen EOCHAIDH ACHTICATHAN
98.   Breas & Nar & Lothar + Clothra (Clotherne) ingen ECHACH
          (THE 3 BOYS' SISTER WHO THEY RAPED)
99.   Lewy `of the Red Circles' of IRELAND + Clothra (Clotherne)
          ingen ECHACH
100.   Criffan Crimthann (Criomthann; II) `Niadh-Nar' MacLUGAID
          + Naira (Mar Tath Chabob) of the PICTS, dau of Loich
          (King) of the PICTS, son of Dareletuis (King) of the
          NORTHERN PICTS
101.   Feredac `the True' MacCRIMTHAINAN NIA NAIRE + Naira

Mar Tath Chabob
102. Fiache II (Fiachaidh IV) Fionnolaidh MacFEREDAIG + Eithne
Nar of ALBA (25? - ?), dau of Elderus (King) of SCOTS (or
PICTS), son of Reutherus (Reude Reutha) (? - 187? BC),
son of Dornadille (Dorvididla) (? - 233? BC), son of
Mainus (? - 261? BC), son of Fergus I of SCOTS (or PICTS)
103. Tuathal (I) TECHTMAR (TEACHTMAR; MacFIACHACH) +
Baine ingen SCAL, dau of Sgaile (Scal) Balbh (Sub-king in
ENGLAND)
104. Felim Rachtmar `the Lawgiver' MacTUATHAL + Ughna
(Ughua Aghna) OLLCHROTHACH (Princess) of
DENMARK, dau of Indearg (King) of DENMARK
105. Conn Ceadchathach MacFEIDEILMID (? - 157?) + Landabaria
na LEINSTER
106. Sarad (Serad) ingen CONN + Conaire (II) MacMOGA LAMA (?
- 165?)
107. Corbred of PICTS, sister of
108. Eochaidh of PICTS, sister of + Athirco (? - 250?)
109. Findochar of PICTS, sister of
110. Thrinklind of PICTS, sister of
111. Fincormach of PICTS + Findacher MacATHIRCO
112. Romaich of PICTS, sister of
113. (NN) of the Picts + Loarn Mor (King) of DALRIADA (436? - ?)
114. Earca ingen LOAIRN (Princess) of DALRIADA + Fergus
Cennfota MacCONAILL
115. Feidhlimidh (Fedlim) MacFEARGUSA + Eithne (Princess) of
LEINSTER
116. Eogan (Eoghan) MacFEIDEILMID
117. Donchad (? - 600+)
118. Cuillum (Colla)
119. Eathach Feighlioch
120. Cartain (Lord) of the ISLES
121. Eirc (Lord) of the ISLES
122. Crimthanne (Lord) of the ISLES
123. Eirc (Lord) of the ISLES
124. Fergus (Lord) of the ISLES
125. Gofraidh (Goffra) (Lord) of the ISLES
126. Maine (Lord) of the ISLES
127. Niallghus (Lord) of the ISLES
128. Suibne (Lord) of the ISLES
129. Maolbruidhe (Lord) of the ISLES ·

130.   Solaimh (Lord) of the ISLES
131.   Gilladomnan (Lord) of the ISLES
132.   Duncan (Thane/Priest) of DULE
133.   Duncan (I) MacDONACHADH (Abthane) of DULE (DULL)
            (920? - 965?)
134.   Duncan (Thane) of ATHOLL
135.   Crinan `the Thane and Lay Abbot' of Dunkeld + Bethoc
            (Beatrix) MacKENNETH of SCOTLAND (984? - ?)
136.   Duncan I `the Gracious' MacCRINAN of SCOTLAND + Bethoc
            MacDUFF (1009? - 1040?), daughter of Malcolm
            MacDUFF (990? - ?), son of Kenneth (III) MacDUFF (14th
            King) of SCOTS
137.   Malcolm III MacCRINAN (19th King) of SCOTS + Margaret
            (Queen; Saint) of SCOTLAND
138.   Matilda (Edith Eagdith) `Atheling' STEWART of SCOTLAND +
            Henry I BEAUCLERC (King) of ENGLAND
139.   Matilda (Maud Augusta) the EMPRESS + Geoffrey V `the Fair'
            (`Plantagenet')
140.   Henry II (King) of ENGLAND + Eleanor (Duchess/Princess) of
            AQUITAINE
141.   John `Lackland' (King) of ENGLAND + Isabella (d'
            ANGOULEME) TAILLEFER
142.   Eleanor (Alianor) of ENGLAND (1215? - 1275) + Simon V de
            MONTFORT (1208 - 4/8/1265)
143.   Eleanor de MONTFORT (1252 - 1282) + Llywellyn (II) ap
            GRUFFYDD (? - 1282)
144.   Catherine verch LLYWELLYN + Philip ap IFOR
145.   Eleanor (of ISCOED; GOCH) verch PHILIP + Thomas ap
            LLEWELLYN
146.   Lowri verch GRUFFUDD FYCHAN + Robert (Sir; of Emral)
            PULESTON (1358? - 1399?)
147.   Angharad PULESTON + Edward TREVOR ap DAFFYD (? -
            1448?)
148.   Otewell Worsley, Sir + Rose (TREVOR) verch EDWART
149.   Joyce Worsley + Richard Lee II
150.   Richard Lee III + Eleanor Burgoine
151.   Geoffrey Lee, MP + Agnes Conyers
152.   Reginald Lee + Dorothy Thurland
153.   Gervase Lee of Nottinghamshire
154.   Thomas Lee, of Ashfield + Margaret Mary Oscroft
155.   Elizabeth Lee + Thomas Hanks

156. Robert Hanks + Margaret NLN
157. Peter Hanks I + Mary Bressie
158. Elinor Hanks + Rober Nelson
159. Rachael Nelson + Timothy Ragan
160. Timothy Reagan + Elizabeth Trigg
161. Richard Bazel Reagan + Cecelia Creppy
162. Richard Reagan + Phoebe Samples
163. Reuben Perry Reagan + Elizabeth Cagle
164. George Reagan + Emaline Garner
165. Marshall Reagan + Emma Rogers
166. Elzie Reagan + Delmar Raines
      ------- Gina Davis
         ------- Jackson Davis
      ------- Patricia Stuart
         ------- Bobby Caldwell
         ------- Jennifer Caldwell
      ------- Mike Raines
         ------- Leah Raines
         ------- Kendra Raines
         ------- Joshua Raines
         ------- Michael Raines
      ------- Frank Raines
         ------- Franklin Cody Raines
         ------- Kip Allen Raines
      ------- Richard Raines
         ------- Tyler Lee
         ------- Devin Lee
         ------- Emma Lundy

19

THE JEWISH LINEAGE

1. Mummu the Creator GOD + Nammu, Goddess of the Sea
2. Apsu, Ocean of Sweet Water + Tiamat, Ocean of Salt Water
3. Lahmu, The Primordial God + Lahamu, the Primordial GODDESS
4. Anshar, the Primordial God + Kishar, the Primordial GODDESS
5. Anu, GOD of the Sky + Ki Urash, GODDESS of the Earth
6. Enlil, GOD of Wind
7. El Shaddai, Supreme GOD of CANAAN + Atiratu, Semitic GODDESS of Fertility
8. Elohim, GOD of Israel
9. Adam, the First Man + Eve, the First Woman
10. Seth + Azura, his sister
11. Enosh (Henos Enos) ADANYA (3769 BC - 2864 BC) + Noham ADANYA, Daughter of Seth and Lilleth the Demoness
12. Cainan (Keinan) + Mualeleth ADANYA
13. Mahalalel ben KENAN + Dinah
14. Jared ben MAHALALEL (ADANYA) + Baraka ADANYA
15. Enoch (Henoch) ben JARED (3382 BC - 3017 BC) + Ednah ADANYA

16. Methusaleh (Mathusale) ben ENOCH + Ednah bint AZRAIL (ADANYA)
17. Laamech ibn METHUSALEH (3130? BC - 2353 BC) + Betenos (Ashmua) ADANYA
18. Noah (Noe) ibn LAMEK (2948? BC - 1998 BC) + Emzara (Coba)
19. Shem (Sceaf Sam Sem) ibn NOAH + Sedeqetelebab
20. Arphaxad (King) of ARRAPACHTIS + Arphaxad (King) of ARRAPACHTIS
21. Cainain the SEMITE + Melka (bint MADAI) of MEDES
22. Shelah (ben CAINAN) of CHALDEA + Mu'ak (Muak) ben KESED
23. Eber ibn NOAH (2454? BC - 277? BC - 1813? BC) + Azurad bint NEBROD
24. Pelag ben EBER (Shinar 2243? BC - 2004? BC) + Lomna bint SINA'AR
25. Heraclim + Shela
26. Abram + NN of UR
27. Edna bat 'ABRAM + Terah (Thare Terih) (King) of AGADE
28. Abraham (Avraham Ibrahim) of GENESIS + Sarai (Sarah) (Princess) bint HARAN
29. Isaac ibn ABRAHAM (1922 BC - 1742 BC) + Rebekah (Rebecca) bint BETHEUL
30. Jacob ibn ISAAC (King of GOSHEN) + Leah (Lia) bint LABAN
31. Judah (Judas Juda) ibn JACOB + Tamar of KADESH (? - 1665? BC)
32. Perez (Phares) + Barayah (bas JACOB?)
33. Hezron ibn PHARES (Prince of JUDAH) + Ephratha bint MACHIR
34. Caleb ben HEZRON + Ephratha bint MACHIR
35. Hur (Jephunneh) ben CALEB + Miriam (the PROPHETESS) bat AMRAM
36. Salma ben HUR
37. Beth-Lehem
38. NNs of BETHLEHEM (some missing generations)
39. Ibzan of BETHLEHEM
40. (NN; 'Edal?; Abrias?) ben IBZAN
41. Abala (Habalith) + Jesse ben OBED (Bethlehem 1078? BC - ?)
42. David (1st King) of JUDAH & ISRAEL + Bathsheba (Bathshua) bat AMMIEL
43. Solomon ben DAVID (2nd King) of ISRAEL (? - 930 BC) +

Nicaule (Nicauli Tashere) of EGYPT
44. Basemath bat SOLOMON + Ahimaaz the NAPHALITE
45. Ana bat AHIMAAZ + Abia (Abijah) (4th King) of JUDAH
46. Asa (Asaph) (5th King) of JUDEA + Azubah (Queen) of JUDEA
47. Jehoshapat (6th King) of JUDAH + daughter of Omri
48. Jehoram (Joram) (7th King) of JUDAH + Athalia of ISRAEL
    (9th Queen) of JUDAH
49. Ozias (Ahaziah Ochozias) (8th King) of JUDAH + Zibiah of
    BEERSHEBA
50. Josiah (I; 10th King) of JUDAH (871 BC - 796 BC) + Jehoaddin
    of JERUSALEM
51. Amaziah (Amasias) (11th King) of JUDAH + Jecoliah of
    JERUSALEM
52. Uzziah (Azariah) (12th King) of JUDAH + Jerusha of ISRAEL
53. Joatham (Jotham) (13th King) of JUDAH + Ahio (Princess) bat
    AZRIKAM
54. Achaz (Ahaz) (14th King) of JUDAH + Abijah bat ZECHARIAH
    (Heiress) of ISRAEL
55. Ezechias (Hezekiah) (15th King) of JUDAH + Hephzibah bat
    ISAIAH
56. Manasses ha-DAVID (Manasseh) (16th King) of JUDAH +
    Meshullemeth bat HARUZ of JOTBAH
57. Amon ha-DAVID (17th King) of JUDAH + Jedidah bat ADAIAH
    of BOZKATH
58. Josias (Josiah) ha-DAVID (18th King) of JUDAH + Zebidah
    (Zebudah; bat PEDAIAH) of RUMAH
59. Johanan (Crown Prince) of JUDAH
60. Tamar (Heiress) of the DAVIDIC Dynasty + Neri (Neriah) ha-
    DAVID
61. Salathial (Shealtiel) ha-DAVID + poss. Hadast (Hetbath)
62. Zorobabel ha-DAVID (Heir) of the DAVIDIC Dynasty +
    Rhodah (Princess) of PERSIA (? - 571? BC)
63. Resa (Reza Rhesa) ha-DAVID
64. Joanna (Joanan Yohannai Jehohanen) ben RESA
65. Judah (Juda Joda Judas) ben JOANNA
66. Joseph (Josech) ben JUDAH
67. Semel ben JOSEPH
68. Mattathias (Mathathias) ben SEMEL + daughter of Simon ha-
    KOHEN
69. Maath ben MATTATHIAS ha-DAVID
70. Nagga ben MAATH

71. Esli ben NAGGA
72. Naum ben ESLI of JUDAH
73. Amos ben NAUM
74. Mattathias (Mathathias Mattathiah) ben AMOS
75. Joseph (Jose) ben MATTATHIAS
76. Janna (Janne Jannai Johanan) ben JOSEPH
77. Melchi (Melki) ben JANNA
78. Levi ben MELCHI
79. Matthat (Mathat) ben LEVI of ARIMATHEA + daughter of
     Eleazar
80. Joseph ben MATTHAT (Saint) of ARIMATHEA + Alyuba
81. Anna (Enygeus) of ARIMATHEA + Mandubratius ap LUD of
     BRITAIN
82. Boadicea (Queen) of ICENIANS (22? - 62?) + Prasutagus
     (King) of ICENIA (? - 61?)
83. Julia (Victoria) verch PRASUTAGUS of the ICENI + Meric
     (Marius Meurig Cyllin) of BRITONS (65? - 125?)
84. Coel I (Cole Coilus) (Old King Cole) King of BRITONS +
     Ystradwl (Stradwawl) of SILURIA
85. Lleurig (Lucius) MAWR (King) of EWYAS + Gladys (Gwladys)
     verch EURGEN of SILURIA
86. Gladys `the Younger' of BRITAIN (190? - ?) + Cadvan of
     CAMBRIA
87. Strada `the Fair' of COMBRIA + Coilus II (Coel Cole) of
     GLOUCESTER (by 232 - 305?)
88. Helena (Augusta) (Saint) of the CROSS + Flavius Valerius
     Constantius I of Rome
89. Constantine `the Great' of ROME + Flavia Maxima Fausta (? -
     326?)
90. Flavia Constantia Augusta (320? - 354?) + Flavius Claudius
     CONSTANTIUS Gallus
91. Anastasia
92. Gallus
93. Anastasia (Arriana) CONSTANTINA + Pompeius of
     DYRRHACHIUM
94. Flavius PAULUS (Consul) (? - 496+) + Magna Sabiniani
95. Flavius PROBUS (Consul) (? - 502+) + daughter of Flavius
     Sabinianus
96. Flavius Anastasius PAULUS PROBUS Sabinianus POMPEIUS +
     Theodora(?), daughter of Theodora
97. Paulus of ARABISSO + Joanna of ARABISSA

98. Maurice (EMPEROR) of the EAST (539? - 27/11/602)
99. Julius of BYZANTIUM
100. Georgia
101. Juliana FLAVIA + Athanagild (II; King) of the VISIGOTHS
102. Ardabast (Count/King) of the VISIGOTHS + Goda of the
BURGUNDIANS
103. Ervik (King) of the VISIGOTHS (? - 687) + Liubigotona
(Liuvigotona) of the VISIGOTHS
104. Aupais (of SPAIN)
105. Charles Martel "The Hammer", Mayor of the Palace +
Rotrude, Duchess of Austrasia
106. Pépin III, King of the Franks + Bertha Broadfoot of Laon
107. CHARLEMAGNE, Carolus 'Magnus', Rex Francorum &
Imperator Romanorum + Hildegard of Vinzgouw
108. "Pépin" Carloman, King of Italy + Mistress of Pepin
109. Bernard, King of Lombardy + Cunigundis (Cunegonde)
(Princess) de VERMANDOIS
110. Pépin II, lord of Péronne + Rothaide de Bobbio
111. Pepin (I; Count) de SENLIS de VALOIS
112. (Miss) de SENLIS de VALOIS (845? - ?) + Berenger (Count) de
RENNES (? - 931)
113. Poppa (Poppaeia) de VALOIS (872? - ?) + Rollo (Hrolf Rollon
Rou Robert) `the Dane' RAGNVALDSSON
114. Guillaume (2nd Duke) of NORMANDY + Sprota de
BRETAGNE (concubine)
115. Richard I `the Fearless' (Count) of NORMANDY + Gunnora
(Gonnor) de CREPON
116. Richard II `the Good' of NORMANDY (963? - 1027) + Judith
(Princess) of BRITTANY
117. Robert II (Duke) of NORMANDY + Herleve (Salburpyr) de
FALAISE (1003? - 1050?)
118. WILLIAM the CONQUEROR (Duke) of NORMANDY + Matilda
(Maud) FLEMING (1032 - 1083 Caan)
119. Henry I BEAUCLERC (King) of ENGLAND + Matilda (Edith
Eagdith) `Atheling' STEWART of SCOTLAND
120. Matilda (Maud Augusta) the EMPRESS + Geoffrey V `the Fair'
(`Plantagenet')
121. Henry II (King) of ENGLAND + Eleanor (Duchess/Princess) of
AQUITAINE
122. John `Lackland' (King) of ENGLAND + Isabella (d'
ANGOULEME) TAILLEFER

123. Eleanor (Alianor) of ENGLAND (1215? - 1275) + Simon V de
      MONTFORT (1208 - 4/8/1265)
124. Eleanor de MONTFORT (1252 - 1282) + Llywellyn (II) ap
      GRUFFYDD (? - 1282)
125. Catherine verch LLYWELLYN + Philip ap IFOR
126. Eleanor (of ISCOED; GOCH) verch PHILIP + Thomas ap
      LLEWELLYN
127. Lowri verch GRUFFUDD FYCHAN + Robert (Sir; of Emral)
      PULESTON (1358? - 1399?)
128. Angharad PULESTON + Edward TREVOR ap DAFFYD (? -
      1448?)
129. Otewell Worsley, Sir + Rose (TREVOR) verch EDWART
130. Joyce Worsley + Richard Lee II
131. Richard Lee III + Eleanor Burgoine
132. Geoffrey Lee, MP + Agnes Conyers
133. Reginald Lee + Dorothy Thurland
134. Gervase Lee of Nottinghamshire
135. Thomas Lee, of Ashfield + Margaret Mary Oscroft
136. Elizabeth Lee + Thomas Hanks
137. Robert Hanks + Margaret NLN
138. Peter Hanks I + Mary Bressie
139. Elinor Hanks + Robert Nelson
140. Rachael Nelson + Timothy Ragan
141. Timothy Reagan + Elizabeth Trigg
142. Richard Bazel Reagan + Cecelia Creppy
143. Richard Reagan + Phoebe Samples
144. Reuben Perry Reagan + Elizabeth Cagle
145. George Reagan + Emaline Garner
146. Marshall Reagan + Emma Rogers
147. Elzie Reagan + Delmar Raines
    ------- Gina Davis
        ------- Jackson Davis
    ------- Patricia Stuart
        ------- Bobby Caldwell
        ------- Jennifer Caldwell
    ------- Mike Raines
        ------- Leah Raines
        ------- Kendra Raines
        ------- Joshua Raines
        ------- Michael Raines
    ------- Frank Raines

------- Franklin Cody Raines
------- Kip Allen Raines
------- Richard Raines
------- Tyler Lee
------- Devin Lee
------- Emma Lundy

20

THE JUTE-SAXON LINEAGE

1. Sesostris + Nefret
2. Amenemhat I Sehetepibre (Founder) of 12th Dynasty + Nefrutotenen
3. Sesotris I Kheperkare (PHARAOH) of EGYPT (? - 1928? BC) + Nefrusheri (Princess) of EGYPT
4. Amenemhat (Ammenemes) II Nubkaure (PHARAOH) of EGYPT + Keminnub (Queen) of EGYPT
5. Sesotris II Khakheperre (PHARAOH) of EGYPT + Nofret of EGYPT
6. Sesotris III Khakaure of EGYPT + Sebekshedty-Neferu (Queen) of EGYPT
7. Amenemhat III Nemare (PHARAOH) of EGYPT + Sebeknefru (Queen) of EGYPT
8. Amenemhat (Ammenemes) IV (PHARAOH) of EGYPT
9. Wegaf (PHARAOH) of 13th Dynasty + daughter of Amenemhet IV
10. Ameny Intef (Inyotef) IV (PHARAOH) of EGYPT
11. Hor (PHARAOH) of EGYPT (? - 1760? BC)
12. Sobekhotep II (PHARAOH) of EGYPT (? - 1750? BC)
13. Khendjer (PHARAOH) of EGYPT (? - 1747? BC)

14. Sobekhotep III (PHARAOH) of EGYPT (? - 1745? BC)
15. Neferhotep I (PHARAOH) of EGYPT
16. Sobekhotep IV Khaneferre (PHARAOH) of 13th Dynasty +
       Tjan
17. Sebekhotep (Princess) of THEBES + Senebhanef, son of
       Renressonb
18. Mentuhotep (Queen) of EGYPT + Sekhemre-Sementawi
       Djehuti (PHARAOH) of EGYPT
19. Sekhemre-Se'ankhtawi Neferhotep (PHARAOH) of EGYPT
20. Sobekemsaf Sekhemre-Shedtawi (PHARAOH) of EGYPT +
       Nubkhas (Queen) of EGYPT
21. Inyotef VII (PHARAOH) at THEBES + Sobkemsaf
       (Sebekamzaf) of EGYPT (1635? BC - ?)
22. Sekenenre Tao I (PHARAOH) at THEBES + Tetisheri of
       THEBES
23. Sekenenre Tao II (King) of THEBES + Ahhotep (Ahotop) I
       (Queen) of EGYPT
24. Ahmose I (1st PHARAOH) of 18th Dynasty + Nefretiri
       (Queen) of EGYPT
25. Amenhotep I Djeserkare (PHARAOH) of EGYPT + Senisonb
       (Seneseneb) of EGYPT
26. Thutmose I (PHARAOH) of EGYPT (? - 1481? BC) + Amhose
       (Aahmes II) (Queen) of EGYPT
27. Hatshepsut (Queen & PHARAOH) of EGYPT (? - 1482 BC) +
       Thutmose (Tuthmosis) II (PHARAOH) of EGYPT
28. Meryetre Hatshepsut of EGYPT + Thutmose III `the Great' of
       EGYPT (Moses of the Bible)
29. Akheperure Amenhotep II THUTMOSID (PHARAOH) of
       EGYPT + Tio (Tiye Tiaa)
30. Menkheprure' Thutmose IV (PHARAOH) of EGYPT +
       Mutemwiya, daughter of Artatama (I; King) of MITANNI
31. Nebma'atre' Amenhotep III (PHARAOH) of EGYPT + Tiye-
       Nefertari (Tiy) of EGYPT (1382 BC - 1344 BC)
32. Akhenaton (Iknaton) (10th PHARAOH) of 18th Dynasty
       EGYPT + Nefertiti (Chief Queen) of EGYPT
33. Meritaten (Royal Daughter) of EGYPT + Judah (Judas Juda)
       ibn JACOB, son of Jacob ibn ISAAC (King of GOSHEN)
34. Zerah (Zehrah Zarah Zare) ibn JUDAH + Electra the PLEIADE
35. Dardanus (Dara) (King) of ACADIA + Batea of TEUCRI
36. Erichthonius (King) of ACADIA (? - 1386? BC) + Astyoche of
       ACADIA

37. Trois of ACADIA + Callirhoe (TEUCRI)
38. Ilus (Ilyus) (King) of TROY (? - 1282? BC) + Eurydice
       (Eurydike) of TROY
39. Laomedan (King) of TROY
40. Tithonius of TROY (? - 1237+ BC)
41. Memnon (Munon) of TROY (? - 1183? BC)
42. Thor (Tror) (King) of THRACE + Sibil (Sif)
43. Loridi (Hloritha) TRORSSON
44. Einridi LORIDESSON
45. Vingethor (Vingethior) EINRIDISSON
46. Vingener VINGETHORSSON
47. Moda (Mode) VINGENERSSON
48. Maji (Magi) MODASSON
49. Seskef (Sceaf Scaef)
50. Bedwig (Bedvig; of SCEAF)
51. Hwala (Hvala Hawala Guala)
52. Hathra (Athra)
53. Itermon (Itormann)
54. Heremod (King) in DENMARK
55. Sceldwa (King) in DENMARK
56. Beaw (Gram) (King) in DENMARK
57. Taetwa (Tatwa Tecti)
58. Jat (Geatwa Geata Geat Gaut Geot Gauti)
59. Godwulf (Gudolfr)
60. Flocwald (of Asgard)
61. Finn (the TROJAN ?) (Asgard 130? - ?)
62. Frithuwulf (the TROJAN ?)
63. Frealaf (Friallaf Froethelaf) (160? - ?)
64. Frithuwald (Bor) (190? - ?)
65. Woden (Wodan Odin) of ASGARD + Frigg (Frigida) of
       ASALAND
66. Wecta (Waegdaeg) the JUTE (280? - 350+)
67. Witta (Vitta Vitgils Witte; II) the JUTE
68. Wihtgils the JUTE
69. Hengest VVIHTGILSING (King) of KENT - First Saxon to
       invade Britain with his brother, Horsa
70. Oeric (King) of KENT (470? - 512?)
71. Octa (Octha) AECING (King) of KENT (? - 540?)
72. Eormenric OCTING (King) of KENT (530? - 560?)
73. Aethelbert I EORMENRICING (Saint; King) of KENT
74. Eadbald (Adolald) AETHELBRYHTING (King) of KENT

75.   Eorcenbert EADBALDING (King) of KENT
76.   Egbert I EARCONBRYHTING (King) of KENT
77.   Wihtred OISCINGA (King) of KENT (673? - 725)
78.   Aethelbert II (co-King) of KENT (700+ - 762)
79.   Alburga(?) AETHELBRYHTING of KENT (? - 803?)
80.   Egbert III `the Great' (1st King) of ENGLAND
81.   Ethelwulf (2nd King) of ENGLAND (806? - 858)
82.   Alfred "the Great" KING OF WESSEX b: 0848 d: 26 OCT 0899
          + Ealhswith OF THE GAINI of Mercia b: 0852 d: 05 DEC
          0905
83.   Edward "the Elder" of Wessex KING OF ENGLAND b: 0871 d:
          AUG 0924 + Ædgifu OF KENT b: 0896 d: 25 AUG 0968
84.   Edmund I "the Magnificent" KING OF ENGLAND b: 0920 d: 26
          MAY 0946 + Ælfgifu OF WESSEX b: 0922 d: 0944
85.   Edgar "the Peaceful" KING OF ENGLAND b: 0943 d: 08 JUL
          0975 + Ælfthryth OF DEVON b: 0945 d: 1000
86.   Æthelred II "the Unready" KING OF ENGLAND b: 0968 d: 23
          APR 1016 + Alfflaed (Elfreda Aelfgifu) GUNNARSDOTTIR
          of NORTHUMBRIA b: ABT 0963 d: 1002
87.   Ælfgifu OF ENGLAND b: 0990 + Uchtred (Ughtred) (Earl) of
          NORTHUMBRIA
88.   Gospatrick FitzUGHTRED of BAMBURGH (? - 1064?)
89.   Uchtred FitzGOSPATRIC
90.   Dunning (FitzUGHTRED) (? - 1092)
91.   Siward FitzDUNNING (1073 - 1095)
92.   Huck (Hucca) de SINGLETON
93.   Uchtred de SINGLETON (? - by 1183)
94.   Matilda de SINGLETON
95.   Maud de PARLES + Richard de WORSLEY (? - by 1233)
96.   Geoffrey de WORSLEY (? - by 1268) + Agnes de WORSLEY
97.   Richard de WORSLEY (? - 1292?) + Maud de WARDLEY
98.   Henry de WORSLEY (? - 1312? (or by '04)) + Margaret
          SCHORESWORTH (? - 1363?)
99.   Robert de Worsley, Lord of Booths + Cecily Margaret
          Bromhall
100.   William de Worsley + Ellen de Huton
101.   Robert Worsley + Isabel de Trafford
102.   Robert de Worsley + Katherine Clark
103.   Otewell Worsley, Sir + Rose verch Edward
104.   Joyce Worsley + Richard Lee II
105.   Richard Lee III + Eleanor Burgoine

106.   Geoffrey Lee, MP + Agnes Conyers
107.   Reginald Lee + Dorothy Thurland
108.   Gervase Lee of Nottinghamshire
109.   Thomas Lee, of Ashfield + Margaret Mary Oscroft
110.   Elizabeth Lee + Thomas Hanks
111.   Robert Hanks + Margaret NLN
112.   Peter Hanks I + Mary Bressie
113.   Elinor Hanks + Rober Nelson
114.   Rachael Nelson + Timothy Ragan
115.   Timothy Reagan + Elizabeth Trigg
116.   Richard Bazel Reagan + Cecelia Creppy
117.   Richard Reagan + Phoebe Samples
118.   Reuben Perry Reagan + Elizabeth Cagle
119.   George Reagan + Emaline Garner
120.   Marshall Reagan + Emma Rogers
121.   Elzie Reagan + Delmar Raines
        ------- Gina Davis
              ------- Jackson Davis
        ------- Patricia Stuart
              ------- Bobby Caldwell
              ------- Jennifer Caldwell
        ------- Mike Raines
              ------- Leah Raines
              ------- Kendra Raines
              ------- Joshua Raines
              ------- Michael Raines
        ------- Frank Raines
              ------- Franklin Cody Raines
              ------- Kip Allen Raines
        ------- Richard Raines
              ------- Tyler Lee
              ------- Devin Lee
              ------- Emma Lundy

21

THE KINGS OF ARCADIA-PELASGIA LINEAGE

1.   Uranus (1st Ruler GOD of the Universe)
2.   Cronos (Kronos) the TITAN + Rhea (Rheia) the TITAN
3.   Zeus the OLYMPIANborn in Cretan cave) + Niobe of ARGOS (ARGUS), daughter of Phoroneus of ARGOS (and Teledice the NYMPH)
4.   Pelasgus (1st King) of the PELASGIANS + Deianirra of the PELASGIANS, daughter of Lycaon of the PELASGIANS, son of Aezeius of the PELASGIANS
5.   Lycaon (King) of ARCADIA + Nonacris of ARCADIA
6.   Aglaia of ARGOS + Abas (II; King) of ARGOS (& Abae)
7.   Acrisius (King) of ARGOS + Eurydice of LACEDAEMON, daughter of Lacedaemon (King) of LACEDAEMON
8.   Evarete of ARGOS + Oenomaus (King) of PISA
9.   Hippodamia of PISA + Pelops (King) of PISA, LYDIA and/or MYCENE
10.   Dias of MYCENAE + Archippe
11.   Cleolla of MYCENAE + Plisthenes (King) of MYCENAE
12.   Agamemnon (King) of MYCENAE + Clytaemnestra of SPARTA
13.   Orestes (King) of ARGOS, MYCENAE & Sparta + Erigone of MYCENAE

14.   Sancus
15.   Sabinus
16.   Son of Sabinus
17.   (NN) | (poss. missing generations)
18.   Demophon + descendant of Parapilius
19.   Pomponius the SABINE + Jullia Prima of ROME
20.   Numa Pompilius (2nd King) of ROME + Egeria the NYMPH or
         CAMENAE
21.   Rehea Silvia + Fethuir (Fetjuir, Fetebir I)
22.   Alanus
23.   Armenon
24.   Irmino (progenitor) of the HERMINONES
25.   (NN) ... (NN) of the HERMINONES | (many missing
         generations)
26.   Askanes (Chief) of the HERMINONES
27.   Ernst
28.   (NN) ... (NN) | (some missing generations)
29.   Teutbal (King) of the TEUTONS (? - 102 BC) + (Miss) of
         SUEBIAN Confederacy
30.   Ariovistus (King) of GERMANIA (? - 49 BC)
31.   (NN) ... (NN) of SUEVICS | (many missing generations)
32.   Hermerich (Prince) of SUEVICS
33.   (NN) of SUEVES
34.   Gueric (Probus/Governor) of REIMS (455? - 494+) + Gunzie
         la FRANQUE
35.   Industria de REIMS (475? - ?) + Tonantius (II) `Vis
         Clarisimus' FERREOLUS
36.   Deoteria de BEZIERS de REIMS
37.   Theodon II (Duke) of BAVARIA + Theodon III of BAVARIA (? -
         565?)
38.   Theodon III of BAVARIA (? - 565?)
39.   Theobald (Theodebert) of BAVARIA
40.   Garibald I (AGILOFINGES ?) of BAVARIA + Waldrada
         (Princess) of the LOMBARDS
41.   Gundwald (Duke) of ASTI (? - 613?) + Harinanda, daughter of
         Rotbert I (King) of LONGOBARDS
42.   Aripert I (Viscount) of LOMBARDY (? - 661?)
43.   Berthari (21st King) of the LANGOBARDS
44.   Kunibert (25th King) of the LANGOBARDS (? - 702?)
45.   Liutpert (26th King) of the LANGOBARDS (? - 712?)
46.   Theoderada (of the LOMBARDS) + Ansbrand (28th King) of

the LANGOBARDS (655? - 712?)
47. Sigiprand of the LOMBARDS
48. Ansbrand of LOMBARDS
49. Ansia of LOMBARDS (? - 774?) + Desiderio (last King) of LOMBARDS (? - 774+)
50. Gerberga of LOMBARDY (? - 774) + Carloman II (Archduke) of AUSTRASIA (747? - 771)
51. Kunigunde (Auberge) of AUSTRASIA + Adelgis (Count) of PARMA (of SPOLETO-PARMA) (? - 836?)
52. Cunegonde (Princess) de VERMANDOIS + Bernard (Bernhard; I) (King) of ITALY (Lombardy)
53. Pépin II, lord of Péronne + Rothaide de Bobbio
54. Héribert I, count of Vermandois + Bertha of Morvois
55. Héribert II, count of Vermandois + Liegarde Hildebrante of France
56. Count Robert de Vermandois, comte de Meaux et de Troyes + Adélaïde-Wera de Bourgogne, Chalon et Troyes
57. Arnulf de Ganelon + Gisia de Ganelon
58. Mathilde Hildeburg, de Condé-sur-Noireau + Guillaume I, 'Talvas' de Belleme, seigneur d'Alençon
59. Guillaume II "Talvas" Comte de Bellême, seigneur d'Alençon + Haberga "Hildeburge" de Beaumont
60. Mabile, dame de Bellême et d'Alençon + Roger Ii de Montgomery, 1st Earl of Shrewsbury
61. Aimeria Emma de Montgomery + Warine "The Sherriff" de Metz
62. Sir Guy Warin "The Bold" de Metz + Baroness Melette (Maud) Maud Peverell, Heiress of Whittington
63. Fulk FitzWarin, Lord of Whittington and Alderbury + Eva Whittington and FitzWarin (of Whittington & Alveston)
64. Warin FitzWarin FitzWarin
65. Warin de Burwardslegh, Lord of Estelegh
66. Alicia de Burwardslegh + Sir Walter Bromley
67. Geoffrey Galffridus Bromley + Philippa Bagot
68. Richard Bromley + Elizabeth Knockton
69. Ranulph Bromley + Agnes de Baddington
70. John de Bromley + Joan de Baddington
71. Cecily Margaret Bromhall + Robert de Worsley, Lord of Booths
72. William de Worsley + Ellen de Huton
73. Robert Worsley + Isabel de Trafford

74.   Robert de Worsley + Katherine Clark
75.   Otewell Worsley, Sir + Rose verch Edward
76.   Joyce Worsley + Richard Lee II
77.   Richard Lee III + Eleanor Burgoine
78.   Geoffrey Lee, MP + Agnes Conyers
79.   Reginald Lee + Dorothy Thurland
80.   Gervase Lee of Nottinghamshire
81.   Thomas Lee, of Ashfield + Margaret Mary Oscroft
82.   Elizabeth Lee + Thomas Hanks
83.   Robert Hanks + Margaret NLN
84.   Peter Hanks I + Mary Bressie
85.   Elinor Hanks + Rober Nelson
86.   Rachael Nelson + Timothy Ragan
87.   Timothy Reagan + Elizabeth Trigg
88.   Richard Bazel Reagan + Cecelia Creppy
89.   Richard Reagan + Phoebe Samples
90.   Reuben Perry Reagan + Elizabeth Cagle
91.   George Reagan + Emaline Garner
92.   Marshall Reagan + Emma Rogers
93.   Elzie Reagan + Delmar Raines
       ------- Gina Davis
              ------- Jackson Davis
       ------- Patricia Stuart
              ------- Bobby Caldwell
              ------- Jennifer Caldwell
       ------- Mike Raines
              ------- Leah Raines
              ------- Kendra Raines
              ------- Joshua Raines
              ------- Michael Raines
       ------- Frank Raines
              ------- Franklin Cody Raines
              ------- Kip Allen Raines
       ------- Richard Raines
              ------- Tyler Lee
              ------- Devin Lee
              ------- Emma Lundy

22

THE KINGS OF ARGOS LINEAGE

1. Ptah, Creator GOD + Sekhmet, GODDESS of Destruction
2. Thoth, GOD of Wisdom + Maat, GODDESS of Universal Order
3. Shu, GOD of Wind + Tefnut, GODDESS of Moisture
4. Geb, GOD of the Earth + Nut, GODDESS of the Sky
5. Osiris, GOD of Egypt + Isis, GODDESS of EGYPT
6. Kenkenes Horus (1st PHARAOH) of EGYPT
7. (NN) ... (NN) in EGYPT | (many missing generations)
8. Telegonus (PHARAOH) of EGYPT + Io (the NYMPH) of ARGOS
9. Epaphus (PHARAOH) of EGYPT + Memphis, daughter of the NILE
10. Libya (Queen) of EGYPT + Poseidon (the OLYMPIAN; GOD of the Sea)
11. Belus (King) of EGYPT + Anchinoe of EGYPT, daughter of NILE
12. Aegyptus (King) of EGYPT + Argyphia
13. Lynceus (I; King) of ARGOS + Hypermnestra the DANAID
14. Abas (II; King) of ARGOS (& Abae) + Aglaia of ARGOS, daughter of Mantineus (King) of MANTINEIA, son of Lycaon (King) of ARCADIA (and Nonacris of ARCADIA)

15.   Acrisius (King) of ARGOS + Eurydice of LACEDAEMON, daughter of Lacedaemon (King) of LACEDAEMON
16.   Evarete of ARGOS + Oenomaus (King) of PISA
17.   Hippodamia of PISA + Pelops (King) of PISA, LYDIA and/or MYCENE
18.   Dias of MYCENAE + Archippe
19.   Cleolla of MYCENAE + Plisthenes (King) of MYCENAE
20.   Agamemnon (King) of MYCENAE + Clytaemnestra of SPARTA
21.   Orestes (King) of ARGOS, MYCENAE & Sparta + Erigone of MYCENAE
22.   Sancus
23.   Sabinus
24.   Son of Sabinus
25.   (NN) | (poss. missing generations)
26.   Demophon + descendant of Parapilius
27.   Pomponius the SABINE + Jullia Prima of ROME
28.   Numa Pompilius (2nd King) of ROME + Egeria the NYMPH or CAMENAE
29.   Rehea Silvia + Fethuir (Fetjuir, Fetebir I)
30.   Alanus
31.   Armenon
32.   Irmino (progenitor) of the HERMINONES
33.   (NN) ... (NN) of the HERMINONES | (many missing generations)
34.   Askanes (Chief) of the HERMINONES
35.   Ernst
36.   (NN) ... (NN) | (some missing generations)
37.   Teutbal (King) of the TEUTONS (? - 102 BC) + (Miss) of SUEBIAN Confederacy
38.   Ariovistus (King) of GERMANIA (? - 49 BC)
39.   (NN) ... (NN) of SUEVICS | (many missing generations)
40.   Hermerich (Prince) of SUEVICS
41.   (NN) of SUEVES
42.   Gueric (Probus/Governor) of REIMS (455? - 494+) + Gunzie la FRANQUE
43.   Industria de REIMS (475? - ?) + Tonantius (II) `Vis Clarisimus' FERREOLUS
44.   Deoteria de BEZIERS de REIMS
45.   Theodon II (Duke) of BAVARIA + Theodon III of BAVARIA (? - 565?)
46.   Theodon III of BAVARIA (? - 565?)

47.   Theobald (Theodebert) of BAVARIA
48.   Garibald I (AGILOFINGES ?) of BAVARIA + Waldrada (Princess) of the LOMBARDS
49.   Gundwald (Duke) of ASTI (? - 613?) + Harinanda, daughter of Rotbert I (King) of LONGOBARDS
50.   Aripert I (Viscount) of LOMBARDY (? - 661?)
51.   Berthari (21st King) of the LANGOBARDS
52.   Kunibert (25th King) of the LANGOBARDS (? - 702?)
53.   Liutpert (26th King) of the LANGOBARDS (? - 712?)
54.   Theoderada (of the LOMBARDS) + Ansbrand (28th King) of the LANGOBARDS (655? - 712?)
55.   Sigiprand of the LOMBARDS
56.   Ansbrand of LOMBARDS
57.   Ansia of LOMBARDS (? - 774?) + Desiderio (last King) of LOMBARDS (? - 774+)
58.   Gerberga of LOMBARDY (? - 774) + Carloman II (Archduke) of AUSTRASIA (747? - 771)
59.   Kunigunde (Auberge) of AUSTRASIA + Adelgis (Count) of PARMA (of SPOLETO-PARMA) (? - 836?)
60.   Cunegonde (Princess) de VERMANDOIS + Bernard (Bernhard; I) (King) of ITALY (Lombardy)
61.   Pépin II, lord of Péronne + Rothaide de Bobbio
62.   Héribert I, count of Vermandois + Bertha of Morvois
63.   Héribert II, count of Vermandois + Liegarde Hildebrante of France
64.   Count Robert de Vermandois, comte de Meaux et de Troyes + Adélaïde-Wera de Bourgogne, Chalon et Troyes
65.   Arnulf de Ganelon + Gisia de Ganelon
66.   Mathilde Hildeburg, de Condé-sur-Noireau + Guillaume I, 'Talvas' de Belleme, seigneur d'Alençon
67.   Guillaume II "Talvas" Comte de Bellême, seigneur d'Alençon + Haberga "Hildeburge" de Beaumont
68.   Mabile, dame de Bellême et d'Alençon + Roger Ii de Montgomery, 1st Earl of Shrewsbury
69.   Aimeria Emma de Montgomery + Warine "The Sherriff" de Metz
70.   Sir Guy Warin "The Bold" de Metz + Baroness Melette (Maud) Maud Peverell, Heiress of Whittington
71.   Fulk FitzWarin, Lord of Whittington and Alderbury + Eva Whittington and FitzWarin (of Whittington & Alveston)
72.   Warin FitzWarin FitzWarin

73.   Warin de Burwardslegh, Lord of Estelegh
74.   Alicia de Burwardslegh + Sir Walter Bromley
75.   Geoffrey Galffridus Bromley + Philippa Bagot
76.   Richard Bromley + Elizabeth Knockton
77.   Ranulph Bromley + Agnes de Baddington
78.   John de Bromley + Joan de Baddington
79.   Cecily Margaret Bromhall + Robert de Worsley, Lord of Booths
80.   William de Worsley + Ellen de Huton
81.   Robert Worsley + Isabel de Trafford
82.   Robert de Worsley + Katherine Clark
83.   Otewell Worsley, Sir + Rose verch Edward
84.   Joyce Worsley + Richard Lee II
85.   Richard Lee III + Eleanor Burgoine
86.   Geoffrey Lee, MP + Agnes Conyers
87.   Reginald Lee + Dorothy Thurland
88.   Gervase Lee of Nottinghamshire
89.   Thomas Lee, of Ashfield + Margaret Mary Oscroft
90.   Elizabeth Lee + Thomas Hanks
91.   Robert Hanks + Margaret NLN
92.   Peter Hanks I + Mary Bressie
93.   Elinor Hanks + Rober Nelson
94.   Rachael Nelson + Timothy Ragan
95.   Timothy Reagan + Elizabeth Trigg
96.   Richard Bazel Reagan + Cecelia Creppy
97.   Richard Reagan + Phoebe Samples
98.   Reuben Perry Reagan + Elizabeth Cagle
99.   George Reagan + Emaline Garner
100.   Marshall Reagan + Emma Rogers
101.   Elzie Reagan + Delmar Raines
    ------- Gina Davis
        ------- Jackson Davis
    ------- Patricia Stuart
        ------- Bobby Caldwell
        ------- Jennifer Caldwell
    ------- Mike Raines
        ------- Leah Raines
        ------- Kendra Raines
        ------- Joshua Raines
        ------- Michael Raines
    ------- Frank Raines

------- Franklin Cody Raines
------- Kip Allen Raines
------- Richard Raines
------- Tyler Lee
------- Devin Lee
------- Emma Lundy

23

THE KINGS OF THESSALY-ITHACA-LATIUM -ALBA LONGA-ROMAN LINEAGE

LINEAGE I

(Common Lineage to Gaius Livius Drusus, Roman Consul)

1. Uranus (1st Ruler GOD of the Universe)
2. Cronos (Kronos) the TITAN
3. Zeus the OLYMPIANborn in Cretan cave)
4. Hephaestus, GOD of Fire
5. Pandora of PTHIA
6. Pyrrha of PTHIA
7. Hellen (King) of the HELLENES + Orseis the NYMPH, daughter of Zeus the OLYMPIAN (and Dino the GRAEAE)
8. Aeolus of THESSALY + Enarete of THESSALY
9. Deioneus (King) of PHOCIS + Diomede of PHOCIS
10. Cephalus of CEPHALLENIA + Procris of ATHENS, daughter of Erechtheus (King) of ATHENS (and Praxithea (II) of ATHENS)
11. Arcisius the ARGONAUT
12. Laertes (King) of ITHACA

13. Odysseus (King) of ITHACA [(Ulysses); many famous exploits
     as leader of the Cephallenians, e.g. construction of the
     Trojan Horse; only man to hear Sirens' song and survive;
     journeyed to Hades; HERO] + Anticlia of PARNASSUS,
     daughter of Autolycus of PARNASSUS (and Amphithea of
     PARNASSUS), son of Chione of PARNASSUS (and Hermes
     the OLYMPIAN; the Messenger GOD), daughter of
     Daedalion (King) of PARNASSUS, son of Eosphorus the
     TITAN + Penelope of SPARTA, daughter of Icarius
     (Prince) of SPARTA (and Periboea the NAIAD), son of
     Oibalos (King) of SPARTA & LACEDAEMON (and Batia
     the NAIAD)
14. Telemachus (King) of ITHACA + Circe (AEAEA) the
     Enchantress, daughter of Aeetes (King) of COLCHIS (and
     Hecate of the UNDERWORLD)
15. daughter of Circe + Faunus (II; King) of LATIUM (? - 1215?
     BC)
16. Latinus (King) of LATIUM + Amata
17. Lavinia of LATIUM + Aeneas `the Dardanian' of LATIUM
     [eponym of the Aeneid , his alleged biography by Virgil;
     aka Aineias, Eneas ysgwyt wyn]
18. Silvius (2nd King) of ALBA LONGA + Odela
19. Aeneas (3rd King) of ALBA LONGA
20. Latinus Silvius (4th King) of ALBA LONGA
21. Alba (5th King) of ALBA LONGA
22. Capetus (6th King) of ALBA LONGA
23. Capys (7th King) of ALBA LONGA
24. Capetus (II; 8th King) of ALBA LONGA
25. Tiberinus Silvius (9th King) of ALBA LONGA
26. Agrippa (10th King) of ALBA LONGA
27. Romulus Silvius of ALBA LONGA
28. Allodius (11th King) of ALBA LONGA
29. Aventinus (12th King) of ALBA LONGA
30. Procas (13th King) of ALBA LONGA
31. Numitor (15th King) of ALBA LONGA
32. Rhea Silvia (Princess) of ALBA LONGA + Ares (the
     OLYMPIAN; GOD of War)
33. Romulus (1st King) of ROME (? - 5/7/716? BC) + Hersilia `the
     Raped' of SABINA, daughter of Titus Tatius (King) of
     SABINA, (NN) ... (NN) the SABINE | (few missing
     generations), Sabinus, eponym of the Sabines

34.   Jullia Prima of ROME + Pomponius the SABINE, descendant
          of colonists from Greece
35.   Numa Pompilius (2nd King) of ROME
36.   Mamericus `Aemilius'
37.   (NN) ... (NN) Aemilius
38.   (NN) ... (NN) Aemilius
39.   (NN) ... (NN) Aemilius
40.   (NN) ... (NN) Aemilius
41.   Marcus AEMILIUS (560? BC - ?)
42.   Lucius Aemilius Mamercus [Roman Consul]
43.   Marcus Aemilius Mamercus [Roman Consul]
44.   Mamercus AEMILIUS Mamercinus (Macerinus) [Roman
          Consul]
45.   Lucius Aemilius MAMERCUS (Mamercinus) [Roman Consul]
46.   Lucius Aemilius Memercinus (? - 363+ BC) [Roman Consul]
47.   Quintus Aemilius Barbula (? - 311+ BC) [Roman Consul]
48.   Marcus Aemilius BARBULA (? - 292+ BC) [Dictator of Rome]
49.   Marcus Aemilius Lepidus ? - 285+ BC) [Roman Consul]
50.   Marcus Aemilius Lepidus (305? BC - ?)
51.   Marcus Aemilius Lepidus ? - 216 BC) [Roman Consul]
52.   Marcus Aemilius LEPIDUS ? - 218+ BC) [Roman Consul;
          Praetor of Sicily] + Calavia
53.   Gaius Livius Drusus [Roman Consul] (? - 147+ BC) + Julia
          CAESARIS (? - 155+ BC), daughter of Gaius JULIUS Caesar

LINEAGE IIA

(From Gaius Livius Drusus, Roman Consul)

161.   Gaius Livius Drusus [Roman Consul] (? - 147+ BC) + Julia
           CAESARIS (? - 155+ BC), daughter of Gaius JULIUS Caesar
162.   Livia + Publius RUTILIUS Rufus, descendant of Turnus (King)
           of the RUTULIANS
163.   Rutilia RUFA + Lucius Aurelius COTTA (? - 119+ BC),
           descendant of Aurelius, progenitor of gens AURELII (of
           Sabine origin)
164.   Aurelia COTTA (? - 54 BC) + Gaius JULIUS Caesar (Praetor) of
           ROME (Governor of Asia)
165.   Julia I Minor + Marcus ATIUS Balbus
166.   Atia Maior of ROME (85? BC - 43? BC) + Gaius (IV) OCTAVIUS
           (Praetor) of ROME

167. Octavia `the Younger' THURINIA + Marcus ANTONIUS
        (Triumvir of ROME)
168. Antonia + Aedd MAWR (King/Duke) of CORNWALL
169. Prydain ap AEDD (Duke/King) of CORNWALL
170. Leil (Lleon) Ici (King) of ICENI
171. Rhun Huidibras of ICENI, son of Antedios (King) of ICENI, son
        of Addedomaros (King) of TRINOVANTES, son of
        Mandubracius (King) of TRINOVANTES, son of
        manuentus (King) of TRINOVANTES
172. Boadicea (Queen) of ICENIANS (22? - 62?) + Prasutagus
        (King) of ICENIA (? - 61?)
173. Julia (Victoria) verch PRASUTAGUS of the ICENI + Meric
        (Marius Meurig Cyllin) of BRITONS (65? - 125?)
174. Coel I (Cole Coilus) (Old King Cole) King of BRITONS +
        Ystradwl (Stradwawl) of SILURIA
175. Althildis (Princess) of BRITAIN (by 105 - ?) + Marcomir IV
        (King) of FRANKS (by 105 - 149?)
176. (Miss) of the FRANKS + Gall Gaodnu of CYMRU
177. Aife (Aoife) of GALL GAEDAL + Fiachaidh (V) Sraibhthine
        (Scrabhtaine) of IRELAND
178. Muireadeach (II) Tirech MacFIACHACH + Muireann ingen
        FIACHAIDH
179. Eochaid (Eochu) Mugmedon of IRELAND + Cairenn
        Chasdubh of BRITAIN
180. Niall Noigiallach MacECHACH [Niall of the Nine Hostages; aka
        Nial Mor NAOIGHIALLACH `of the Nine Hostages'; 1st
        King (but reckoned 126th MONARCH) of IRELAND;
        conquered nine countries (incl. part of France); eponym
        & progenitor of O'NEILL; Born: ? Died: abt. 405 Boulogne,
        slain by Prince of Leinster]
181. Conall Gulban MacNEILL (? - 464?)
182. Fergus Cennfota MacCONAILL
183. Feidhlimidh (Fedlim) MacFEARGUSA + Eithne (Princess) of
        LEINSTER
184. Eogan (Eoghan) MacFEIDEILMID
185. Donchad (? - 600+)
186. Cuillum (Colla)
187. Eathach `Feighlioch
188. Cartain (Lord) of the ISLES
189. Eirc (Lord) of the ISLES
190. Crimthanne (Lord) of the ISLES

191. Eirc (Lord) of the ISLES
192. Fergus (Lord) of the ISLES
193. Gofraidh (Goffra) (Lord) of the ISLES
194. Maine (Lord) of the ISLES
195. Niallghus (Lord) of the ISLES
196. Suibne (Lord) of the ISLES
197. Maolbruidhe (Lord) of the ISLES
198. Solaimh (Lord) of the ISLES
199. Gilladomnan (Lord) of the ISLES
200. Duncan (Thane/Priest) of DULE
201. Duncan (I) MacDONACHADH (Abthane) of DULE (DULL) (920? - 965?)
202. Duncan (Thane) of ATHOLL
203. Crinan `the Thane and Lay Abbot' of Dunkeld + Bethoc (Beatrix) MacKENNETH of SCOTLAND (984? - ?)
204. Duncan I `the Gracious' MacCRINAN of SCOTLAND + Bethoc MacDUFF (1009? - 1040?), daughter of Malcolm MacDUFF (990? - ?), son of Kenneth (III) MacDUFF (14th King) of SCOTS
205. Malcolm III MacCRINAN (19th King) of SCOTS + Margaret (Queen; Saint) of SCOTLAND
206. Matilda (Edith Eagdith) `Atheling' STEWART of SCOTLAND + Henry I BEAUCLERC (King) of ENGLAND
207. Matilda (Maud Augusta) the EMPRESS + Geoffrey V `the Fair' (`Plantagenet')
208. Henry II (King) of ENGLAND + Eleanor (Duchess/Princess) of AQUITAINE
209. John `Lackland' (King) of ENGLAND + Isabella (d' ANGOULEME) TAILLEFER
210. Eleanor (Alianor) of ENGLAND (1215? - 1275) + Simon V de MONTFORT (1208 - 4/8/1265)
211. Eleanor de MONTFORT (1252 - 1282) + Llywellyn (II) ap GRUFFYDD (? - 1282)
212. Catherine verch LLYWELLYN + Philip ap IFOR
213. Eleanor (of ISCOED; GOCH) verch PHILIP + Thomas ap LLEWELLYN
214. Lowri verch GRUFFUDD FYCHAN + Robert (Sir; of Emral) PULESTON (1358? - 1399?)
215. Angharad PULESTON + Edward TREVOR ap DAFFYD (? - 1448?)
216. Otewell Worsley, Sir + Rose (TREVOR) verch EDWART

217. Joyce Worsley + Richard Lee II
218. Richard Lee III + Eleanor Burgoine
219. Geoffrey Lee, MP + Agnes Conyers
220. Reginald Lee + Dorothy Thurland
221. Gervase Lee of Nottinghamshire
222. Thomas Lee, of Ashfield + Margaret Mary Oscroft
223. Elizabeth Lee + Thomas Hanks
224. Robert Hanks + Margaret NLN
225. Peter Hanks I + Mary Bressie
226. Elinor Hanks + Rober Nelson
227. Rachael Nelson + Timothy Ragan
228. Timothy Reagan + Elizabeth Trigg
229. Richard Bazel Reagan + Cecelia Creppy
230. Richard Reagan + Phoebe Samples
231. Reuben Perry Reagan + Elizabeth Cagle
232. George Reagan + Emaline Garner
233. Marshall Reagan + Emma Rogers
234. Elzie Reagan + Delmar Raines
  ------- Gina Davis
    ------- Jackson Davis
  ------- Patricia Stuart
    ------- Bobby Caldwell
    ------- Jennifer Caldwell
  ------- Mike Raines
    ------- Leah Raines
    ------- Kendra Raines
    ------- Joshua Raines
    ------- Michael Raines
  ------- Frank Raines
    ------- Franklin Cody Raines
    ------- Kip Allen Raines
  ------- Richard Raines
    ------- Tyler Lee
    ------- Devin Lee
    ------- Emma Lundy

LINEAGE IIB

(From Gaius Livius Drusus, Roman Consul)

1. Gaius Livius Drusus [Roman Consul] (? - 147+ BC) + Julia

CAESARIS (? - 155+ BC), daughter of Gaius JULIUS Caesar

2.   Marcus Livius (II) DRUSUS `the Elder' (? - 109? BC) [Roman Consul and Censor) + Cornelia Scipionis of ROME (? - 89? BC), daughter of Publius Cornelius SCIPIO Nasica SERAPIO, son of Publius CORNELIUS Scipio Nasica CORCULUM, son of Publius Cornelius NASICA (? - 171+ BC), son of Cneius Cornelius Scipio Calvus, son of Lucius Cornelius Scipio (? - 258+ BC), son of Lucius Cornelius Scipio BARBATUS (? - 293+ BC), son of Cnaeus Cornelius Scipio

3.   Marcus LIVIUS (III) Drusus [Roman Tribune] + Servilia CAEPIONIS Major (? - 35? BC), daughter of Quintus Servilius CAEPIO [Roman Quaestor], son of Quintus SERVILIUS Caepio (? - 87? BC) [son of Quintus SERVILIUS Caepio (? - 87? BC) {Roman Consul}, son of Gnaeus Servilius CAEPIO (? - 123? BC) {Roman Consul}, son of Gnaeus Servilius Caepio (? - 155? BC) {Roman Consul}, son of Gnaeus CAEPIO (? - 203+ BC) {Roman Consul}] (and Metalla Terentia Varae (? - 114+ BC) [daughter of Marcus Terentius VARUS (and Sempronia, daughter of Gaius SEMPRONIUS Tuditanus [Roman Praetor], son of Gaius Sempronius TUDITANUS [Roman Pontifex], son of Marcus SEMPRONIUS [Roman Consul], son of Gaius SEMPRONIUS, son of Marcus SEMPRONIUS])

4.   Marcus Livius Drusus CLAUDIANUS + Alfidia

5.   Luvia (Livia) DRUSILLA (? - 30) + Tiberius Claudius NERO, son of Tiberius Claudius NERO (105? BC - 67 BC) [Roman Pontiff], son of Appius Claudius NERO, son of Tiberius Claudius NERO (105? BC - 67 BC) [Roman Praetor], son of Tiberius Claudius Nero (145? BC - ?), son of Appius Claudius NERO (170? BC - ?), son of Tiberius Claudius Nero (? - 167+ BC) [Roman Praetor for Sicilia], son of Appius CLAUDIUS Nero (? - 195+ BC) [Roman Quaestor], son of Publius Claudius Nero (260? BC - ?), son of Tiberius Claudius NERO (290? BC - ?), son of Appius Claudius CAECUS (340? BC - 273 BC) [Roman Consul; Dictator of ROME; extended democratic rights, builder & eponym of Via Appia & Aqua Appia , etc., said `every man is the architect of his own fortune'], son of Gaius CLAUDIUS Crassus (? - 337+ BC), son of Appius Claudius CRASSUS (425? BC - ?), son of Appius CLAUDIUS

CRASSUS (460? BC - ?), son of Appius Claudius Crassus Regillensis SABINUS, son of Appius Claudius Sabinus REGILLENSIS, son of Appius Claudius Sabinus Inregillensis

6.   Nero Claudius DRUSUS (Germanicus) [Roman General; Governor of Gaul]

7.   Antonia Minor `the Younger' Augusta (36? BC - 37?)

8.   Claudius I (EMPEROR) of ROME [aka Tiberius Claudius Nero Germanicus; aka Tiberius Nero DRUSUS; murdered by wife] + Aemilia LEPIDA (? - 26), daughter of Julia (Minor; IV) Vipsania (12? BC - 33?), Julia Augusta CAESONIA (? - 15?) (and Marcus VIPSANIUS Agrippa (62 BC - 12 BC)), daughter of Gaius Octavius Augustus (1st EMPEROR) of ROME [aka Caesar Augustus; eponym of month August; (considered one of the Wealthiest autocrats ever); C. (Gaius) Octavius Gaii f. (born, 63 BC); C. Iulius Gaii f. Caesar Octavianus (after posthumous adoption by Julius Caesar, 44); C. Iulius Divi f. Caesar Octavianus (after deification of stepfather, 42); Imperator Gaius Iulius Divi f. Caesar Octavianus (made Imperator, 31); Imperator Caesar Divi f. Augustus (made Augustus by Senate, 27 BC)]

9.   Genuissa (Venessa Julia) Claudia of ROME (? - 50?) + Aviragus (King) of the BRITONS (15? - 74? Avalon?)

10.   Meric (Marius Meurig Cyllin) of BRITONS (65? - 125?) + Julia (Victoria) verch PRASUTAGUS of the ICENI

11.   Coel I (Cole Coilus) (Old King Cole) King of BRITONS + Ystradwl (Stradwawl) of SILURIA

12.   Lleurig (Lucius) MAWR (King) of EWYAS + Gladys (Gwladys) verch EURGEN of SILURIA

13.   Gladys `the Younger' of BRITAIN (190? - ?) + Cadvan of CAMBRIA

14.   Strada `the Fair' of COMBRIA + Coilus II (Coel Cole) of GLOUCESTER (by 232 - 305?)

15.   Helena (Augusta) (Saint) of the CROSS + Flavius Valerius Constantius I of Rome

16.   Constantine `the Great' of ROME + Flavia Maxima Fausta (? - 326?)

17.   Flavia Constantia Augusta (320? - 354?) + Flavius Claudius CONSTANTIUS Gallus

18.   Anastasia

19.   Gallus
20.   Anastasia (Arriana) CONSTANTINA + Pompeius of
          DYRRHACHIUM
21.   Flavius PAULUS (Consul) (? - 496+) + Magna Sabiniani
22.   Flavius PROBUS (Consul) (? - 502+) + daughter of Flavius
          Sabinianus
23.   Flavius Anastasius PAULUS PROBUS Sabinianus POMPEIUS +
          Theodora(?), daughter of Theodora
24.   Paulus of ARABISSO + Joanna of ARABISSA
25.   Maurice (EMPEROR) of the EAST (539? - 27/11/602)
26.   Julius of BYZANTIUM
27.   Georgia
28.   Juliana FLAVIA + Athanagild (II; King) of the VISIGOTHS
29.   Ardabast (Count/King) of the VISIGOTHS + Goda of the
          BURGUNDIANS
30.   Ervik (King) of the VISIGOTHS (? - 687) + Liubigotona
          (Liuvigotona) of the VISIGOTHS
31.   Aupais (of SPAIN)
32.   Charles Martel "The Hammer", Mayor of the Palace +
          Rotrude, Duchess of Austrasia
33.   Pépin III, King of the Franks + Bertha Broadfoot of Laon
34.   CHARLEMAGNE, Carolus 'Magnus', Rex Francorum &
          Imperator Romanorum + Hildegard of Vinzgouw
35.   "Pépin" Carloman, King of Italy + Mistress of Pepin
36.   Bernard, King of Lombardy + Cunigundis (Cunegonde)
          (Princess) de VERMANDOIS
37.   Pépin II, lord of Péronne + Rothaide de Bobbio
38.   Pepin (I; Count) de SENLIS de VALOIS
39.   (Miss) de SENLIS de VALOIS (845? - ?) + Berenger (Count) de
          RENNES (? - 931)
40.   Poppa (Poppaeia) de VALOIS (872? - ?) + Rollo (Hrolf Rollon
          Rou Robert) 'the Dane' RAGNVALDSSON
41.   Guillaume (2nd Duke) of NORMANDY + Sprota de
          BRETAGNE (concubine)
42.   Richard I 'the Fearless' (Count) of NORMANDY + Gunnora
          (Gonnor) de CREPON
43.   Richard II 'the Good' of NORMANDY (963? - 1027) + Judith
          (Princess) of BRITTANY
44.   Robert II (Duke) of NORMANDY + Herleve (Salburpyr) de
          FALAISE (1003? - 1050?)
45.   WILLIAM the CONQUEROR (Duke) of NORMANDY + Matilda

(Maud) FLEMING (1032 - 1083 Caan)
46. Henry I BEAUCLERC (King) of ENGLAND + Matilda (Edith Eagdith) `Atheling' STEWART of SCOTLAND
47. Matilda (Maud Augusta) the EMPRESS + Geoffrey V `the Fair' (`Plantagenet')
48. Henry II (King) of ENGLAND + Eleanor (Duchess/Princess) of AQUITAINE
49. John `Lackland' (King) of ENGLAND + Isabella (d' ANGOULEME) TAILLEFER
50. Eleanor (Alianor) of ENGLAND (1215? - 1275) + Simon V de MONTFORT (1208 - 4/8/1265)
51. Eleanor de MONTFORT (1252 - 1282) + Llywellyn (II) ap GRUFFYDD (? - 1282)
52. Catherine verch LLYWELLYN + Philip ap IFOR
53. Eleanor (of ISCOED; GOCH) verch PHILIP + Thomas ap LLEWELLYN
54. Lowri verch GRUFFUDD FYCHAN + Robert (Sir; of Emral) PULESTON (1358? - 1399?)
55. Angharad PULESTON + Edward TREVOR ap DAFFYD (? - 1448?)
56. Otewell Worsley, Sir + Rose (TREVOR) verch EDWART
57. Joyce Worsley + Richard Lee II
58. Richard Lee III + Eleanor Burgoine
59. Geoffrey Lee, MP + Agnes Conyers
60. Reginald Lee + Dorothy Thurland
61. Gervase Lee of Nottinghamshire
62. Thomas Lee, of Ashfield + Margaret Mary Oscroft
63. Elizabeth Lee + Thomas Hanks
64. Robert Hanks + Margaret NLN
65. Peter Hanks I + Mary Bressie
66. Elinor Hanks + Robert Nelson
67. Rachael Nelson + Timothy Ragan
68. Timothy Reagan + Elizabeth Trigg
69. Richard Bazel Reagan + Cecelia Creppy
70. Richard Reagan + Phoebe Samples
71. Reuben Perry Reagan + Elizabeth Cagle
72. George Reagan + Emaline Garner
73. Marshall Reagan + Emma Rogers
74. Elzie Reagan + Delmar Raines
------- Gina Davis
------- Jackson Davis

------- Patricia Stuart
     ------- Bobby Caldwell
     ------- Jennifer Caldwell
------- Mike Raines
     ------- Leah Raines
     ------- Kendra Raines
     ------- Joshua Raines
     ------- Michael Raines
------- Frank Raines
     ------- Franklin Cody Raines
     ------- Kip Allen Raines
------- Richard Raines
     ------- Tyler Lee
     ------- Devin Lee
     ------- Emma Lundy

24

THE LOMBARDIAN LINEAGE

1. Uranus (1st Ruler GOD of the Universe) + Gaia (Gaea) the Earth GODDESS
2. Cronos (Kronos) the TITAN + Rhea (Rheia) the TITAN
3. Zeus the OLYMPIAN (born in Cretan cave) + Europa of PHOENICIA
4. Minos `the Elder' (King) of CRETE + Itone of CRETE
5. Lycastus of CRETE + Ide of CRETE
6. Minos II, King of CRETE + Pasiphae of CORINTH
7. Catreus (King) of CRETE
8. Aerope of CRETE + Atreus (King) of MYCENAE in ARGOS
9. Plisthenes (King) of MYCENAE + Cleolla of MYCENAE
10. Agamemnon (King) of MYCENAE + Clytaemnestra of SPARTA
11. Orestes (King) of ARGOS, MYCENAE & Sparta
12. (NN) ... (NN) (about five missing generations)
13. Sabinus
14. son of Sabinus
15. Demophon
16. Pomponius the SABINE + Jullia Prima of ROME
17. Numa Pompilius (2nd King) of ROME + Tatia (Princess) of SABINES

18.   Pompilla + Marcius II
19.   Ancus Marcius (4th King) of ROME (? - 616 BC)
20.   (NN) ... (NN) MARCIUS (some missing generations)
21.   Gaius Marcius + Artoria
22.   Quintus Marcius Barea Soranus (10? BC - 42) + Caepionia
          Crispina
23.   Quintus Marcius Barea Sura (12? - 63+) + Antonia Furnilla
24.   Marcia + Marcus Ulpius Traianus the Elder (? - by 100)
25.   Trajan (EMPEROR) of ROME (? - 117) + Pompeia Plotina
          Domitia Lucilla
26.   Domitia Lucilla Trajanus + Annius Verus
27.   Marcus Aurelius Antonius (EMPEROR) of ROME + Annia
          Galeria FAUSTINA (130 - 175), daughter of Antoninus
          Pius (EMPEROR) of ROME
28.   Severus Antoninus
29.   Marcus Annius Severus + Silvana
30.   Fabia Orestilla + Gordian I (Marcellus) (EMPEROR) of ROME
31.   Maecia Faustina GORDIANA (? - 241?) + Junius Licinius
          BALBUS (? - 238+)
32.   Gordian III (EMPEROR) of ROME + Furia Sabinia
          TRANQUILLINA (Greece)
33.   Furia GORDIANA + Marcus Maecius ORFITUS
34.   Maceia CETHEGILLA + Gaius Memmius Caecilianus
          PLACIDUS
35.   Placida + Cornelius SEVERUS
36.   Cornelia Severa + Quintus FLAVIUS Egnatius Lollianus
          Mavortius
37.   Quintus FLAVIUS Egnatius Placidus SEVERUS + Antonia
          Marcianilla
38.   Egnatia Avita (Major) SEVERA + Flavius Eparchius Philagrius
          (? - 382+)
39.   Agricola (Consul) of ROME (? - 421+) + Magna Major of
          ROME
40.   Marcus Maecilius (Eparchius) AVITUS
41.   Papinilla (Papianilla Pampanilla) AVITUS of ROME +
          Tonantius (I) FERREOLUS (by 418 - 476)
42.   Tonantius (II) `Vis Clarisimus' FERREOLUS + Industria de
          REIMS (475? - ?)
43.   Deoteria de BEZIERS (505? - 548?) + Theodon II (Duke) of
          BAVARIA (? - 537?)
44.   Theodon III of BAVARIA

45.   Theobald (Theodebert) of BAVARIA
46.   Garibald I (AGILOFINGES ?) of BAVARIA + Waldrada
            (Princess) of the LOMBARDS
47.   Gundwald (Duke) of ASTI (? - 613?) + Harinanda, daughter of
            Rotbert I (King) of LONGOBARDS
48.   Aripert I (Viscount) of LOMBARDY (? - 661?)
49.   Berthari (21st King) of the LANGOBARDS
50.   Kunibert (25th King) of the LANGOBARDS (? - 702?)
51.   Liutpert (26th King) of the LANGOBARDS (? - 712?)
52.   Theoderada (of the LOMBARDS) + Ansbrand (28th King) of
            the LANGOBARDS (655? - 712?)
53.   Sigiprand of the LOMBARDS
54.   Ansbrand of LOMBARDS
55.   Ansia of LOMBARDS (? - 774?) + Desiderio (last King) of
            LOMBARDS (? - 774+)
56.   Gerberga of LOMBARDY (? - 774) + Carloman II (Archduke)
            of AUSTRASIA (747? - 771)
57.   Kunigunde (Auberge) of AUSTRASIA + Adelgis (Count) of
            PARMA (of SPOLETO-PARMA) (? - 836?)
58.   Cunegonde (Princess) de VERMANDOIS + Bernard
            (Bernhard; I) (King) of ITALY (Lombardy)
59.   Pépin II, lord of Péronne + Rothaide de Bobbio
60.   Pepin (I; Count) de SENLIS de VALOIS
61.   (Miss) de SENLIS de VALOIS (845? - ?) + Berenger (Count) de
            RENNES (? - 931)
62.   Poppa (Poppaeia) de VALOIS (872? - ?) + Rollo (Hrolf Rollon
            Rou Robert) `the Dane' RAGNVALDSSON
63.   Guillaume (2nd Duke) of NORMANDY + Sprota de
            BRETAGNE (concubine)
64.   Richard I `the Fearless' (Count) of NORMANDY + Gunnora
            (Gonnor) de CREPON
65.   Richard II `the Good' of NORMANDY (963? - 1027) + Judith
            (Princess) of BRITTANY
66.   Robert II (Duke) of NORMANDY + Herleve (Salburpyr) de
            FALAISE (1003? - 1050?)
67.   WILLIAM the CONQUEROR (Duke) of NORMANDY + Matilda
            (Maud) FLEMING (1032 - 1083 Caan)
68.   Henry I BEAUCLERC (King) of ENGLAND + Matilda (Edith
            Eagdith) `Atheling' STEWART of SCOTLAND
69.   Matilda (Maud Augusta) the EMPRESS + Geoffrey V `the Fair'
            (`Plantagenet')

70.   Henry II (King) of ENGLAND + Eleanor (Duchess/Princess) of
            AQUITAINE
71.   John `Lackland' (King) of ENGLAND + Isabella (d'
            ANGOULEME) TAILLEFER
72.   Eleanor (Alianor) of ENGLAND (1215? - 1275) + Simon V de
            MONTFORT (1208 - 4/8/1265)
73.   Eleanor de MONTFORT (1252 - 1282) + Llywellyn (II) ap
            GRUFFYDD (? - 1282)
74.   Catherine verch LLYWELLYN + Philip ap IFOR
75.   Eleanor (of ISCOED; GOCH) verch PHILIP + Thomas ap
            LLEWELLYN
76.   Lowri verch GRUFFUDD FYCHAN + Robert (Sir; of Emral)
            PULESTON (1358? - 1399?)
77.   Angharad PULESTON + Edward TREVOR ap DAFFYD (? -
            1448?)
78.   Otewell Worsley, Sir + Rose (TREVOR) verch EDWART
79.   Joyce Worsley + Richard Lee II
80.   Richard Lee III + Eleanor Burgoine
81.   Geoffrey Lee, MP + Agnes Conyers
82.   Reginald Lee + Dorothy Thurland
83.   Gervase Lee of Nottinghamshire
84.   Thomas Lee, of Ashfield + Margaret Mary Oscroft
85.   Elizabeth Lee + Thomas Hanks
86.   Robert Hanks + Margaret NLN
87.   Peter Hanks I + Mary Bressie
88.   Elinor Hanks + Robert Nelson
89.   Rachael Nelson + Timothy Ragan
90.   Timothy Reagan + Elizabeth Trigg
91.   Richard Bazel Reagan + Cecelia Creppy
92.   Richard Reagan + Phoebe Samples
93.   Reuben Perry Reagan + Elizabeth Cagle
94.   George Reagan + Emaline Garner
95.   Marshall Reagan + Emma Rogers
96.   Elzie Reagan + Delmar Raines
            ------- Gina Davis
                ------- Jackson Davis
            ------- Patricia Stuart
                ------- Bobby Caldwell
                ------- Jennifer Caldwell
            ------- Mike Raines
                ------- Leah Raines

------- Kendra Raines
------- Joshua Raines
------- Michael Raines
------- Frank Raines
------- Franklin Cody Raines
------- Kip Allen Raines
------- Richard Raines
------- Tyler Lee
------- Devin Lee
------- Emma Lundy

25

THE MACEDONIAN KINGS LINEAGE

1. Chronos (Primordial GOD)
2. Chaos (PRIMORDIAL)
3. Erebus (Primordial GOD)
4. Aether (the Upper Sky; PRIMORDIAL)
5. Uranus (1st Ruler GOD of the Universe)
6. Cronos (Kronos) the TITAN
7. Zeus the OLYMPIANborn in Cretan cave)
8. Apollo the OLYMPIAN
9. Melaneus (King) of the DRYOPIANS
10. Eurytus (Prince) of OECHALIA
11. Iole of OECHALIA
12. Cleodaeos the HERACLIDE
13. Aristomachos (of THEBES)
14. Temenos (King) of ARGOS
15. Ceisus (King) of ARGOS
16. Maron
17. Thestrus
18. Acous
19. Aristodamidas the HERACLIDE
20. Caranus ARGEAD (1st King) of MACEDONIA

21.   Coenus ARGEAD (2nd King) of MACEDONIA
22.   Tyrimmas (3rd King) of MACEDONIA
23.   Perdiccas I (4th King) of MACEDONIA
24.   Argaeus I (King) of MACEDONIA (? - 611 BC), grandson of
            Gordios (1st King) of PHRYGIA (the son of a poor farmer)
25.   Philip I (King) of MACEDONIA (? - 578 BC)
26.   Aeropus I (King) of MACEDONIA (600? BC - 558 BC)
-       Alcetas I (King) of MACEDONIA
27.   Amyntas TEMENID (I; King) of MACEDONIA
28.   Alexander I (King) of MACEDONIA
29.   Amyntas TEMENID of MACEDONIA (? - 411? BC)
30.   Arrhidaeus (Prince) of MACEDONIA
31.   Amyntas III (King) of MACEDONIA (? - 370? BC)
32.   Philip II (King) of MACEDONIA (382? BC - 336 BC) +
            Olympias of the MOLOSSIANS (375 BC - 316 BC)
33.   Alexander III `the Great' (King) of MACEDONIA
34.   Percefus, Greek Governor in Britain
35.   Bethides (Governor) in BRITAIN
36.   Barsine of MACEDONIA
37.   Caecilia Metellus Macedonicus
38.   Lucius Julius Caesar (? - 183+ BC)
39.   Lucius JULIUS Caesar (? - 166 BC)
40.   Sextus Julius CAESAR (? - 147 BC)
41.   Sextus Julius CAESAR (? - 147+ BC)
42.   Lucius Julius (II) CAESAR (Sextus) (? - 124? BC)
43.   Lucius JULIUS (III) CAESAR, son of Popillia (Major)
            LAENATUM, grandson of Popillius Laenas
44.   Julia Caesia Caesonia of ROME (103? BC - ?)
45.   Marcus ANTONIUS (Mark Antony, Triumvir of ROME)
46.   Antonia
47.   Prydain ap AEDD (Duke/King) of CORNWALL
48.   Dyfnarth (Cynfarch Cyfnarch) (Duke/King) of CORNWALL
49.   Crydon (Krydon) the CAMBRIAN
50.   Cerwydr the CAMBRIAN, descendant of Hamilcar and
            Hannibal, Kings of Carthage
51.   Capoir of the DRUIDS (King) of BRITONS
52.   Manogan
53.   Penardim (Penardun)
54.   Bran Fendigaid `the Blessed' (King) of SILURIA
55.   Caradoc (King) of BRITAIN
56.   Guidgen (? - 85)

57.   Art `Cois'
58.   Quintus (5th King) of PICTS
59.   Corvus (1st King) of DUMBARTON
60.   Art `Vroisc' (King) of DUMBARTON
61.   Fer `Fi' (King) of DUMBARTON
62.   Duibne `Mor' (King) of DUMBARTON
63.   Art `Og' (King) of DUMBARTON
64.   Con (Confer)
65.   Fer (King) of DUMBARTON
66.   Cursalem (King) of DUMBARTON
67.   Cluim (Clemens Clium Cluian) of ROME
68.   Cinhil (Quintillian) of the DAMNONII
69.   Cynlop (Cynllwyb Cynloup Cynloyp) of the DAMNONII
70.   Ceredig WLEDIG (King) of STRATHCLYDE
71.   Erp (Erbin Seirb) ap CERETIC (? - 480?)
72.   Geraint ap ERP
73.   (Miss) verch GERAINT
74.   Erb MacDRUST (? - 529)
75.   Nechtan (Neiton; II; III; MAWR) MacERB (? - 621?)
76.   Beli (I; King) of STRATHCLYDE
77.   daughter of Beli
78.   Spondana ingen ENFIDAIG (Princess) of the PICTS
79.   Eochaid (III) Angbaid (Angbhadh; MacECHACH) of ARGYLL
80.   Fergus (II) MacECHACH (King) of DALRIADA
81.   Constantine (67th/101th King) of PICTS (? - 820+)
82.   Drust IX (69th/103rd King) of PICTS, sister of + Alpin
        MacEOCHAID (King) of KINTYRE (778? - 834)
83.   Kenneth I (Cinaed) MacALPIN (1st King) of SCOTS; united
        Scots & Picts in 846; aka Ciniod (mac Ailpin) II (77th
        King) of PICTS; aka Kenneth `the Hardy'; `the Raven
        Feeder'; the CONQUEROR + daughter of Donald Anicom,
        Lord of the Isles [Note: Scholars generally treat the
        stories and ancestry given for Kenneth to be partly
        fictional. Defeated Picts in battle in 841 (acquiring
        nickname `Raven Feeder'); invited Pictish royal family to
        a great banquet and massacred them; became King of
        both Scots & Picts in 846. The Scots moved their capital
        to Scone, sacred heart of the Pictish Kingdom, and sat on
        a stone throne which, in legend, had come from Spain
        with the 1st Milesian monarch and spent centuries at
        Dunstaffnage Castle in Tara. Although the Picts had ruled

much of northern Britain for over 1000 years, within a century after MacAlpin's Treason Pictish culture and language had almost disappeared.]

84. Constantine I `the Wine-Bountiful' of ALBA (3rd King) of SCOTS (836? - 877, beheaded by the Norse) + Nesta verch RHODRI MAWR (840? - ?)

85. Donald II Dasachtach (6th King) of SCOTS (King of ALBA); aka Domnall mac Causantin; `the Madman' (abt. 862-900, killed in Battle against Danes) + Unknown

86. Malcolm I MacALPIN of ALBA, 8th King of SCOTS; aka Maol Chaluim mac Ailpin; `the Dangerous Red' (897-954, slain by men of Moray) + Unknown

87. Kenneth II MacALPIN of ALBA, 12th King of SCOTS (murdered by his own men) + Unknown

88. Malcolm II MacKENNETH of ALBA, 15th King of SCOTS; aka Mael-Coluim, Melkolf, Malbrigdeson, `the Destroyer' + Aefgifu, Irish Woman of OSSORY

89. Bethoc (Beatrix) MacKENNETH of SCOTLAND (984? - ?) + Crinan of Dunkeld, Abthane of ATHOLL (976? - 1045)

90. Duncan I `the Gracious' MacCRINAN of SCOTLAND + Bethoc MacDUFF (1009? - 1040?)

91. Malcolm III MacCRINAN (CANMORE) (19th King) of SCOTS + Margaret (Queen; Saint) of SCOTLAND

92. Matilda (Edith Eagdith) `Atheling' STEWART of SCOTLAND + Henry I BEAUCLERC (King) of ENGLAND

93. Matilda (Maud Augusta) the EMPRESS + Geoffrey V `the Fair' (`Plantagenet')

94. Henry II (King) of ENGLAND + Eleanor (Duchess/Princess) of AQUITAINE

95. John `Lackland' (King) of ENGLAND + Isabella (d' ANGOULEME) TAILLEFER

96. Eleanor (Alianor) of ENGLAND (1215? - 1275) + Simon V de MONTFORT (1208 - 4/8/1265)

97. Eleanor de MONTFORT (1252 - 1282) + Llywellyn (II) ap GRUFFYDD (? - 1282)

98. Catherine verch LLYWELLYN + Philip ap IFOR

99. Eleanor (of ISCOED; GOCH) verch PHILIP + Thomas ap LLEWELLYN

100. Lowri verch GRUFFUDD FYCHAN + Robert (Sir; of Emral) PULESTON (1358? - 1399?)

101. Angharad PULESTON + Edward TREVOR ap DAFFYD (? -

1448?)

102. Otewell Worsley, Sir + Rose (TREVOR) verch EDWART
103. Joyce Worsley + Richard Lee II
104. Richard Lee III + Eleanor Burgoine
105. Geoffrey Lee, MP + Agnes Conyers
106. Reginald Lee + Dorothy Thurland
107. Gervase Lee of Nottinghamshire
108. Thomas Lee, of Ashfield + Margaret Mary Oscroft
109. Elizabeth Lee + Thomas Hanks
110. Robert Hanks + Margaret NLN
111. Peter Hanks I + Mary Bressie
112. Elinor Hanks + Rober Nelson
113. Rachael Nelson + Timothy Ragan
114. Timothy Reagan + Elizabeth Trigg
115. Richard Bazel Reagan + Cecelia Creppy
116. Richard Reagan + Phoebe Samples
117. Reuben Perry Reagan + Elizabeth Cagle
118. George Reagan + Emaline Garner
119. Marshall Reagan + Emma Rogers
120. Elzie Reagan + Delmar Raines

------- Gina Davis
    ------- Jackson Davis
------- Patricia Stuart
    ------- Bobby Caldwell
    ------- Jennifer Caldwell
------- Mike Raines
    ------- Leah Raines
    ------- Kendra Raines
    ------- Joshua Raines
    ------- Michael Raines
------- Frank Raines
    ------- Franklin Cody Raines
    ------- Kip Allen Raines
------- Richard Raines
    ------- Tyler Lee
    ------- Devin Lee
    ------- Emma Lundy

26

THE MEROVINGIAN LINEAGE

1.   Sesostris + Nefret
2.   Amenemhat I Sehetepibre (Founder) of 12th Dynasty +
        Nefrutotenen
3.   Sesotris I Kheperkare (PHARAOH) of EGYPT (? - 1928? BC) +
        Nefrusheri (Princess) of EGYPT
4.   Amenemhat (Ammenemes) II Nubkaure (PHARAOH) of
        EGYPT + Keminnub (Queen) of EGYPT
5.   Sesotris II Khakheperre (PHARAOH) of EGYPT + Nofret of
        EGYPT
6.   Sesotris III Khakaure of EGYPT + Sebekshedty-Neferu
        (Queen) of EGYPT
7.   Amenemhat III Nemare (PHARAOH) of EGYPT + Sebeknefru
        (Queen) of EGYPT
8.   Amenemhat (Ammenemes) IV (PHARAOH) of EGYPT
9.   Wegaf (PHARAOH) of 13th Dynasty + daughter of
        Amenemhet IV
10. Ameny Intef (Inyotef) IV (PHARAOH) of EGYPT
11. Hor (PHARAOH) of EGYPT (? - 1760? BC)
12. Sobekhotep II (PHARAOH) of EGYPT (? - 1750? BC)
13. Khendjer (PHARAOH) of EGYPT (? - 1747? BC)

14. Sobekhotep III (PHARAOH) of EGYPT (? - 1745? BC)
15. Neferhotep I (PHARAOH) of EGYPT
16. Sobekhotep IV Khaneferre (PHARAOH) of 13th Dynasty + Tjan
17. Sebekhotep (Princess) of THEBES + Senebhanef, son of Renressonb
18. Mentuhotep (Queen) of EGYPT + Sekhemre-Sementawi Djehuti (PHARAOH) of EGYPT
19. Sekhemre-Se'ankhtawi Neferhotep (PHARAOH) of EGYPT
20. Sobekemsaf Sekhemre-Shedtawi (PHARAOH) of EGYPT + Nubkhas (Queen) of EGYPT
21. Inyotef VII (PHARAOH) at THEBES + Sobkemsaf (Sebekamzaf) of EGYPT (1635? BC - ?)
22. Sekenenre Tao I (PHARAOH) at THEBES + Tetisheri of THEBES
23. Sekenenre Tao II (King) of THEBES + Ahhotep (Ahotop) I (Queen) of EGYPT
24. Ahmose I (1st PHARAOH) of 18th Dynasty + Nefretiri (Queen) of EGYPT
25. Amenhotep I Djeserkare (PHARAOH) of EGYPT + Senisonb (Seneseneb) of EGYPT
26. Thutmose I (PHARAOH) of EGYPT (? - 1481? BC) + Amhose (Aahmes II) (Queen) of EGYPT
27. Hatshepsut (Queen & PHARAOH) of EGYPT (? - 1482 BC) + Thutmose (Tuthmosis) II (PHARAOH) of EGYPT
28. Meryetre Hatshepsut of EGYPT + Thutmose III `the Great' of EGYPT (Moses of the Bible)
29. Akheperure Amenhotep II THUTMOSID (PHARAOH) of EGYPT + Tio (Tiye Tiaa)
30. Menkheprure' Thutmose IV (PHARAOH) of EGYPT + Mutemwiya, daughter of Artatama (I; King) of MITANNI
31. Nebma'atre' Amenhotep III (PHARAOH) of EGYPT + Tiye Nefertari (Tiy) of EGYPT (1382 BC - 1344 BC)
32. Akhenaton (Iknaton) (10th PHARAOH) of 18th Dynasty EGYPT + Nefertiti (Chief Queen) of EGYPT
33. Meritaten (Royal Daughter) of EGYPT + Judah (Judas Juda) ibn JACOB, son of Jacob ibn ISAAC (King of GOSHEN)
34. Zerah (Zehrah Zarah Zare) ibn JUDAH + Electra the PLEIADE
35. Dardanus (Dara) (King) of ACADIA + Batea of TEUCRI
36. Erichthonius (King) of ACADIA (? - 1386? BC) + Astyoche of ACADIA

37.   Trois of ACADIA + Callirhoe (TEUCRI)
38.   Ilus (Ilyus) (King) of TROY (? - 1282? BC) + Eurydice (Eurydike) of TROY
39.   Priam Podarces (High King) of TROY (? - 1183? BC) + Hecuba (Hecabe) of PHRYGIA
40.   Helenus of TROY (King of the SCYTHIANS) + daughter of Scythes (1st King) of SCYTHIA
41.   Genger of the SCYTHIANS
42.   Esdron the TROJAN
43.   Gelio the TROJAN
44.   Bosabiliano (Basabelian I) the TROJAN
45.   Plaserio (Plaserius I) the TROJAN
46.   Plesron (King of CIMMERIANS)
47.   Eliacor the TROJAN
48.   Gaberiano (Zaberian) the TROJAN
49.   Plaserius II the TROJAN
50.   Antenor I the TROJAN
51.   Priam II Trianus the TROJAN
52.   Helenus II the TROJAN
53.   Plesron II the TROJAN
54.   Basabelian (Basabiliano) II the TROJAN
55.   Alexandre the TROJAN
56.   Priam III of the CIMMERIANS
57.   Gentilanor (Prince) of the CIMMERIANS
58.   Almadius (King) of the CIMMERIANS
59.   Dilulius I (King) of the CIMMERIANS
60.   Helenus III (King) of the CIMMERIANS
61.   Plaserius (Plaserio) III (King) of the CIMMERIANS
62.   Dilulius (Diluglio) II (King) of the CIMMERIANS
63.   Marcomir (King) of the CIMMERIANS
64.   Priam IV (King) of the CIMMERIANS
65.   Helenus IV (King) of the CIMMERIANS
66.   Antenor I (II; King) of the CIMMERIANS (? - 433? BC)
67.   Marcomir I (King) of SICAMBRI (? - 412? BC)
68.   Antenor II (III; King) of SICAMBRI (? - 384? BC) + Cambra
69.   Priamus (V; Priam) (King) of SICAMBRI (? - 358? BC)
70.   Helenus V (King) of SICAMBRI
71.   Diocles (King) of SICAMBRI
72.   Bassanus Magnus (King) of SICAMBRI
73.   Clodimir I (King) of SICAMBRI
74.   Nicanor I (King) of SICAMBRI

75.   Marcomir II (King) of SICAMBRI + (Princess NN), daughter of
       Elidure (Chieftain) in BRITAIN
76.   Clodius I (King) of SICAMBRI
77.   Antenor III (King) of SICAMBRI
78.   Clodimir II (King) of SICAMBRI (? - 123? BC)
79.   Merodachus (King) of SICAMBRI (? - 95? BC)
80.   Cassander (King) of SICAMBRI
81.   Antharius (King) of the SICAMBRI (77? BC - 36? BC)
82.   Francus (King) of the WEST FRANKS (57? BC - 5?)
83.   Clodius II (King) of the FRANKS (37? BC - 20?)
84.   Marcomir III (King) of the FRANKS (17? BC - 50?)
85.   Clodomir III (King) of the FRANKS
86.   Antenor IV (King) of the WEST FRANKS
87.   Ratherius (King) of the FRANKS
88.   Richemer I (King) of FRANKS + Ascyla of the FRANKS
89.   Odomir (Odomar) (King) of FRANKS
90.   Marcomir IV (King) of FRANKS + Althildis (Princess) of
       BRITAIN
91.   Clodimir IV (King) of FRANKS + Hafilda (Princess) of the
       RUGIJ
92.   Farabert (King) of FRANKS (by 145 - 186?)
93.   Sunno (Huano Hunno) (King) of FRANKS
94.   Childeric (Hilderic) (King) of FRANKS
95.   Bartherus (King) of FRANKS (? - 272)
96.   Clodius (III) of FRANKS (225? - 298?)
97.   Walter (King) of the EAST FRANKS (by 245 - 306?)
98.   Dagobert I (King) of FRANKS (? - 317?)
99.   Genebald (I; 1st Duke) of the EAST FRANKS (262+ - 358) +
       Athildis
100.   Dagobert II (Duke) of EAST FRANKS
101.   Clodius (I; IV; Duke) of EAST FRANKS
102.   Marcomir I (VI; V; Duke) of EAST FRANKS + Hatilde(?) of the
       FRANKS (351? - ?)
103.   Pharamond (Faramond) (King) of WESTPHALIA + Argotta
       (Princess) of the SALIC FRANKS (376? - 406?) Daughter
       of Genebald
104.   Clodius V (King) of WESTPHALIA (388? - 448?) + Basina of
       THURINGIA (by 398 - ?)
105.   Merovech (I; King) of (Salic) Franks (MEROVINGIAN) +
       Chlodoswintha des FRANCS RIPUAIRES
106.   Childeric I (King) of FRANKS (of YSSEL) + Basina Andovera

107.   (Saint?) of THURINGIA
107.   Clovis `the Great' (1st King) of All FRANKS + Clothilde (Saint; Princess) of BURGUNDY
108.   Chlothar I (2nd King) of All FRANKS (497? - 561) + Ildegonde of the FRANKS
109.   Sigebert (Siegbert) (I; King) of COLOGNE
110.   Cloderic `the Parricide' (King) of COLOGNE + Agilofinginne of the AGILOFING
111.   Munderic of VITRY-EN-PERTHOIS + Arthemia(?) of GENEVA (503? - 530+)
112.   Mummolin des FRANCS RIPUAIRES (505? - 558?)
113.   Baudgise II (Duke) of AQUITAINE + Oda (Saint) of SAVOY (562? - 611+)
114.   Saint Arnoul, bishop of Metz + Saint Dode (Clotilde) of Metz
115.   Ansigisel of Metz, Mayor of the Palace of Austrasia + Saint Beggue of Austrasia
116.   Pépin ll "the Fat"; d'Héristal, Mayor of the Palace of Austrasia + Alpaïde (Alpais)
117.   Charles Martel "The Hammer", Mayor of the Palace + Rotrude, Duchess of Austrasia
118.   Pépin III, King of the Franks + Bertha Broadfoot of Laon
119.   CHARLEMAGNE, Carolus 'Magnus', Rex Francorum & Imperator Romanorum + Hildegard of Vinzgouw
120.   "Pépin" Carloman, King of Italy + Mistress of Pepin
121.   Bernard, King of Lombardy + Cunigundis (Cunegonde) (Princess) de VERMANDOIS
122.   Pépin II, lord of Péronne + Rothaide de Bobbio
123.   Pepin (I; Count) de SENLIS de VALOIS
124.   (Miss) de SENLIS de VALOIS (845? - ?) + Berenger (Count) de RENNES (? - 931)
125.   Poppa (Poppaeia) de VALOIS (872? - ?) + Rollo (Hrolf Rollon Rou Robert) `the Dane' RAGNVALDSSON
126.   Guillaume (2nd Duke) of NORMANDY + Sprota de BRETAGNE (concubine)
127.   Richard I `the Fearless' (Count) of NORMANDY + Gunnora (Gonnor) de CREPON
128.   Richard II `the Good' of NORMANDY (963? - 1027) + Judith (Princess) of BRITTANY
129.   Robert II (Duke) of NORMANDY + Herleve (Salburpyr) de FALAISE (1003? - 1050?)
130.   WILLIAM the CONQUEROR (Duke) of NORMANDY + Matilda

(Maud) FLEMING (1032 - 1083 Caan)

131. Henry I BEAUCLERC (King) of ENGLAND + Matilda (Edith Eagdith) `Atheling' STEWART of SCOTLAND

132. Matilda (Maud Augusta) the EMPRESS + Geoffrey V `the Fair' (`Plantagenet')

133. Henry II (King) of ENGLAND + Eleanor (Duchess/Princess) of AQUITAINE

134. John `Lackland' (King) of ENGLAND + Isabella (d' ANGOULEME) TAILLEFER

135. Eleanor (Alianor) of ENGLAND (1215? - 1275) + Simon V de MONTFORT (1208 - 4/8/1265)

136. Eleanor de MONTFORT (1252 - 1282) + Llywellyn (II) ap GRUFFYDD (? - 1282)

137. Catherine verch LLYWELLYN + Philip ap IFOR

138. Eleanor (of ISCOED; GOCH) verch PHILIP + Thomas ap LLEWELLYN

139. Lowri verch GRUFFUDD FYCHAN + Robert (Sir; of Emral) PULESTON (1358? - 1399?)

140. Angharad PULESTON + Edward TREVOR ap DAFFYD (? - 1448?)

141. Otewell Worsley, Sir + Rose (TREVOR) verch EDWART

142. Joyce Worsley + Richard Lee II

143. Richard Lee III + Eleanor Burgoine

144. Geoffrey Lee, MP + Agnes Conyers

145. Reginald Lee + Dorothy Thurland

146. Gervase Lee of Nottinghamshire

147. Thomas Lee, of Ashfield + Margaret Mary Oscroft

148. Elizabeth Lee + Thomas Hanks

149. Robert Hanks + Margaret NLN

150. Peter Hanks I + Mary Bressie

151. Elinor Hanks + Robert Nelson

152. Rachael Nelson + Timothy Ragan

153. Timothy Reagan + Elizabeth Trigg

154. Richard Bazel Reagan + Cecelia Creppy

155. Richard Reagan + Phoebe Samples

156. Reuben Perry Reagan + Elizabeth Cagle

157. George Reagan + Emaline Garner

158. Marshall Reagan + Emma Rogers

159. Elzie Reagan + Delmar Raines

------- Gina Davis

------- Jackson Davis

------- Patricia Stuart
     ------- Bobby Caldwell
     ------- Jennifer Caldwell
------- Mike Raines
     ------- Leah Raines
     ------- Kendra Raines
     ------- Joshua Raines
     ------- Michael Raines
------- Frank Raines
     ------- Franklin Cody Raines
     ------- Kip Allen Raines
------- Richard Raines
     ------- Tyler Lee
     ------- Devin Lee
     ------- Emma Lundy

27

THE MESOPOTAMIAN LINEAGE

1. Mummu the Creator GOD + Nammu, Goddess of the Sea
2. Apsu, Ocean of Sweet Water + Tiamat, Ocean of Salt Water
3. Lahmu, The Primordial God + Lahamu, the Primordial GODDESS
4. Anshar, the Primordial God + Kishar, the Primordial GODDESS
5. Anu, GOD of the Sky + Anatu GODDESS
6. Enki (Ea), GOD OF WISDOM + Ninhursag, Mother GODDESS
7. Alulim (1st King) of ERIDU
8. Alalgar
9. Kidunnu
10. Alimma
11. Enmenluanna
12. Dumuzi
13. Ensipazianna
14. En-men-dur-anna
15. Urbar-Tutu of SHURRUPAK
16. Ziu-sudra (last King) of BABEL
17. Mashkakatu (1st King) of KISH
18. Kullassina-Bel (King) of KISH

19.   Nangislishima (King) of KISH
20.   Endaranna (King) of KISH
21.   Babum (King) of KISH
22.   Puannum (King) of KISH
23.   Kalibum of KISH
24.   Qalumun (King) of KISH
25.   Zuqaqip (King) of KISH
26.   Atab (King) of KISH
27.   Mashda (King) of KISH
28.   Arwium (King) of KISH
29.   Etana `the Shepherd' (King) of KISH (? - 2831 BC)
30.   Balih (King) of KISH
31.   Emennuna (King) of KISH
32.   Melam-Kish of KISH
33.   Hia-Kish of KISH
34.   Meskiaggasher (1st King) of URUK
35.   Enmerker (2nd King) of URUK + Inanna Ishtar (Queen) of
          HEAVEN
36.   Lugalbanda (3rd King) of URUK
37.   Gilgamesh (5th King) of URUK
38.   Nimrod (King) of ASSYRIA & BABYLON + Hept Ishtar
39.   Azurad bint NEBROD + Eber ibn SHELAH (2277? BC - 1813?
          BC)
40.   Pelag ben EBERShinar 2243? BC - 2004? BC) + Lomna bint
          SINA'AR
41.   Heraclim + Shela
42.   Abram + (Miss) de UR
43.   'Edna bat 'ABRAM + Ierah (Thare Terih) (King?) of AGADE
44.   Abraham (Avraham Ibrahim) of GENESIS + Sarai (Sarah)
          (Princess) bint HARAN
45.   Isaac ibn ABRAHAM (1922 BC - 1742 BC) + Rebekah
          (Rebecca) bint BETHEUL
46.   Jacob ibn ISAAC (King of GOSHEN) + Leah (Lia) bint LABAN
47.   Judah (Judas Juda) ibn JACOB + Tamar of KADESH (? - 1665?
          BC)
48.   Perez (Phares) + Barayah (bas JACOB?)
49.   Hezron ibn PHARES (Prince of JUDAH) + Ephratha bint
          MACHIR
50.   Caleb ben HEZRON + Ephratha bint MACHIR
51.   Hur (Jephunneh) ben CALEB + Miriam (the PROPHETESS)
          bat AMRAM

52. Salma ben HUR
53. Beth-Lehem
54. NNs of BETHLEHEM (some missing generations)
55. Ibzan of BETHLEHEM
56. (NN; 'Edal?; Abrias?) ben IBZAN
57. Abala (Habalith) + Jesse ben OBED (Bethlehem 1078? BC - ?)
58. David (1st King) of JUDAH & ISRAEL + Bathsheba (Bathshua) bat AMMIEL
59. Solomon ben DAVID (2nd King) of ISRAEL (? - 930 BC) + Nicaule (Nicauli Tashere) of EGYPT
60. Basemath bat SOLOMON + Ahimaaz the NAPHALITE
61. Ana bat AHIMAAZ + Abia (Abijah) (4th King) of JUDAH
62. Asa (Asaph) (5th King) of JUDEA + Azubah (Queen) of JUDEA
63. Jehoshapat (6th King) of JUDAH + daughter of Omri
64. Jehoram (Joram) (7th King) of JUDAH + Athalia of ISRAEL (9th Queen) of JUDAH
65. Ozias (Ahaziah Ochozias) (8th King) of JUDAH + Zibiah of BEERSHEBA
66. Josiah (I; 10th King) of JUDAH (871 BC - 796 BC) + Jehoaddin of JERUSALEM
67. Amaziah (Amasias) (11th King) of JUDAH + Jecoliah of JERUSALEM
68. Uzziah (Azariah) (12th King) of JUDAH + Jerusha of ISRAEL
69. Joatham (Jotham) (13th King) of JUDAH + Ahio (Princess) bat AZRIKAM
70. Achaz (Ahaz) (14th King) of JUDAH + Abijah bat ZECHARIAH (Heiress) of ISRAEL
71. Ezechias (Hezekiah) (15th King) of JUDAH + Hephzibah bat ISAIAH
72. Manasses ha-DAVID (Manasseh) (16th King) of JUDAH + Meshullemeth bat HARUZ of JOTBAH
73. Amon ha-DAVID (17th King) of JUDAH + Jedidah bat ADAIAH of BOZKATH
74. Josias (Josiah) ha-DAVID (18th King) of JUDAH + Zebidah (Zebudah; bat PEDAIAH) of RUMAH
75. Johanan (Crown Prince) of JUDAH
76. Tamar (Heiress) of the DAVIDIC Dynasty + Neri (Neriah) ha-DAVID
77. Salathial (Shealtiel) ha-DAVID + poss. Hadast (Hetbath)
78. Zorobabel ha-DAVID (Heir) of the DAVIDIC Dynasty + Rhodah (Princess) of PERSIA (? - 571? BC)

79.   Resa (Reza Rhesa) ha-DAVID
80.   Joanna (Joanan Yohannai Jehohanen) ben RESA
81.   Judah (Juda Joda Judas) ben JOANNA
82.   Joseph (Josech) ben JUDAH
83.   Semel ben JOSEPH
84.   Mattathias (Mathathias) ben SEMEL + daughter of Simon ha-
         KOHEN
85.   Maath ben MATTATHIAS ha-DAVID
86.   Nagga ben MAATH
87.   Esli ben NAGGA
88.   Naum ben ESLI of JUDAH
89.   Amos ben NAUM
90.   Mattathias (Mathathias Mattathiah) ben AMOS
91.   Joseph (Jose) ben MATTATHIAS
92.   Janna (Janne Jannai Johanan) ben JOSEPH
93.   Melchi (Melki) ben JANNA
94.   Levi ben MELCHI
95.   Matthat (Mathat) ben LEVI of ARIMATHEA + daughter of
         Eleazar
96.   Joseph ben MATTHAT (Saint) of ARIMATHEA + Alyuba
97.   Anna (Enygeus) of ARIMATHEA + Mandubratius ap LUD of
         BRITAIN
98.   Boadicea (Queen) of ICENIANS (22? - 62?) + Prasutagus
         (King) of ICENIA (? - 61?)
99.   Julia (Victoria) verch PRASUTAGUS of the ICENI + Meric
         (Marius Meurig Cyllin) of BRITONS (65? - 125?)
100.   Coel I (Cole Coilus) (Old King Cole) King of BRITONS +
         Ystradwl (Stradwawl) of SILURIA
101.   Lleurig (Lucius) MAWR (King) of EWYAS + Gladys (Gwladys)
         verch EURGEN of SILURIA
102.   Gladys `the Younger' of BRITAIN (190? - ?) + Cadvan of
         CAMBRIA
103.   Strada `the Fair' of COMBRIA + Coilus II (Coel Cole) of
         GLOUCESTER (by 232 - 305?)
104.   Helena (Augusta) (Saint) of the CROSS + Flavius Valerius
         Constantius I of Rome
105.   Constantine `the Great' of ROME + Flavia Maxima Fausta (? -
         326?)
106.   Flavia Constantia Augusta (320? - 354?) + Flavius Claudius
         CONSTANTIUS Gallus
107.   Anastasia

108. Gallus
109. Anastasia (Arriana) CONSTANTINA + Pompeius of
        DYRRHACHIUM
110. Flavius PAULUS (Consul) (? - 496+) + Magna Sabiniani
111. Flavius PROBUS (Consul) (? - 502+) + daughter of Flavius
        Sabinianus
112. Flavius Anastasius PAULUS PROBUS Sabinianus POMPEIUS +
        Theodora(?), daughter of Theodora
113. Paulus of ARABISSO + Joanna of ARABISSA
114. Maurice (EMPEROR) of the EAST (539? - 27/11/602)
115. Julius of BYZANTIUM
116. Georgia
117. Juliana FLAVIA + Athanagild (II; King) of the VISIGOTHS
118. Ardabast (Count/King) of the VISIGOTHS + Goda of the
        BURGUNDIANS
119. Ervik (King) of the VISIGOTHS (? - 687) + Liubigotona
        (Liuvigotona) of the VISIGOTHS
120. Aupais (of SPAIN)
121. Charles Martel "The Hammer", Mayor of the Palace +
        Rotrude, Duchess of Austrasia
122. Pépin III, King of the Franks + Bertha Broadfoot of Laon
123. CHARLEMAGNE, Carolus 'Magnus', Rex Francorum &
        Imperator Romanorum + Hildegard of Vinzgouw
124. "Pépin" Carloman, King of Italy + Mistress of Pepin
125. Bernard, King of Lombardy + Cunigundis (Cunegonde)
        (Princess) de VERMANDOIS
126. Pépin II, lord of Péronne + Rothaide de Bobbio
127. Pepin (I; Count) de SENLIS de VALOIS
128. (Miss) de SENLIS de VALOIS (845? - ?) + Berenger (Count) de
        RENNES (? - 931)
129. Poppa (Poppaeia) de VALOIS (872? - ?) + Rollo (Hrolf Rollon
        Rou Robert) 'the Dane' RAGNVALDSSON
130. Guillaume (2nd Duke) of NORMANDY + Sprota de
        BRETAGNE (concubine)
131. Richard I `the Fearless' (Count) of NORMANDY + Gunnora
        (Gonnor) de CREPON
132. Richard II `the Good' of NORMANDY (963? - 1027) + Judith
        (Princess) of BRITTANY
133. Robert II (Duke) of NORMANDY + Herleve (Salburpyr) de
        FALAISE (1003? - 1050?)
    134. WILLIAM the CONQUEROR (Duke) of NORMANDY +

Matilda (Maud) FLEMING (1032 - 1083 Caan)
135. Henry I BEAUCLERC (King) of ENGLAND + Matilda (Edith
      Eagdith) `Atheling' STEWART of SCOTLAND
136. Matilda (Maud Augusta) the EMPRESS + Geoffrey V `the
      Fair' (`Plantagenet')
137. Henry II (King) of ENGLAND + Eleanor (Duchess/Princess)
      of AQUITAINE
138. John `Lackland' (King) of ENGLAND + Isabella (d'
      ANGOULEME) TAILLEFER
139. Eleanor (Alianor) of ENGLAND (1215? - 1275) + Simon V
      de MONTFORT (1208 - 4/8/1265)
140. Eleanor de MONTFORT (1252 - 1282) + Llywellyn (II) ap
      GRUFFYDD (? - 1282)
141. Catherine verch LLYWELLYN + Philip ap IFOR
142. Eleanor (of ISCOED; GOCH) verch PHILIP + Thomas ap
      LLEWELLYN
143. Lowri verch GRUFFUDD FYCHAN + Robert (Sir; of Emral)
      PULESTON (1358? - 1399?)
144. Angharad PULESTON + Edward TREVOR ap DAFFYD (? -
      1448?)
145. Otewell Worsley, Sir + Rose (TREVOR) verch EDWART
146. Joyce Worsley + Richard Lee II
147. Richard Lee III + Eleanor Burgoine
148. Geoffrey Lee, MP + Agnes Conyers
149. Reginald Lee + Dorothy Thurland
150. Gervase Lee of Nottinghamshire
151. Thomas Lee, of Ashfield + Margaret Mary Oscroft
152. Elizabeth Lee + Thomas Hanks
153. Robert Hanks + Margaret NLN
154. Peter Hanks I + Mary Bressie
155. Elinor Hanks + Robert Nelson
156. Rachael Nelson + Timothy Ragan
157.   Timothy Reagan + Elizabeth Trigg
158. Richard Bazel Reagan + Cecelia Creppy
159. Richard Reagan + Phoebe Samples
160. Reuben Perry Reagan + Elizabeth Cagle
161. George Reagan + Emaline Garner
162. Marshall Reagan + Emma Rogers
163. Elzie Reagan + Delmar Raines
      ------- Gina Davis
           ------- Jackson Davis

------- Patricia Stuart
     ------- Bobby Caldwell
     ------- Jennifer Caldwell
------- Mike Raines
     ------- Leah Raines
     ------- Kendra Raines
     ------- Joshua Raines
     ------- Michael Raines
------- Frank Raines
     ------- Franklin Cody Raines
     ------- Kip Allen Raines
------- Richard Raines
     ------- Tyler Lee
     ------- Devin Lee
     ------- Emma Lundy

28

THE MINOAN-CRETAN-MYCENAEN LINEAGE

1.   Uranus (1st Ruler GOD of the Universe)
2.   Cronos (Kronos) the TITAN + Rhea (Rheia) the TITAN
3.   Zeus the OLYMPIANborn in Cretan cave) + Europa of
          PHOENICIA
4.   Minos `the Elder' (King) of CRETE + Itone of CRETE
5.   Lycastus of CRETE + Ide of CRETE
6.   Minos (II; King) of CRETE + Pasiphae of CORINTH
7.   Catreus (King) of CRETE
8.   Aerope of CRETE + Atreus (King) of MYCENAE in ARGOS
9.   Plisthenes (King) of MYCENAE + Cleolla of MYCENAE
10.   Agamemnon (King) of MYCENAE + Clytaemnestra of SPARTA
11.   Orestes (King) of ARGOS, MYCENAE & Sparta + Erigone of
          MYCENAE
12.   Sancus
13.   Sabinus
14.   Son of Sabinus
15.   (NN) | (poss. missing generations)
16.   Demophon + descendant of Parapilius
17.   Pomponius the SABINE + Jullia Prima of ROME
18.   Numa Pompilius (2nd King) of ROME + Egeria the NYMPH or

CAMENAE

19. Rehea Silvia + Fethuir (Fetjuir, Fetebir I)
20. Alanus
21. Armenon
22. Irmino (progenitor) of the HERMINONES
23. (NN) ... (NN) of the HERMINONES | (many missing generations)
24. Askanes (Chief) of the HERMINONES
25. Ernst
26. (NN) ... (NN) | (some missing generations)
27. Teutbal (King) of the TEUTONS (? - 102 BC) + (Miss) of SUEBIAN Confederacy
28. Ariovistus (King) of GERMANIA (? - 49 BC)
29. (NN) ... (NN) of SUEVICS | (many missing generations)
30. Hermerich (Prince) of SUEVICS
31. (NN) of SUEVES
32. Gueric (Probus/Governor) of REIMS (455? - 494+) + Gunzie la FRANQUE
33. Industria de REIMS (475? - ?) + Tonantius (II) `Vis Clarisimus' FERREOLUS
34. Deoteria de BEZIERS de REIMS
35. Theodon II (Duke) of BAVARIA + Theodon III of BAVARIA (? - 565?)
36. Theodon III of BAVARIA (? - 565?)
37. Theobald (Theodebert) of BAVARIA
38. Garibald I (AGILOFINGES ?) of BAVARIA + Waldrada (Princess) of the LOMBARDS
39. Gundwald (Duke) of ASTI (? - 613?) + Harinanda, daughter of Rotbert I (King) of LONGOBARDS
40. Aripert I (Viscount) of LOMBARDY (? - 661?)
41. Berthari (21st King) of the LANGOBARDS
42. Kunibert (25th King) of the LANGOBARDS (? - 702?)
43. Liutpert (26th King) of the LANGOBARDS (? - 712?)
44. Theoderada (of the LOMBARDS) + Ansbrand (28th King) of the LANGOBARDS (655? - 712?)
45. Sigiprand of the LOMBARDS
46. Ansbrand of LOMBARDS
47. Ansia of LOMBARDS (? - 774?) + Desiderio (last King) of LOMBARDS (? - 774+)
48. Gerberga of LOMBARDY (? - 774) + Carloman II (Archduke) of AUSTRASIA (747? - 771)

49. Kunigunde (Auberge) of AUSTRASIA + Adelgis (Count) of PARMA (of SPOLETO-PARMA) (? - 836?)
50. Cunegonde (Princess) de VERMANDOIS + Bernard (Bernhard; I) (King) of ITALY (Lombardy)
51. Pépin II, lord of Péronne + Rothaide de Bobbio
52. Héribert I, count of Vermandois + Bertha of Morvois
53. Héribert II, count of Vermandois + Liegarde Hildebrante of France
54. Count Robert de Vermandois, comte de Meaux et de Troyes + Adélaïde-Wera de Bourgogne, Chalon et Troyes
55. Arnulf de Ganelon + Gisia de Ganelon
56. Mathilde Hildeburg, de Condé-sur-Noireau + Guillaume I, 'Talvas' de Belleme, seigneur d'Alençon
57. Guillaume II "Talvas" Comte de Bellême, seigneur d'Alençon + Haberga "Hildeburge" de Beaumont
58. Mabile, dame de Bellême et d'Alençon + Roger Ii de Montgomery, 1st Earl of Shrewsbury
59. Aimeria Emma de Montgomery + Warine "The Sherriff" de Metz
60. Sir Guy Warin "The Bold" de Metz + Baroness Melette (Maud) Maud Peverell, Heiress of Whittington
61. Fulk FitzWarin, Lord of Whittington and Alderbury + Eva Whittington and FitzWarin (of Whittington & Alveston)
62. Warin FitzWarin FitzWarin
63. Warin de Burwardslegh, Lord of Estelegh
64. Alicia de Burwardslegh + Sir Walter Bromley
65. Geoffrey Galffridus Bromley + Philippa Bagot
66. Richard Bromley + Elizabeth Knockton
67. Ranulph Bromley + Agnes de Baddington
68. John de Bromley + Joan de Baddington
69. Cecily Margaret Bromhall + Robert de Worsley, Lord of Booths
70. William de Worsley + Ellen de Huton
71. Robert Worsley + Isabel de Trafford
72. Robert de Worsley + Katherine Clark
73. Otewell Worsley, Sir + Rose verch Edward
74. Joyce Worsley + Richard Lee II
75. Richard Lee III + Eleanor Burgoine
76. Geoffrey Lee, MP + Agnes Conyers
77. Reginald Lee + Dorothy Thurland
78. Gervase Lee of Nottinghamshire

79. Thomas Lee, of Ashfield + Margaret Mary Oscroft
80. Elizabeth Lee + Thomas Hanks
81. Robert Hanks + Margaret NLN
82. Peter Hanks I + Mary Bressie
83. Elinor Hanks + Rober Nelson
84. Rachael Nelson + Timothy Ragan
85. Timothy Reagan + Elizabeth Trigg
86. Richard Bazel Reagan + Cecelia Creppy
87. Richard Reagan + Phoebe Samples
88. Reuben Perry Reagan + Elizabeth Cagle
89. George Reagan + Emaline Garner
90. Marshall Reagan + Emma Rogers
91. Elzie Reagan + Delmar Raines
------- Gina Davis
    ------- Jackson Davis
------- Patricia Stuart
    ------- Bobby Caldwell
    ------- Jennifer Caldwell
------- Mike Raines
    ------- Leah Raines
    ------- Kendra Raines
    ------- Joshua Raines
    ------- Michael Raines
------- Frank Raines
    ------- Franklin Cody Raines
    ------- Kip Allen Raines
------- Richard Raines
    ------- Tyler Lee
    ------- Devin Lee
    ------- Emma Lundy

29

THE NORSE-DANISH LINEAGE

1. Sesostris + Nefret
2. Amenemhat I Sehetepibre (Founder) of 12th Dynasty + Nefrutotenen
3. Sesotris I Kheperkare (PHARAOH) of EGYPT (? - 1928? BC) + Nefrusheri (Princess) of EGYPT
4. Amenemhat (Ammenemes) II Nubkaure (PHARAOH) of EGYPT + Keminnub (Queen) of EGYPT
5. Sesotris II Khakheperre (PHARAOH) of EGYPT + Nofret of EGYPT
6. Sesotris III Khakaure of EGYPT + Sebekshedty-Neferu (Queen) of EGYPT
7. Amenemhat III Nemare (PHARAOH) of EGYPT + Sebeknefru (Queen) of EGYPT
8. Amenemhat (Ammenemes) IV (PHARAOH) of EGYPT
9. Wegaf (PHARAOH) of 13th Dynasty + daughter of Amenemhet IV
10. Ameny Intef (Inyotef) IV (PHARAOH) of EGYPT
11. Hor (PHARAOH) of EGYPT (? - 1760? BC)
12. Sobekhotep II (PHARAOH) of EGYPT (? - 1750? BC)

13. Khendjer (PHARAOH) of EGYPT (? - 1747? BC)
14. Sobekhotep III (PHARAOH) of EGYPT (? - 1745? BC)
15. Neferhotep I (PHARAOH) of EGYPT
16. Sobekhotep IV Khaneferre (PHARAOH) of 13th Dynasty +
     Tjan
17. Sebekhotep (Princess) of THEBES + Senebhanef, son of
     Renressonb
18. Mentuhotep (Queen) of EGYPT + Sekhemre-Sementawi
     Djehuti (PHARAOH) of EGYPT
19. Sekhemre-Se'ankhtawi Neferhotep (PHARAOH) of EGYPT
20. Sobekemsaf Sekhemre-Shedtawi (PHARAOH) of EGYPT +
     Nubkhas (Queen) of EGYPT
21. Inyotef VII (PHARAOH) at THEBES + Sobkemsaf
     (Sebekamzaf) of EGYPT (1635? BC - ?)
22. Sekenenre Tao I (PHARAOH) at THEBES + Tetisheri of
     THEBES
23. Sekenenre Tao II (King) of THEBES + Ahhotep (Ahotop) I
     (Queen) of EGYPT
24. Ahmose I (1st PHARAOH) of 18th Dynasty + Nefretiri
     (Queen) of EGYPT
25. Amenhotep I Djeserkare (PHARAOH) of EGYPT + Senisonb
     (Seneseneb) of EGYPT
26. Thutmose I (PHARAOH) of EGYPT (? - 1481? BC) + Amhose
     (Aahmes II) (Queen) of EGYPT
27. Hatshepsut (Queen & PHARAOH) of EGYPT (? - 1482 BC) +
     Thutmose (Tuthmosis) II (PHARAOH) of EGYPT
28. Meryetre Hatshepsut of EGYPT + Thutmose III `the Great' of
     EGYPT (Moses of the Bible)
29. Akheperure Amenhotep II THUTMOSID (PHARAOH) of
     EGYPT + Tio (Tiye Tiaa)
30. Menkheprure' Thutmose IV (PHARAOH) of EGYPT +
     Mutemwiya, daughter of Artatama (I; King) of MITANNI
31. Nebma'atre' Amenhotep III (PHARAOH) of EGYPT + Tiye-
     Nefertari (Tiy) of EGYPT (1382 BC - 1344 BC)
32. Akhenaton (Iknaton) (10th PHARAOH) of 18th Dynasty
     EGYPT + Nefertiti (Chief Queen) of EGYPT
33. Meritaten (Royal Daughter) of EGYPT + Judah (Judas Juda)
     ibn JACOB, son of Jacob ibn ISAAC (King of GOSHEN)
34. Zerah (Zehrah Zarah Zare) ibn JUDAH + Electra the PLEIADE
35. Dardanus (Dara) (King) of ACADIA + Batea of TEUCRI
36. Erichthonius (King) of ACADIA (? - 1386? BC) + Astyoche of

ACADIA
37. Trois of ACADIA + Callirhoe (TEUCRI)
38. Ilus (Ilyus) (King) of TROY (? - 1282? BC) + Eurydice
        (Eurydike) of TROY
39. Priam Podarces (High King) of TROY (? - 1183? BC) + Hecuba
        (Hecabe) of PHRYGIA
40. Troana Iluim of TROY + Memnon (Munon) of TROY (? - 1183?
        BC)
41. Thor (Tror) (King) of THRACE + Sibil (Sif)
42. Einridi LORIDESSON
43. Vingethor (Vingethior) EINRIDISSON
44. Moda (Mode) VINGENERSSON
45. Maji (Magi) MODASSON
46. Seskef (Sceaf Scaef)
47. Bedwig (Bedvig; of SCEAF)
48. Hwala (Hvala Hawala Guala)
49. Hathra (Athra)
50. Itermon (Itormann)
51. Heremod (King) in DENMARK
52. Sceldwa (King) in DENMARK
53. Beaw (Gram) (King) in DENMARK
54. Taetwa (Tatwa Tecti)
55. Jat (Geatwa Geata Geat Gaut Geot Gauti)
56. Godwulf (Gudolfr)
57. Flocwald (of ASGARD ?)
58. Finn (the TROJAN ?) (Asgard 130? - ?)
59. Frithuwulf (the TROJAN ?)
60. Frealaf (Friallaf Froethelaf) (160? - ?)
61. Frithuwald (Bor) (190? - ?) + Beltsea (Beltsa) of ASGARD
62. Odin (Wodan Woden) of ASGARD + Frigg (Frigida) of
        ASALAND
63. Skjoldr of the AESIR (1st King) of the DANES + Geitir
64. Fridleif SKJOLDSSON (King) of the DANES + Signe
        HULMULSDOTTER
65. Frodi FRIDLEIFSSON (King) of the DANES (281? - ?) + Inga
        (Queen in DENMARK)
66. Fridleif FRODASON (King in DENMARK)
67. Havar FRIDLEIFSSON (King in DENMARK)
68. Frodi HAVARSSON (King of DENMARK) (347? - ?)
69. Vermund `the Sage' FRODASON (King of DENMARK)
70. Olaf (Uffe) `the Mild' VERMUNDSSON (391? - ?) + Danpi

(Queen of DENMARK) (Denmark 395? - ?)
71. Frodi OLAFSSON (Denmark 433? - ?) + Inga YNGVESDOTTIR
72. Fridleif (III) FRODASON (456? - ?)
73. Frodi (Froda; VII; IV) FRIDLEIFSSON + Hilda of the VANDALS
74. Halfdan `the Tall' FRODASON (King) of DENMARK + Sigris (of DENMARK ?)
75. Hrothgar II the SKJOLDING (King) in DENMARK [aka Hroar (Hrodgar Roar) HALFDANSSON; built Heorot; his Kingdom was rescued from Grendel by Beowulf, q.v.]+ Ogne (Princess) of NORTHUMBRIA
76. Valdar (King of ROESKILDE) HROARSSON + Hildis (Princess) of the VANDALS
77. Harold VALDARSSON (Jutland 568? - ?) + Hildur HEIDREKSDATTIR
78. Halfdan HAROLDSSON (Jutland 590? - ?) + Moalde `Digri' (KINRIKSDOTTER ?), daughter of Cynric (Centric) (King) of WESSEX (525? - 581?)
79. Ivar `Wide Fathom' HALFDANSSON of SCANE (612? - 647?) + Gauthild (Gothilda) ALFSDOTTER
80. Audur IVARSDOTTIR (Queen) of HOLMGARD + Radbart (King) of GARDGARIGE
81. Randver RADBARDSSON of LETHRA (? - 770?) + Signy of ESSEX
82. Sigurd Ring (King of DENMARK) RANVERSSON + Brynhild BUDLASDATTER
83. Halfdan SIGURDSSON (750+ - ?) + Asberga (Aslaug) SIGURDSDOTTIR
84. Ragnar `Lothbrock' of Uppsala HALFDANSSON + Asberga (Aslaug) SIGURDSDOTTIR
85. Bjorn `Ironside' RAGNARSSON
86. Refil BJORNSSON (poss. co-King of SWEDES)
87. Erik (III; V) REFILSSON (BJORNSSON ?)
88. Edmund (Anund) (I) ERIKSSON (832? - 873?)
89. Erik (V; VI) EDMUNDSSON (King) of SWEDEN (& Goten)
90. Bjorn (III) `the Old' (`a Haugi') ERIKSSON + Ingeborg (? - 934+)
91. Erik VII `Segersall' the Victorious (King) of SWEDEN (930? - 995?) + Sigrid (Sigrith) STORRADA (Queen) of DENMARK
92. Olaf III (II; King; Skot-konig) of SWEDEN + Astrid (Princess) of the OBOTRITES
93. Ingegarda (Ingrid) OLAFSDOTTIR (1001? - 1050) + Jaroslav

(Yaroslav Laroslav) I WLADIMIROWWITSCH

94. Agatha (RURIKID) (? - 1066+) + Edward `the OutLaw' of ENGLAND (1016? - 1057?)

95. Margaret (Queen; Saint) of SCOTLAND + Malcolm III MacCrinan (Erinus) (CANMORE) (19th King) of SCOTS

96. Matilda (Edith Eagdith) `Atheling' STEWART of SCOTLAND + Henry I BEAUCLERC (King) of ENGLAND

97. Matilda (Maud Augusta) the EMPRESS + Geoffrey V `the Fair' (`Plantagenet')

98. Henry II (King) of ENGLAND + Eleanor (Duchess/Princess) of AQUITAINE

99. John `Lackland' (King) of ENGLAND + Isabella (d' ANGOULEME) TAILLEFER

100. Eleanor (Alianor) of ENGLAND (1215? - 1275) + Simon V de MONTFORT (1208 - 4/8/1265)

101. Eleanor de MONTFORT (1252 - 1282) + Llywellyn (II) ap GRUFFYDD (? - 1282)

102. Catherine verch LLYWELLYN + Philip ap IFOR

103. Eleanor (of ISCOED; GOCH) verch PHILIP + Thomas ap LLEWELLYN

104. Lowri verch GRUFFUDD FYCHAN + Robert (Sir; of Emral) PULESTON (1358? - 1399?)

105. Angharad PULESTON + Edward TREVOR ap DAFFYD (? - 1448?)

106. Otewell Worsley, Sir + Rose (TREVOR) verch EDWART

107. Joyce Worsley + Richard Lee II

108. Richard Lee III + Eleanor Burgoine

109. Geoffrey Lee, MP + Agnes Conyers

110. Reginald Lee + Dorothy Thurland

111. Gervase Lee of Nottinghamshire

112. Thomas Lee, of Ashfield + Margaret Mary Oscroft

113. Elizabeth Lee + Thomas Hanks

114. Robert Hanks + Margaret NLN

115. Peter Hanks I + Mary Bressie

116. Elinor Hanks + Rober Nelson

117. Rachael Nelson + Timothy Ragan

118. Timothy Reagan + Elizabeth Trigg

119. Richard Bazel Reagan + Cecelia Creppy

120. Richard Reagan + Phoebe Samples

121. Reuben Perry Reagan + Elizabeth Cagle

122. George Reagan + Emaline Garner

123.	Marshall Reagan + Emma Rogers
124.	Elzie Reagan + Delmar Raines
	------- Gina Davis
		------- Jackson Davis
	------- Patricia Stuart
		------- Bobby Caldwell
		------- Jennifer Caldwell
	------- Mike Raines
		------- Leah Raines
		------- Kendra Raines
		------- Joshua Raines
		------- Michael Raines
	------- Frank Raines
		------- Franklin Cody Raines
		------- Kip Allen Raines
	------- Richard Raines
		------- Tyler Lee
		------- Devin Lee
		------- Emma Lundy

30

THE NORSE-SAXON LINEAGE

1. Sesostris + Nefret
2. Amenemhat I Sehetepibre (Founder) of 12th Dynasty + Nefrutotenen
3. Sesotris I Kheperkare (PHARAOH) of EGYPT (? - 1928? BC) + Nefrusheri (Princess) of EGYPT
4. Amenemhat (Ammenemes) II Nubkaure (PHARAOH) of EGYPT + Keminnub (Queen) of EGYPT
5. Sesotris II Khakheperre (PHARAOH) of EGYPT + Nofret of EGYPT
6. Sesotris III Khakaure of EGYPT + Sebekshedty-Neferu (Queen) of EGYPT
7. Amenemhat III Nemare (PHARAOH) of EGYPT + Sebeknefru (Queen) of EGYPT
8. Amenemhat (Ammenemes) IV (PHARAOH) of EGYPT
9. Wegaf (PHARAOH) of 13th Dynasty + daughter of Amenemhet IV
10. Ameny Intef (Inyotef) IV (PHARAOH) of EGYPT
11. Hor (PHARAOH) of EGYPT (? - 1760? BC)
12. Sobekhotep II (PHARAOH) of EGYPT (? - 1750? BC)

13.   Khendjer (PHARAOH) of EGYPT (? - 1747? BC)
14.   Sobekhotep III (PHARAOH) of EGYPT (? - 1745? BC)
15.   Neferhotep I (PHARAOH) of EGYPT
16.   Sobekhotep IV Khaneferre (PHARAOH) of 13th Dynasty +
         Tjan
17.   Sebekhotep (Princess) of THEBES + Senebhanef, son of
         Renressonb
18.   Mentuhotep (Queen) of EGYPT + Sekhemre-Sementawi
         Djehuti (PHARAOH) of EGYPT
19.   Sekhemre-Se'ankhtawi Neferhotep (PHARAOH) of EGYPT
20.   Sobekemsaf Sekhemre-Shedtawi (PHARAOH) of EGYPT +
         Nubkhas (Queen) of EGYPT
21.   Inyotef VII (PHARAOH) at THEBES + Sobkemsaf
         (Sebekamzaf) of EGYPT (1635? BC - ?)
22.   Sekenenre Tao I (PHARAOH) at THEBES + Tetisheri of
         THEBES
23.   Sekenenre Tao II (King) of THEBES + Ahhotep (Ahotop) I
         (Queen) of EGYPT
24.   Ahmose I (1st PHARAOH) of 18th Dynasty + Nefretiri
         (Queen) of EGYPT
25.   Amenhotep I Djeserkare (PHARAOH) of EGYPT + Senisonb
         (Seneseneb) of EGYPT
26.   Thutmose I (PHARAOH) of EGYPT (? - 1481? BC) + Amhose
         (Aahmes II) (Queen) of EGYPT
27.   Hatshepsut (Queen & PHARAOH) of EGYPT (? - 1482 BC) +
         Thutmose (Tuthmosis) II (PHARAOH) of EGYPT
28.   Meryetre Hatshepsut of EGYPT + Thutmose III `the Great' of
         EGYPT (Moses of the Bible)
29.   Akheperure Amenhotep II THUTMOSID (PHARAOH) of
         EGYPT + Tio (Tiye Tiaa)
30.   Menkheprure' Thutmose IV (PHARAOH) of EGYPT +
         Mutemwiya, daughter of Artatama (I; King) of MITANNI
31.   Nebma'atre' Amenhotep III (PHARAOH) of EGYPT + Tiye-
         Nefertari (Tiy) of EGYPT (1382 BC - 1344 BC)
32.   Akhenaton (Iknaton) (10th PHARAOH) of 18th Dynasty
         EGYPT + Nefertiti (Chief Queen) of EGYPT
33.   Meritaten (Royal Daughter) of EGYPT + Judah (Judas Juda)
         ibn JACOB, son of Jacob ibn ISAAC (King of GOSHEN)
34.   Zerah (Zehrah Zarah Zare) ibn JUDAH + Electra the PLEIADE
35.   Dardanus (Dara) (King) of ACADIA + Batea of TEUCRI
36.   Erichthonius (King) of ACADIA (? - 1386? BC) + Astyoche of

ACADIA
37. Trois of ACADIA + Callirhoe (TEUCRI)
38. Ilus (Ilyus) (King) of TROY (? - 1282? BC) + Eurydice
       (Eurydike) of TROY
39. Priam Podarces (High King) of TROY (? - 1183? BC) + Hecuba
       (Hecabe) of PHRYGIA
40. Troana Iluim of TROY + Memnon (Munon) of TROY (? - 1183?
       BC)
41. Thor (Tror) (King) of THRACE + Sibil (Sif)
42. Einridi LORIDESSON
43. Vingethor (Vingethior) EINRIDISSON
44. Moda (Mode) VINGENERSSON
45. Maji (Magi) MODASSON
46. Seskef (Sceaf Scaef)
47. Bedwig (Bedvig; of SCEAF)
48. Hwala (Hvala Hawala Guala)
49. Hathra (Athra)
50. Itermon (Itormann)
51. Heremod (King) in DENMARK
52. Sceldwa (King) in DENMARK
53. Beaw (Gram) (King) in DENMARK
54. Taetwa (Tatwa Tecti)
55. Jat (Geatwa Geata Geat Gaut Geot Gauti)
56. Godwulf (Gudolfr)
57. Flocwald (of Asgard)
58. Finn (the TROJAN ?) (Asgard 130? - ?)
59. Frithuwulf (the TROJAN ?)
60. Frealaf (Friallaf Froethelaf) (160? - ?)
61. Frithuwald (Bor) (190? - ?) + Beltsea (Beltsa) of ASGARD
62. Odin (Woden, Wodan) of ASGARD + Frigg (Frigida) of
       ASALAND
63. Wecta (Waegdaeg) the JUTE (280? - 350+)
64. Witta (II) the JUTE
65. Wihtgils the JUTE
66. Hengest VVIHTGILSING (King) of KENT
67. Hartwake (Prince) of the SAXONS
68. Hathwigate (Prince) of the SAXONS
69. Hulderick (King) of the SAXONS (472? - 540?)
70. Bodicus (Prince) of the SAXONS (? - 568?)
71. poss. Berthold of the SAXONS (547? - 633?)
72. Sighard (Sigehard Sigismund) (King) of the SAXONS

73. Willehari + Dobiogera (Dobzogera) von WENDEN
74. Dietrich (King) of SAXONS
75. Hersuinde (Hereswintha) of SAXONY (705? - ?) + Nebi (Hnabi) (Count/Duke/King) of ALAMANNIA
76. Emma of SWABIA (736? - 789?) + Gerold I (Duke) of ALLEMANIA (? - 779+)
77. Hildegarde of VINZGAU (SWABIA) + CHARLEMAGNE, Carolus 'Magnus', Rex Francorum & Imperator Romanorum (King) of the FRANKS
78. "Pépin" Carloman, King of Italy + Mistress of Pepin
79. Bernard, King of Lombardy + Cunigundis (Cunegonde) (Princess) de VERMANDOIS
80. Pépin II, lord of Péronne + Rothaide de Bobbio
81. Pepin (I; Count) de SENLIS de VALOIS
82. (Miss) de SENLIS de VALOIS (845? - ?) + Berenger (Count) de RENNES (? - 931)
83. Poppa (Poppaeia) de VALOIS (872? - ?) + Rollo (Hrolf Rollon Rou Robert) `the Dane' RAGNVALDSSON
84. Guillaume (2nd Duke) of NORMANDY + Sprota de BRETAGNE (concubine)
85. Richard I `the Fearless' (Count) of NORMANDY + Gunnora (Gonnor) de CREPON
86. Richard II `the Good' of NORMANDY (963? - 1027) + Judith (Princess) of BRITTANY
87. Robert II (Duke) of NORMANDY + Herleve (Salburpyr) de FALAISE (1003? - 1050?)
88. WILLIAM the CONQUEROR (Duke) of NORMANDY + Matilda (Maud) FLEMING (1032 - 1083 Caan)
89. Henry I BEAUCLERC (King) of ENGLAND + Matilda (Edith Eagdith) `Atheling' STEWART of SCOTLAND
90. Matilda (Maud Augusta) the EMPRESS + Geoffrey V `the Fair' (`Plantagenet')
91. Henry II (King) of ENGLAND + Eleanor (Duchess/Princess) of AQUITAINE
92. John `Lackland' (King) of ENGLAND + Isabella (d' ANGOULEME) TAILLEFER
93. Eleanor (Alianor) of ENGLAND (1215? - 1275) + Simon V de MONTFORT (1208 - 4/8/1265)
94. Eleanor de MONTFORT (1252 - 1282) + Llywellyn (II) ap GRUFFYDD (? - 1282)
95. Catherine verch LLYWELLYN + Philip ap IFOR

96.   Eleanor (of ISCOED; GOCH) verch PHILIP + Thomas ap
        LLEWELLYN
97.   Lowri verch GRUFFUDD FYCHAN + Robert (Sir; of Emral)
        PULESTON (1358? - 1399?)
98.   Angharad PULESTON + Edward TREVOR ap DAFFYD (? -
        1448?)
99.   Otewell Worsley, Sir + Rose (TREVOR) verch EDWART
100.   Joyce Worsley + Richard Lee II
101.   Richard Lee III + Eleanor Burgoine
102.   Geoffrey Lee, MP + Agnes Conyers
103.   Reginald Lee + Dorothy Thurland
104.   Gervase Lee of Nottinghamshire
105.   Thomas Lee, of Ashfield + Margaret Mary Oscroft
106.   Elizabeth Lee + Thomas Hanks
107.   Robert Hanks + Margaret NLN
108.   Peter Hanks I + Mary Bressie
109.   Elinor Hanks + Robert Nelson
110.   Rachael Nelson + Timothy Ragan
111.   Timothy Reagan + Elizabeth Trigg
112.   Richard Bazel Reagan + Cecelia Creppy
113.   Richard Reagan + Phoebe Samples
114.   Reuben Perry Reagan + Elizabeth Cagle
115.   George Reagan + Emaline Garner
116.   Marshall Reagan + Emma Rogers
117.   Elzie Reagan + Delmar Raines
       ------- Gina Davis
          ------- Jackson Davis
       ------- Patricia Stuart
          ------- Bobby Caldwell
          ------- Jennifer Caldwell
       ------- Mike Raines
          ------- Leah Raines
          ------- Kendra Raines
          ------- Joshua Raines
          ------- Michael Raines
       ------- Frank Raines
          ------- Franklin Cody Raines
          ------- Kip Allen Raines
       ------- Richard Raines
          ------- Tyler Lee
          ------- Devin Lee

A BARDIC TALE OF THE ANCIENT LINEAGES OF THE REAGAN FAMILY

------- Emma Lundy

223

31

THE OSTRAGOTH LINEAGE

1. Sesostris + Nefret
2. Amenemhat I Sehetepibre (Founder) of 12th Dynasty + Nefrutotenen
3. Sesotris I Kheperkare (PHARAOH) of EGYPT (? - 1928? BC) + Nefrusheri (Princess) of EGYPT
4. Amenemhat (Ammenemes) II Nubkaure (PHARAOH) of EGYPT + Keminnub (Queen) of EGYPT
5. Sesotris II Khakheperre (PHARAOH) of EGYPT + Nofret of EGYPT
6. Sesotris III Khakaure of EGYPT + Sebekshedty-Neferu (Queen) of EGYPT
7. Amenemhat III Nemare (PHARAOH) of EGYPT + Sebeknefru (Queen) of EGYPT
8. Amenemhat (Ammenemes) IV (PHARAOH) of EGYPT
9. Wegaf (PHARAOH) of 13th Dynasty + daughter of Amenemhet IV
10. Ameny Intef (Inyotef) IV (PHARAOH) of EGYPT
11. Hor (PHARAOH) of EGYPT (? - 1760? BC)
12. Sobekhotep II (PHARAOH) of EGYPT (? - 1750? BC)
13. Khendjer (PHARAOH) of EGYPT (? - 1747? BC)

14. Sobekhotep III (PHARAOH) of EGYPT (? - 1745? BC)
15. Neferhotep I (PHARAOH) of EGYPT
16. Sobekhotep IV Khaneferre (PHARAOH) of 13th Dynasty + Tjan
17. Sebekhotep (Princess) of THEBES + Senebhanef, son of Renressonb
18. Mentuhotep (Queen) of EGYPT + Sekhemre-Sementawi Djehuti (PHARAOH) of EGYPT
19. Sekhemre-Se'ankhtawi Neferhotep (PHARAOH) of EGYPT
20. Sobekemsaf Sekhemre-Shedtawi (PHARAOH) of EGYPT + Nubkhas (Queen) of EGYPT
21. Inyotef VII (PHARAOH) at THEBES + Sobkemsaf (Sebekamzaf) of EGYPT (1635? BC - ?)
22. Sekenenre Tao I (PHARAOH) at THEBES + Tetisheri of THEBES
23. Sekenenre Tao II (King) of THEBES + Ahhotep (Ahotop) I (Queen) of EGYPT
24. Ahmose I (1st PHARAOH) of 18th Dynasty + Nefretiri (Queen) of EGYPT
25. Amenhotep I Djeserkare (PHARAOH) of EGYPT + Senisonb (Seneseneb) of EGYPT
26. Thutmose I (PHARAOH) of EGYPT (? - 1481? BC) + Amhose (Aahmes II) (Queen) of EGYPT
27. Hatshepsut (Queen & PHARAOH) of EGYPT (? - 1482 BC) + Thutmose (Tuthmosis) II (PHARAOH) of EGYPT
28. Meryetre Hatshepsut of EGYPT + Thutmose III `the Great' of EGYPT (Moses of the Bible)
29. Akheperure Amenhotep II THUTMOSID (PHARAOH) of EGYPT + Tio (Tiye Tiaa)
30. Menkheprure' Thutmose IV (PHARAOH) of EGYPT + Mutemwiya, daughter of Artatama (I; King) of MITANNI
31. Nebma'atre' Amenhotep III (PHARAOH) of EGYPT + Tiye-Nefertari (Tiy) of EGYPT (1382 BC - 1344 BC)
32. Akhenaton (Iknaton) (10th PHARAOH) of 18th Dynasty EGYPT + Nefertiti (Chief Queen) of EGYPT
33. Meritaten (Royal Daughter) of EGYPT + Judah (Judas Juda) ibn JACOB, son of Jacob ibn ISAAC (King of GOSHEN)
34. Zerah (Zehrah Zarah Zare) ibn JUDAH + Electra the PLEIADE
35. Dardanus (Dara) (King) of ACADIA + Batea of TEUCRI
36. Erichthonius (King) of ACADIA (? - 1386? BC) + Astyoche of ACADIA

37. Trois of ACADIA + Callirhoe (TEUCRI)
38. Ilus (Ilyus) (King) of TROY (? - 1282? BC) + Eurydice
       (Eurydike) of TROY
39. Priam Podarces (High King) of TROY (? - 1183? BC) + Hecuba
       (Hecabe) of PHRYGIA
40. Troana Iluim of TROY + Memnon (Munon) of TROY (? - 1183?
       BC)
41. Thor (Tror) (King) of THRACE + Sibil (Sif)
42. Einridi LORIDESSON
43. Vingethor (Vingethior) EINRIDISSON
44. Vingener VINGETHORSSON
45. Moda (Mode) VINGENERSSON
46. Maji (Magi) MODASSON
47. Seskef (Sceaf Scaef)
48. Bedwig (Bedvig; of SCEAF)
49. Hwala (Hvala Hawala Guala)
50. Hathra (Athra)
51. Itermon (Itormann)
52. Heremod (King) in DENMARK
53. Sceldwa (King) in DENMARK
54. Beaw (Gram) (King) in DENMARK
55. Taetwa (Tatwa Tecti)
56. Jat (Geatwa Geata Geat Gaut Geot Gauti)
57. Helmul of the GOTHS (? - 105?)
58. Augis (Argis Aragis) of the GOTHS
59. Amal (Amala) of the GOTHS
60. Hisarna (Isama) of GOTHS
61. Ostrogotha (King) of the GOTHS
62. Hunuil of GOTHS (210? - ?)
63. Athal of GOTHS
64. Achiulf of GOTHS
65. Wultwulf (Vulthulf) (Prince) of GOTHS (300? - 378?)
66. Walaravans (Prince) of (East) GOTHS (330? - 409?)
67. Winithar (King) of the OSTROGOTHS (? - 400+)
68. Wandalar (King) of the OSTROGOTHS
69. Theudemir (King) of the OSTAGOTHS (413? - 474+) +
       Erelicia, a concubine
70. Theodoric (I; King) of the OSTROGOTHS + Audofledis
       (Audefleda) des FRANCS SALIENS
71. (Miss) of the EAST FRANKS + Elemund (King) of the
       GEPIDAE (? - 491?)

72. Ostragotha (Austrigusa) of the GEPIDAE + Wacho (9th King)
of the LOMBARDS (490? - 539?)
73. Waldrada (Princess) of the LOMBARDS (528? - 571?) +
Garibald I (AGILOFINGES ?) of BAVARIA
74. Theudelinde of BAVARIA + Agilolf of the LOMBARDS
75. (Miss) of TURIN + Rotbert I (King) of LONGOBARDS
76. Gundwald (Duke) of ASTI (? - 613?) + Harinanda, daughter of
Rotbert I (King) of LONGOBARDS + Gundwald (Duke) of
ASTI (? - 613?)
77. Aripert I (Viscount) of LOMBARDY (? - 661?)
78. Berthari (21st King) of the LANGOBARDS
79. Kunibert (25th King) of the LANGOBARDS (? - 702?)
80. Liutpert (26th King) of the LANGOBARDS (? - 712?)
81. Theoderada (of the LOMBARDS) + Ansbrand (28th King) of
the LANGOBARDS (655? - 712?)
82. Sigiprand of the LOMBARDS
83. Ansbrand of LOMBARDS
84. Ansia of LOMBARDS (? - 774?) + Desiderio (last King) of
LOMBARDS (? - 774+)
85. Gerberga of LOMBARDY (? - 774) + Carloman II (Archduke)
of AUSTRASIA (747? - 771)
86. Kunigunde (Auberge) of AUSTRASIA + Adelgis (Count) of
PARMA (of SPOLETO-PARMA) (? - 836?)
87. Cunegonde (Princess) de VERMANDOIS + Bernard
(Bernhard; I) (King) of ITALY (Lombardy)
88. Pépin II, lord of Péronne + Rothaide de Bobbio
89. Pepin (I; Count) de SENLIS de VALOIS
90. (Miss) de SENLIS de VALOIS (845? - ?) + Berenger (Count) de
RENNES (? - 931)
91. Poppa (Poppaeia) de VALOIS (872? - ?) + Rollo (Hrolf Rollon
Rou Robert) `the Dane' RAGNVALDSSON
92. Guillaume (2nd Duke) of NORMANDY + Sprota de
BRETAGNE (concubine)
93. Richard I `the Fearless' (Count) of NORMANDY + Gunnora
(Gonnor) de CREPON
94. Richard II `the Good' of NORMANDY (963? - 1027) + Judith
(Princess) of BRITTANY
95. Robert II (Duke) of NORMANDY + Herleve (Salburpyr) de
FALAISE (1003? - 1050?)
96. William the CONQUEROR (Duke) of NORMANDY + Matilda
(Maud) FLEMING (1032 - 1083 Caan)

97. Matilda (Edith Eagdith) `Atheling' STEWART of SCOTLAND + Henry I BEAUCLERC (King) of ENGLAND
98. Matilda (Maud Augusta) the EMPRESS + Geoffrey V `the Fair' (`Plantagenet')
99. Henry II (King) of ENGLAND + Eleanor (Duchess/Princess) of AQUITAINE
100. John `Lackland' (King) of ENGLAND + Isabella (d' ANGOULEME) TAILLEFER
101. Eleanor (Alianor) of ENGLAND (1215? - 1275) + Simon V de MONTFORT (1208 - 4/8/1265)
102. Eleanor de MONTFORT (1252 - 1282) + Llywellyn (II) ap GRUFFYDD (? - 1282)
103. Catherine verch LLYWELLYN + Philip ap IFOR
104. Eleanor (of ISCOED; GOCH) verch PHILIP + Thomas ap LLEWELLYN
105. Lowri verch GRUFFUDD FYCHAN + Robert (Sir; of Emral) PULESTON (1358? - 1399?)
106. Angharad PULESTON + Edward TREVOR ap DAFFYD (? - 1448?)
107. Otewell Worsley, Sir + Rose (TREVOR) verch EDWART
108. Joyce Worsley + Richard Lee II
109. Richard Lee III + Eleanor Burgoine
110. Geoffrey Lee, MP + Agnes Conyers
111. Reginald Lee + Dorothy Thurland
112. Gervase Lee of Nottinghamshire
113. Thomas Lee, of Ashfield + Margaret Mary Oscroft
114. Elizabeth Lee + Thomas Hanks
115. Robert Hanks + Margaret NLN
116. Peter Hanks I + Mary Bressie
117. Elinor Hanks + Rober Nelson
118. Rachael Nelson + Timothy Ragan
119. Timothy Reagan + Elizabeth Trigg
120. Richard Bazel Reagan + Cecelia Creppy
121. Richard Reagan + Phoebe Samples
122. Reuben Perry Reagan + Elizabeth Cagle
123. George Reagan + Emaline Garner
124. Marshall Reagan + Emma Rogers
125. Elzie Reagan + Delmar Raines
------- Gina Davis
     ------- Jackson Davis
------- Patricia Stuart

------- Bobby Caldwell
------- Jennifer Caldwell
------- Mike Raines
------- Leah Raines
------- Kendra Raines
------- Joshua Raines
------- Michael Raines
------- Frank Raines
------- Franklin Cody Raines
------- Kip Allen Raines
------- Richard Raines
------- Tyler Lee
------- Devin Lee
------- Emma Lundy

32

THE PHOENICIAN (TYRIAN-CARTHAGIAN) LINEAGE

1. Nimrod (King) of ASSYRIA & BABYLON + Semiramis (Queen) of BABYLON, daughter of Mizraim (1st PHARAOH of ZOANITE Dynasty)
2. Baal of TYRE
3. (NN) ... (NN) (many missing generations)
4. Melqart (1st King) of TYRE
5. (NN) ... (NN) (some missing generations)
6. Hiram I (King) of BYBLOS
7. Abibaal (King) of TYRE (& SIDON)
8. Hiram II (King) of TYRE
9. Baal-Eser (I; King) of TYRE (? - 927? BC)
10. Abdastratus (King) of TYRE
11. Methusastartus (King) of TYRE (? - 906+ BC)
12. Astarymus (King) of TYRE
13. Ahiram Astartus (King) of TYRE
14. Ithobaal I (King) of TYRE
15. Baal-Eser II (King) of TYRE
16. Mattan (I; King) of TYRE (? - 821? BC)
17. Elissa Dido (Founder & 1st Queen) of CARTHAGE + Acestes (King) of SICILY & Lower ITALY

18. Malchus I (King) of CARTHAGE (? - 750+ BC)
19. Kerthodonus (King) of CARTHAGE
20. (NN) ... (NN) of CARTHAGE (about five missing generations)
21. Malchus II (King) of CARTHAGE (? - 550+ BC)
22. Mago I (King) of CARTHAGE (? - 530+ BC)
23. Hannibal I (King) of CARTHAGE
24. Hamilcar I (King) of CARTHAGE
25. Himilco (1st King) of CORNWALL
26. (NN) ... (NN) of CORNWALL (many missing generations)
27. Cerwydr the CAMBRIAN
28. Capoir of the DRUIDS
29. Digueillus (King) of BRITONS
30. Heli I (King) of BRITONS
31. Cas `the Exile'
32. Hu the MIGHTY
33. Lugh II `the Shining One' (? - 103 BC)
34. Heli II (? - 55 BC)
35. Caswallon ap BELI (King) of the CATUVELLAUNI (? - 47 BC)
36. Andocoveros (Duke in BRITAIN)
37. Tenacius (King) of the CATUVELLAUNI (BRITONS)
38. Cymbeline (King) of BRITONS (25 BC - 17?)
39. Aviragus (King) of the BRITONS (15? - 74? Avalon?)
40. Meric (Marius Meurig Cyllin) of BRITONS (65? - 125?) + Julia
       (Victoria) verch PRASUTAGUS of the ICENI
41. Coel I (Cole Coilus) (Old King Cole) King of BRITONS +
       Ystradwl (Stradwawl) of SILURIA
42. Lleurig (Lucius) MAWR (King) of EWYAS + Gladys (Gwladys)
       verch EURGEN of SILURIA
43. Gladys `the Younger' of BRITAIN (190? - ?) + Cadvan of
       CAMBRIA
44. Strada `the Fair' of COMBRIA + Coilus II (Coel Cole) of
       GLOUCESTER (by 232 - 305?)
45. Helena (Augusta) (Saint) of the CROSS + Flavius Valerius
       Constantius I of Rome
46. Constantine `the Great' of ROME + Flavia Maxima Fausta (? -
       326?)
47. Flavia Constantia Augusta (320? - 354?) + Flavius Claudius
       CONSTANTIUS Gallus
48. Anastasia
49. Gallus
50. Anastasia (Arriana) CONSTANTINA + Pompeius of

DYRRHACHIUM
51. Flavius PAULUS (Consul) (? - 496+) + Magna Sabiniani
52. Flavius PROBUS (Consul) (? - 502+) + daughter of Flavius
       Sabinianus
53. Flavius Anastasius PAULUS PROBUS Sabinianus POMPEIUS +
       Theodora(?), daughter of Theodora
54. Paulus of ARABISSO + Joanna of ARABISSA
55. Maurice (EMPEROR) of the EAST (539? - 27/11/602)
56. Julius of BYZANTIUM
57. Georgia
58. Juliana FLAVIA + Athanagild (II; King) of the VISIGOTHS
59. Ardabast (Count/King) of the VISIGOTHS + Goda of the
       BURGUNDIANS
60. Ervik (King) of the VISIGOTHS (? - 687) + Liubigotona
       (Liuvigotona) of the VISIGOTHS
61. Aupais (of SPAIN)
62. Charles Martel "The Hammer", Mayor of the Palace +
       Rotrude, Duchess of Austrasia
63. Pépin III, King of the Franks + Bertha Broadfoot of Laon
64. CHARLEMAGNE, Carolus 'Magnus', Rex Francorum &
       Imperator Romanorum + Hildegard of Vinzgouw
65. "Pépin" Carloman, King of Italy + Mistress of Pepin
66. Bernard, King of Lombardy + Cunigundis (Cunegonde)
       (Princess) de VERMANDOIS
67. Pépin II, lord of Péronne + Rothaide de Bobbio
68. Pepin (I; Count) de SENLIS de VALOIS
69. (Miss) de SENLIS de VALOIS (845? - ?) + Berenger (Count) de
       RENNES (? - 931)
70. Poppa (Poppaeia) de VALOIS (872? - ?) + Rollo (Hrolf Rollon
       Rou Robert) `the Dane' RAGNVALDSSON
71. Guillaume (2nd Duke) of NORMANDY + Sprota de
       BRETAGNE (concubine)
72. Richard I `the Fearless' (Count) of NORMANDY + Gunnora
       (Gonnor) de CREPON
73. Richard II `the Good' of NORMANDY (963? - 1027) + Judith
       (Princess) of BRITTANY
74. Robert II (Duke) of NORMANDY + Herleve (Salburpyr) de
       FALAISE (1003? - 1050?)
75. WILLIAM the CONQUEROR (Duke) of NORMANDY + Matilda
       (Maud) FLEMING (1032 - 1083 Caan)
76. Henry I BEAUCLERC (King) of ENGLAND + Matilda (Edith

Eagdith) `Atheling' STEWART of SCOTLAND
77. Matilda (Maud Augusta) the EMPRESS + Geoffrey V `the Fair' (`Plantagenet')
78. Henry II (King) of ENGLAND + Eleanor (Duchess/Princess) of AQUITAINE
79. John `Lackland' (King) of ENGLAND + Isabella (d' ANGOULEME) TAILLEFER
80. Eleanor (Alianor) of ENGLAND (1215? - 1275) + Simon V de MONTFORT (1208 - 4/8/1265)
81. Eleanor de MONTFORT (1252 - 1282) + Llywellyn (II) ap GRUFFYDD (? - 1282)
82. Catherine verch LLYWELLYN + Philip ap IFOR
83. Eleanor (of ISCOED; GOCH) verch PHILIP + Thomas ap LLEWELLYN
84. Lowri verch GRUFFUDD FYCHAN + Robert (Sir; of Emral) PULESTON (1358? - 1399?)
85. Angharad PULESTON + Edward TREVOR ap DAFFYD (? - 1448?)
86. Otewell Worsley, Sir + Rose (TREVOR) verch EDWART
87. Joyce Worsley + Richard Lee II
88. Richard Lee III + Eleanor Burgoine
89. Geoffrey Lee, MP + Agnes Conyers
90. Reginald Lee + Dorothy Thurland
91. Gervase Lee of Nottinghamshire
92. Thomas Lee, of Ashfield + Margaret Mary Oscroft
93. Elizabeth Lee + Thomas Hanks
94. Robert Hanks + Margaret NLN
95. Peter Hanks I + Mary Bressie
96. Elinor Hanks + Robert Nelson
97. Rachael Nelson + Timothy Ragan
98. Timothy Reagan + Elizabeth Trigg
99. Richard Bazel Reagan + Cecelia Creppy
100. Richard Reagan + Phoebe Samples
101. Reuben Perry Reagan + Elizabeth Cagle
102. George Reagan + Emaline Garner
103. Marshall Reagan + Emma Rogers
104. Elzie Reagan + Delmar Raines
------- Gina Davis
------- Jackson Davis
------- Patricia Stuart
------- Bobby Caldwell

------- Jennifer Caldwell
------- Mike Raines
------- Leah Raines
------- Kendra Raines
------- Joshua Raines
------- Michael Raines
------- Frank Raines
------- Franklin Cody Raines
------- Kip Allen Raines
------- Richard Raines
------- Tyler Lee
------- Devin Lee
------- Emma Lundy

33

THE PHRYGIAN (LYDIAN) LINEAGE

1. Uranus (1st Ruler GOD of the Universe)
2. Cronos (Kronos) the TITAN + Rhea (Rheia) the TITAN
3. Zeus the OLYMPIANborn in Cretan cave) + Hera the
    OLYMPIAN (Queen of the GODS)
4. Ares (the OLYMPIAN; GOD of War) + Theogone
5. Tmolus (King) of LYDIA
6. Tantalus (King) of PHRYGIA (LYDIA) + Dione the HYADE
7. Pelops (King) of PISA, LYDIA and/or MYCENE + Hippodamia
    of PISA, daughter of Oenomaus (King) of PISA (and
    Evarete of ARGOS, daughter of Acrisius (King) of ARGOS)
8. Dias of MYCENAE + Archippe
9. Cleolla of MYCENAE + Plisthenes (King) of MYCENAE
10. Agamemnon (King) of MYCENAE + Clytaemnestra of SPARTA
11. Orestes (King) of ARGOS, MYCENAE & Sparta + Erigone of
    MYCENAE
12. Sancus
13. Sabinus
14. Son of Sabinus
15. (NN) | (poss. missing generations)
16. Demophon + descendant of Parapilius

17.	Pomponius the SABINE + Jullia Prima of ROME
18.	Numa Pompilius (2nd King) of ROME + Egeria the NYMPH or
	CAMENAE
19.	Rehea Silvia + Fethuir (Fetjuir, Fetebir I)
20.	Alanus
21.	Armenon
22.	Irmino (progenitor) of the HERMINONES
23.	(NN) ... (NN) of the HERMINONES | (many missing
	generations)
24.	Askanes (Chief) of the HERMINONES
25.	Ernst
26.	(NN) ... (NN) | (some missing generations)
27.	Teutbal (King) of the TEUTONS (? - 102 BC) + (Miss) of
	SUEBIAN Confederacy
28.	Ariovistus (King) of GERMANIA (? - 49 BC)
29.	(NN) ... (NN) of SUEVICS | (many missing generations)
30.	Hermerich (Prince) of SUEVICS
31.	(NN) of SUEVES
32.	Gueric (Probus/Governor) of REIMS (455? - 494+) + Gunzie
	la FRANQUE
33.	Industria de REIMS (475? - ?) + Tonantius (II) `Vis
	Clarisimus' FERREOLUS
34.	Deoteria de BEZIERS de REIMS
35.	Theodon II (Duke) of BAVARIA + Theodon III of BAVARIA (? -
	565?)
36.	Theodon III of BAVARIA (? - 565?)
37.	Theobald (Theodebert) of BAVARIA
38.	Garibald I (AGILOFINGES ?) of BAVARIA + Waldrada
	(Princess) of the LOMBARDS
39.	Gundwald (Duke) of ASTI (? - 613?) + Harinanda, daughter of
	Rotbert I (King) of LONGOBARDS
40.	Aripert I (Viscount) of LOMBARDY (? - 661?)
41.	Godepert (King) of the LOMBARDS (? - 662+) + Ragnatrude
	of EAST ANGLIA
42.	Reginpert (Duke) of TURIN
43.	Aripert (Aribert Ansprand) II (27th King) of the LOMBARDS
44.	Sigiprand of the LOMBARDS
45.	Ansbrand of LOMBARDS
46.	Ansia of LOMBARDS (? - 774?) + Desiderio (last King) of
	LOMBARDS (? - 774+)
47.	Gerberga of LOMBARDY (? - 774) + Carloman II (Archduke)

of AUSTRASIA (747? - 771)

48. Kunigunde (Auberge) of AUSTRASIA + Adelgis (Count) of PARMA (of SPOLETO-PARMA) (? - 836?)
49. Cunegonde (Princess) de VERMANDOIS + Bernard (Bernhard; I) (King) of ITALY (Lombardy)
50. Pépin II, lord of Péronne + Rothaide de Bobbio
51. Héribert I, count of Vermandois + Bertha of Morvois
52. Héribert II, count of Vermandois + Liegarde Hildebrante of France
53. Count Robert de Vermandois, comte de Meaux et de Troyes + Adélaïde-Wera de Bourgogne, Chalon et Troyes
54. Arnulf de Ganelon + Gisia de Ganelon
55. Mathilde Hildeburg, de Condé-sur-Noireau + Guillaume I, 'Talvas' de Belleme, seigneur d'Alençon
56. Guillaume II "Talvas" Comte de Bellême, seigneur d'Alençon + Haberga "Hildeburge" de Beaumont
57. Mabile, dame de Bellême et d'Alençon + Roger Ii de Montgomery, 1st Earl of Shrewsbury
58. Aimeria Emma de Montgomery + Warine "The Sherriff" de Metz
59. Sir Guy Warin "The Bold" de Metz + Baroness Melette (Maud) Maud Peverell, Heiress of Whittington
60. Fulk FitzWarin, Lord of Whittington and Alderbury + Eva Whittington and FitzWarin (of Whittington & Alveston)
61. Warin FitzWarin FitzWarin
62. Warin de Burwardslegh, Lord of Estelegh
63. Alicia de Burwardslegh + Sir Walter Bromley
64. Geoffrey Galffridus Bromley + Philippa Bagot
65. Richard Bromley + Elizabeth Knockton
66. Ranulph Bromley + Agnes de Baddington
67. John de Bromley + Joan de Baddington
68. Cecily Margaret Bromhall + Robert de Worsley, Lord of Booths
69. William de Worsley + Ellen de Huton
70. Robert Worsley + Isabel de Trafford
71. Robert de Worsley + Katherine Clark
72. Otewell Worsley, Sir + Rose verch Edward
73. Joyce Worsley + Richard Lee II
74. Richard Lee III + Eleanor Burgoine
75. Geoffrey Lee, MP + Agnes Conyers
76. Reginald Lee + Dorothy Thurland

77.   Gervase Lee of Nottinghamshire
78.   Thomas Lee, of Ashfield + Margaret Mary Oscroft
79.   Elizabeth Lee + Thomas Hanks
80.   Robert Hanks + Margaret NLN
81.   Peter Hanks I + Mary Bressie
82.   Elinor Hanks + Rober Nelson
83.   Rachael Nelson + Timothy Ragan
84.   Timothy Reagan + Elizabeth Trigg
85.   Richard Bazel Reagan + Cecelia Creppy
86.   Richard Reagan + Phoebe Samples
87.   Reuben Perry Reagan + Elizabeth Cagle
88.   George Reagan + Emaline Garner
89.   Marshall Reagan + Emma Rogers
90.   Elzie Reagan + Delmar Raines
        ------- Gina Davis
               ------- Jackson Davis
        ------- Patricia Stuart
               ------- Bobby Caldwell
               ------- Jennifer Caldwell
        ------- Mike Raines
               ------- Leah Raines
               ------- Kendra Raines
               ------- Joshua Raines
               ------- Michael Raines
        ------- Frank Raines
               ------- Franklin Cody Raines
               ------- Kip Allen Raines
        ------- Richard Raines
               ------- Tyler Lee
               ------- Devin Lee
               ------- Emma Lundy

34

THE POLISH-SLAVIC LINEAGE

1. (NN), progenitor of SLAVS
2. Lech I, Father of POLES (POLAND)
3. Krakus (Duke) of POLAND
4. Lech II (Duke) of POLAND
5. daughter of Lech II
6. Leszko I (Duke) of POLAND
7. Leszko II (Duke) of POLAND
8. Leszko III (Duke) of POLAND
9. Popiel I (Duke) of POLAND
10. Popiel II (Duke) of POLAND
11. daughter of Popiel II
12. Piast (Chroscieszko) (Duke) of POLAND (? - 892), son of
      Choscisko Pazt (Duke) of POLAND (? - 830+), son of
      Chosisconisu of POLAND
13. Ziemowit (Siemowit) av PIAST (Duke/King) of POLAND
14. Leszek (Lestek Lestko) PIAST (Duke/King) of POLAND
15. Ziemonislaw PIAST (Duke/King) of POLAND + Gorka z
      POLSKA
16. Mieszko (Burislaf ?) I PIAST (Duke/Prince) of POLAND +
      Dubrawka (Princess) of BOHEMIA

17.   Boleslaw I `the Brave' (King) of POLAND + Emnilde (Princess) of WESTERN SLAVS

18.   Mieszko II Lambert PIAST (King) of POLAND + Richeza (Richenza Rixa) of PFALZ-LORRAINE

19.   Agatha (RURIKID) (Agatha of POLAND) (? - 1066+) + Edward `the OutLaw' of ENGLAND (1016? - 1057?)

20.   Margaret (Queen; Saint) of SCOTLAND + Malcolm III MacCRINAN (CANMORE)(19th King) of SCOTS

21.   Matilda (Edith Eagdith) `Atheling' STEWART of SCOTLAND + Henry I BEAUCLERC (King) of ENGLAND

22.   Matilda (Maud Augusta) the EMPRESS + Geoffrey V `the Fair' (`Plantagenet')

23.   Henry II (King) of ENGLAND + Eleanor (Duchess/Princess) of AQUITAINE

24.   John `Lackland' (King) of ENGLAND + Isabella (d' ANGOULEME) TAILLEFER

25.   Eleanor (Alianor) of ENGLAND (1215? - 1275) + Simon V de MONTFORT (1208 - 4/8/1265)

26.   Eleanor de MONTFORT (1252 - 1282) + Llywellyn (II) ap GRUFFYDD (? - 1282)

27.   Catherine verch LLYWELLYN + Philip ap IFOR

28.   Eleanor (of ISCOED; GOCH) verch PHILIP + Thomas ap LLEWELLYN

29.   Lowri verch GRUFFUDD FYCHAN + Robert (Sir; of Emral) PULESTON (1358? - 1399?)

30.   Angharad PULESTON + Edward TREVOR ap DAFFYD (? - 1448?)

31.   Otewell Worsley, Sir + Rose (TREVOR) verch EDWART

32.   Joyce Worsley + Richard Lee II

33.   Richard Lee III + Eleanor Burgoine

34.   Geoffrey Lee, MP + Agnes Conyers

35.   Reginald Lee + Dorothy Thurland

36.   Gervase Lee of Nottinghamshire

37.   Thomas Lee, of Ashfield + Margaret Mary Oscroft

38.   Elizabeth Lee + Thomas Hanks

39.   Robert Hanks + Margaret NLN

40.   Peter Hanks I + Mary Bressie

41.   Elinor Hanks + Robert Nelson

42.   Rachael Nelson + Timothy Ragan

43.   Timothy Reagan + Elizabeth Trigg

44.   Richard Bazel Reagan + Cecelia Creppy

45.   Richard Reagan + Phoebe Samples
46.   Reuben Perry Reagan + Elizabeth Cagle
47.   George Reagan + Emaline Garner
48.   Marshall Reagan + Emma Rogers
49.   Elzie Reagan + Delmar Raines
------- Gina Davis
    ------- Jackson Davis
------- Patricia Stuart
    ------- Bobby Caldwell
    ------- Jennifer Caldwell
------- Mike Raines
    ------- Leah Raines
    ------- Kendra Raines
    ------- Joshua Raines
    ------- Michael Raines
------- Frank Raines
    ------- Franklin Cody Raines
    ------- Kip Allen Raines
------- Richard Raines
    ------- Tyler Lee
    ------- Devin Lee
    ------- Emma Lundy

35

THE SCOTTISH KINGS LINEAGE

LINEAGE I

(Jewish)

1.   Mummu the Creator GOD + Nammu, Goddess of the Sea
2.   Apsu, Ocean of Sweet Water + Tiamat, Ocean of Salt Water
3.   Lahmu, The Primordial God + Lahamu, the Primordial GODDESS
4.   Anshar, the Primordial God + Kishar, the Primordial GODDESS
5.   Anu, GOD of the Sky + Ki Urash, GODDESS of the Earth
6.   Enlil, GOD of Wind
7.   El Shaddai, Supreme GOD of CANAAN + Atiratu, Semitic GODDESS of Fertility
8.   Elohim, GOD of Israel
9.   Adam, the First Man + Eve, the First Woman
10.   Seth + Azura, his sister
11.   Enosh (Henos Enos) ADANYA (3769 BC - 2864 BC) + Noham ADANYA, Daughter of Seth and Lilleth the Demoness
12.   Cainan (Keinan) + Mualeleth ADANYA

13. Mahalalel ben KENAN + Dinah
14. Jared ben MAHALALEL (ADANYA) + Baraka ADANYA
15. Enoch (Henoch) ben JARED (3382 BC - 3017 BC) + Ednah
       ADANYA
16. Methusaleh (Mathusale) ben ENOCH + Ednah bint AZRAIL
       (ADANYA)
17. Laamech ibn METHUSALEH (3130? BC - 2353 BC) + Betenos
       (Ashmua) ADANYA
18. Noah (Noe) ibn LAMEK (2948? BC - 1998 BC) + Emzara
       (Coba)
19. Japhet (Iaphet) ibn NOAH2452+ BC - ?)
20. Magog ben JAPHETH
21. Jobhath (Johnath)
22. Fraimaint
23. Easru
24. Sru
25. Seara (Sera)
26. Tait (Tat)
27. Paim (Pamp)
28. Agnoman (Adnamhain) of SCYTHIA
29. Nemedius Machta
30. Jarbhainiel Faidh
31. Beothach (Bethach) MacIARBONEL FAIDH
32. Iobath MacBEOTHACH
33. Baath MacEBATH
34. Enna MacIOBATH
35. Tavarn MacENNA
36. Tat MacTABARN
37. Allaoi (Aldui) MacTAT
38. Ordam
39. Etarlam (I) MacORDAM
40. Echtach (Eochaid) MacETARLAM
41. Nuada Fuildon (Elcmar) AIRGETLAM MacEOCHAID
42. poss. Nemain, Frenzied Havoc of War
43. Delbaeth MacNEIT
44. Elatha (King) of FOMORIANS
45. Ogma MacELADA
46. Tuireann of the TUATHA de Danaans
47. Fiachna MacDELBAETH
48. Anann (Morrigan) ingen FIACHNA
49. Kinne

50.   Bruithne
51.   Cait
52.   Debbecan
53.   Ofinecta
54.   Guididgaedercach
55.   Feth
56.   Gestgurtich
57.   Urguist
58.   Brudebant
59.   Urpant
60.   Bruduileo
61.   Urleo
62.   Brudegant
63.   Urgrant
64.   Brudegnith
65.   Urgnith
66.   Brude Feachtair
67.   Urfeachtair
68.   Brudecal
69.   Urcal
70.   Brudecint
71.   Urcint
72.   Urfeta
73.   Gartnait Bolg (18th King) of PICTS
74.   Ver
75.   Beru (poss. 19th King) of PICTS
76.   Vipog (20th King) of PICTS
77.   Fiacha Albus (21st King) of PICTS
78.   Canututumel (22nd King) of PICTS
79.   Dovernach Vetalec (poss. 25th King) of PICTS
80.   Verdaich Vetla (poss. 26th King) of PICTS
81.   poss. Garnot Diuperr (28th King) of PICTS
82.   Archiuir
83.   Aniel
84.   Talorg I (29th King) of PICTS, sister of
85.   Geraint ap ERP
86.   (Miss) verch GERAINT
87.   Erb MacDRUST (? - 529)
88.   Nechtan (Neiton; II; III; MAWR) MacERB
89.   Beli (I; King) of STRATHCLYDE? - by 641)
90.   daughter of Beli

91.   Spondana ingen ENFIDAIG (Princess) of the PICTS
92.   Eochaid (III) Angbaid (Angbhadh; MacECHACH) of ARGYLL
93.   Aid (Aedh) of ARGYLL FINN (714? - 778+)
94.   Eochaid IV (Annuine) `the Venomous' ARGYLL
95.   Alpin MacEOCHAID (King) of KINTYRE (778? - 834)
96.   Kenneth I (Cinaed) MacALPIN (1st King) of SCOTS; united
       Scots & Picts in 846; aka Ciniod (mac Ailpin) II (77th
       King) of PICTS; aka Kenneth `the Hardy'; `the Raven
       Feeder'; the CONQUEROR + daughter of Donald Anicom,
       Lord of the Isles [Note: Scholars generally treat the
       stories and ancestry given for Kenneth to be partly
       fictional. Defeated Picts in battle in 841 (acquiring
       nickname `Raven Feeder'); invited Pictish royal family to
       a great banquet and massacred them; became King of
       both Scots & Picts in 846. The Scots moved their capital
       to Scone, sacred heart of the Pictish Kingdom, and sat on
       a stone throne which, in legend, had come from Spain
       with the 1st Milesian monarch and spent centuries at
       Dunstaffnage Castle in Tara. Although the Picts had ruled
       much of northern Britain for over 1000 years, within a
       century after MacAlpin's Treason Pictish culture and
       language had almost disappeared.]
97.   Constantine I `the Wine-Bountiful' of ALBA (3rd King) of
       SCOTS (836? - 877, beheaded by the Norse) + Nesta
       verch RHODRI MAWR (840? - ?)
98.   Donald II Dasachtach (6th King) of SCOTS (King of ALBA);
       aka Domnall mac Causantin; `the Madman' (abt. 862-900,
       killed in Battle against Danes) + Unknown
99.   Malcolm I MacALPIN of ALBA, 8th King of SCOTS; aka Maol
       Chaluim mac Ailpin; `the Dangerous Red' (897-954, slain
       by men of Moray) + Unknown
100.   Kenneth II MacALPIN of ALBA, 12th King of SCOTS
       (murdered by his own men) + Unknown
101.   Malcolm II MacKENNETH of ALBA, 15th King of SCOTS; aka
       Mael-Coluim, Melkolf, Malbrigdeson, `the Destroyer' +
       Aefgifu, Irish Woman of OSSORY
102.   Bethoc (Beatrix) MacKENNETH of SCOTLAND (984? - ?) +
       Crinan of Dunkeld, Abthane of ATHOLL (976? - 1045)
103.   Duncan I `the Gracious' MacCRINAN of SCOTLAND + Bethoc
       MacDUFF (1009? - 1040?)
104.   Malcolm III MacCRINAN (CANMORE) (19th King) of SCOTS +

Margaret (Queen; Saint) of SCOTLAND
105. Matilda (Edith Eagdith) `Atheling' STEWART of SCOTLAND + Henry I BEAUCLERC (King) of ENGLAND
106. Matilda (Maud Augusta) the EMPRESS + Geoffrey V `the Fair' (`Plantagenet')
107. Henry II (King) of ENGLAND + Eleanor (Duchess/Princess) of AQUITAINE
108. John `Lackland' (King) of ENGLAND + Isabella (d' ANGOULEME) TAILLEFER
109. Eleanor (Alianor) of ENGLAND (1215? - 1275) + Simon V de MONTFORT (1208 - 4/8/1265)
110. Eleanor de MONTFORT (1252 - 1282) + Llywellyn (II) ap GRUFFYDD (? - 1282)
111. Catherine verch LLYWELLYN + Philip ap IFOR
112. Eleanor (of ISCOED; GOCH) verch PHILIP + Thomas ap LLEWELLYN
113. Lowri verch GRUFFUDD FYCHAN + Robert (Sir; of Emral) PULESTON (1358? - 1399?)
114. Angharad PULESTON + Edward TREVOR ap DAFFYD (? - 1448?)
115. Otewell Worsley, Sir + Rose (TREVOR) verch EDWART
116. Joyce Worsley + Richard Lee II
117. Richard Lee III + Eleanor Burgoine
118. Geoffrey Lee, MP + Agnes Conyers
119. Reginald Lee + Dorothy Thurland
120. Gervase Lee of Nottinghamshire
121. Thomas Lee, of Ashfield + Margaret Mary Oscroft
122. Elizabeth Lee + Thomas Hanks
123. Robert Hanks + Margaret NLN
124. Peter Hanks I + Mary Bressie
125. Elinor Hanks + Rober Nelson
126. Rachael Nelson + Timothy Ragan
127. Timothy Reagan + Elizabeth Trigg
128. Richard Bazel Reagan + Cecelia Creppy
129. Richard Reagan + Phoebe Samples
130. Reuben Perry Reagan + Elizabeth Cagle
131. George Reagan + Emaline Garner
132. Marshall Reagan + Emma Rogers
133. Elzie Reagan + Delmar Raines
------- Gina Davis
------- Jackson Davis

------- Patricia Stuart
    ------- Bobby Caldwell
    ------- Jennifer Caldwell
------- Mike Raines
    ------- Leah Raines
    ------- Kendra Raines
    ------- Joshua Raines
    ------- Michael Raines
------- Frank Raines
    ------- Franklin Cody Raines
    ------- Kip Allen Raines
------- Richard Raines
    ------- Tyler Lee
    ------- Devin Lee
    ------- Emma Lundy

LINEAGE II

(Greek Athenian; Celtic Damnonii & Romano-British Strathclyde)

1. Uranus (1st Ruler GOD of the Universe)
2. Cronos (Kronos) the TITAN
3. Zeus the OLYMPIANborn in Cretan cave)
4. Hephaestus, GOD of Fire
5. Pandora of PTHIA
6. Pyrrha of PTHIA
7. Hellen (King) of the HELLENES
8. Aeolus of THESSALY
9. Melanippe (Arne)
10. Boeotus (eponym of the BOEOTIANS)
11. Ogyges (King) of OGYGIA & the HECTENES
12. Porphyrion (King) of ATTICA
13. Actaeus (1st King) of ATHENS
14. Aglaurus of ATHENS
15. Pandrosos, daughter of Cecropes I, 1st King of Athens
16. Cranaus (King) of ATHENS
17. Kranaos (King) of ATHENS
18. Atthis of ATHENS
19. Pandion I (King) of ATHENS
20. Erechtheus (King) of ATHENS
21. Cecrops II (King) of ATHENS

22.   Pandion II (King) of ATHENS & MEGARA
23.   Aegeus (King) of ATHENS (? - ? Aegean Sea)
24.   Theseus (greatest King) of ATHENS
25.   Demophon of ATHENS (279? BC - ?)
26.   Pandrasus (King) of GREECE
27.   Ignoge (Innogen) of GREECE
28.   Locrinus (Lochrinus) of the BRITONS (? - 1081? BC)
29.   Madog of the BRITONS (? - 1026? BC)
30.   Mymbyr of the BRITONS
31.   Efrog GADARN of the BRITONS
32.   Brutus Darianlas of the BRITONS
33.   Lleon (Lliwelydd) of the BRITONS
34.   Rhun BALADR-BRAS of the BRITONS
35.   Bleidudd (Bleidud Bladud) King in BRITAIN
36.   Llyr (Lear Leir Lyr) of the BRITONS
37.   Regan (Rhagaw) verch LLYR (860? BC - ?)
38.   Cunedda (King) in BRITAIN (? - 772? BC)
39.   Rhiwallon (King) in BRITAIN
40.   Gwrwst (King) in BRITAIN (? - 735? BC)
41.   Seisyll (Sisillius I) (King) in BRITAIN
42.   Antonius (King/Duke) of CORNWALL
43.   Aedd MAWR (King/Duke) of CORNWALL
44.   Prydain ap AEDD (Duke/King) of CORNWALL
45.   Dyfnarth (Duke/King) of CORNWALL
46.   Cloten (Clydno Klydno)
47.   Dunvallo (Dunuallo) Molmutius (King) in BRITAIN
48.   Belinus (Beli) (King) in BRITAIN
49.   Gurguint (Gurguit) Barbtruc (King) in BRITAIN
50.   Guithelin (King) in BRITAIN
51.   Sisillius (II; King) in BRITAIN
52.   Danius (King) in BRITAIN
53.   Morvidus (King) in BRITAIN
54.   Elidurus (King) in BRITAIN
55.   (NN) ... (NN) (several missing generations)
56.   Arthafel (King) in BRITAIN
57.   Eidol (King) in BRITAIN
58.   Rydon (King) in BRITAIN
59.   Rytherch (King) in BRITAIN
60.   Sawl Benisel (King) in BRITAIN
61.   Pyr (ap SAWL) (King) in BRITAIN
62.   Capoir of the DRUIDS

63. Manogan
64. Penardim (Penardun) + Lear (Llediatha) (King) of BRITAIN
        (King Lear)
65. Bran Fendigaid 'the Blessed' (King) of SILURIA + Enygeus of
        ARIMATHEA, daughter of Joseph ben MATTHAT (Saint)
        of ARIMATHEA (? - 82?)
66. Caradoc (ap BRAN) (King) of BRITAIN [Caradoc fought
        Roman legions successfully for nine years, was betrayed
        by Queen Cartimandua of Brigantes, displayed in Rome in
        chains with family, reprieved as a result of his famous
        noble oration; nevertheless his capture in 51 A.D. marked
        the end of the millenium-long Celtic ascendancy in
        Europe.] + Cartismandua (Queen) of BRIGANTES
        (and/or) Eurgain (and/or) Tegau
67. Guidgen (? - 85) [aka Gwyddien ap CARADOG; led resistance
        against Romans]
68. Art 'Cois' + Sister of Tarain (2nd King) of PICTS
69. Quintus (Ciniad Cinit Cuned) (5th King) of PICTS
70. Corvus (1st King) of DUMBARTON [(Corb Corbred Corbed
        Carvorst); 9th King of PICTS in ALBANY]
71. Art 'Vroisc' (King) of DUMBARTON (14th King of PICTS)
72. Fer 'Fi' (King) of DUMBARTON
73. Duibne 'Mor' (King) of DUMBARTON
74. Art 'Og' (King) of DUMBARTON
75. Con (Confer)
76. Fer (King) of DUMBARTON
77. Cursalem (King) of DUMBARTON (General under
        Constantine the Great)
78. Cluim (Clemens Clium Cluian) of ROME (Roman General)
79. Cinhil (Quintillian) of the DAMNONII
80. Cynlop (Cynllwyb Cynloup Cynloyp) of the DAMNONII
81. Ceredig WLEDIG (King) of STRATHCLYDE [aka Caradog
        (Coroticus Ceretic) GULETIC (King) of ALCLUD
        (DUMBARTON); of the DAMNONII]
82. Erp (Erbin Seirb) ap CERETIC (? - 480?) (King) of
        STRATHCLYDE
83. Geraint ap ERP
84. (Miss) verch GERAINT
85. Erb MacDRUST (? - 529)
86. Nechtan (Neiton; II; III; MAWR) MacERB (? - 621?)
87. Beli (I; King) of STRATHCLYDE

88. Daughter of Beli + Entifidach
89. Spondana ingen ENFIDAIG (Princess) of the PICTS [aka sister
       of Talorcen (Tarachin Taran) (54th King) of PICTS] +
       Eochaid II `Crook-Nose' of ARGYLL
90. Eochaid (III) Angbaid (Angbhadh; MacECHACH) of ARGYLL
91. Fergus (II) MacECHACH (King) of DALRIADA
92. Constantine (67th/101th King) of PICTS (? - 820+)
93. Drust IX (69th/103rd King) of PICTS, sister of + Alpin
       MacEOCHAID (King) of KINTYRE (778? - 834)
94. Kenneth I (Cinaed) MacALPIN (1st King) of SCOTS; united
       Scots & Picts in 846; aka Ciniod (mac Ailpin) II (77th
       King) of PICTS; aka Kenneth `the Hardy'; `the Raven
       Feeder'; the CONQUEROR + daughter of Donald Anicom,
       Lord of the Isles [Note: Scholars generally treat the
       stories and ancestry given for Kenneth to be partly
       fictional. Defeated Picts in battle in 841 (acquiring
       nickname `Raven Feeder'); invited Pictish royal family to
       a great banquet and massacred them; became King of
       both Scots & Picts in 846. The Scots moved their capital
       to Scone, sacred heart of the Pictish Kingdom, and sat on
       a stone throne which, in legend, had come from Spain
       with the 1st Milesian monarch and spent centuries at
       Dunstaffnage Castle in Tara. Although the Picts had ruled
       much of northern Britain for over 1000 years, within a
       century after MacAlpin's Treason Pictish culture and
       language had almost disappeared.]
95. Constantine I `the Wine-Bountiful' of ALBA (3rd King) of
       SCOTS (836? - 877, beheaded by the Norse) + Nesta
       verch RHODRI MAWR (840? - ?)
96. Donald II Dasachtach (6th King) of SCOTS (King of ALBA);
       aka Domnall mac Causantin; `the Madman' (abt. 862-900,
       killed in Battle against Danes) + Unknown
97. Malcolm I MacALPIN of ALBA, 8th King of SCOTS; aka Maol
       Chaluim mac Ailpin; `the Dangerous Red' (897-954, slain
       by men of Moray) + Unknown
98. Kenneth II MacALPIN of ALBA, 12th King of SCOTS
       (murdered by his own men) + Unknown
99. Malcolm II MacKENNETH of ALBA, 15th King of SCOTS; aka
       Mael-Coluim, Melkolf, Malbrigdeson, `the Destroyer' +
       Aefgifu, Irish Woman of OSSORY
100. Bethoc (Beatrix) MacKENNETH of SCOTLAND (984? - ?) +

Crinan of Dunkeld, Abthane of ATHOLL (976? - 1045)
101. Duncan I `the Gracious' MacCRINAN of SCOTLAND + Bethoc
MacDUFF (1009? - 1040?)
102. Malcolm III MacCRINAN (CANMORE) (19th King) of SCOTS +
Margaret (Queen; Saint) of SCOTLAND
103. Matilda (Edith Eagdith) `Atheling' STEWART of SCOTLAND +
Henry I BEAUCLERC (King) of ENGLAND
104. Matilda (Maud Augusta) the EMPRESS + Geoffrey V `the Fair'
(`Plantagenet')
105. Henry II (King) of ENGLAND + Eleanor (Duchess/Princess) of
AQUITAINE
106. John `Lackland' (King) of ENGLAND + Isabella (d'
ANGOULEME) TAILLEFER
107. Eleanor (Alianor) of ENGLAND (1215? - 1275) + Simon V de
MONTFORT (1208 - 4/8/1265)
108. Eleanor de MONTFORT (1252 - 1282) + Llywellyn (II) ap
GRUFFYDD (? - 1282)
109. Catherine verch LLYWELLYN + Philip ap IFOR
110. Eleanor (of ISCOED; GOCH) verch PHILIP + Thomas ap
LLEWELLYN
111. Lowri verch GRUFFUDD FYCHAN + Robert (Sir; of Emral)
PULESTON (1358? - 1399?)
112. Angharad PULESTON + Edward TREVOR ap DAFFYD (? -
1448?)
113. Otewell Worsley, Sir + Rose (TREVOR) verch EDWART
114. Joyce Worsley + Richard Lee II
115. Richard Lee III + Eleanor Burgoine
116. Geoffrey Lee, MP + Agnes Conyers
117. Reginald Lee + Dorothy Thurland
118. Gervase Lee of Nottinghamshire
119. Thomas Lee, of Ashfield + Margaret Mary Oscroft
120. Elizabeth Lee + Thomas Hanks
121. Robert Hanks + Margaret NLN
122. Peter Hanks I + Mary Bressie
123. Elinor Hanks + Robert Nelson
124. Rachael Nelson + Timothy Ragan
125. Timothy Reagan + Elizabeth Trigg
126. Richard Bazel Reagan + Cecelia Creppy
127. Richard Reagan + Phoebe Samples
128. Reuben Perry Reagan + Elizabeth Cagle
129. George Reagan + Emaline Garner

130.   Marshall Reagan + Emma Rogers
131.   Elzie Reagan + Delmar Raines
        ------- Gina Davis
                ------- Jackson Davis
        ------- Patricia Stuart
                ------- Bobby Caldwell
                ------- Jennifer Caldwell
        ------- Mike Raines
                ------- Leah Raines
                ------- Kendra Raines
                ------- Joshua Raines
                ------- Michael Raines
        ------- Frank Raines
                ------- Franklin Cody Raines
                ------- Kip Allen Raines
        ------- Richard Raines
                ------- Tyler Lee
                ------- Devin Lee
                ------- Emma Lundy

36

THE TROJAN-CIMMERIAN-SICAMBRIAN LINEAGE

1. Sesostris + Nefret
2. Amenemhat I Sehetepibre (Founder) of 12th Dynasty + Nefrutotenen
3. Sesotris I Kheperkare (PHARAOH) of EGYPT (? - 1928? BC) + Nefrusheri (Princess) of EGYPT
4. Amenemhat (Ammenemes) II Nubkaure (PHARAOH) of EGYPT + Keminnub (Queen) of EGYPT
5. Sesotris II Khakheperre (PHARAOH) of EGYPT + Nofret of EGYPT
6. Sesotris III Khakaure of EGYPT + Sebekshedty-Neferu (Queen) of EGYPT
7. Amenemhat III Nemare (PHARAOH) of EGYPT + Sebeknefru (Queen) of EGYPT
8. Amenemhat (Ammenemes) IV (PHARAOH) of EGYPT
9. Wegaf (PHARAOH) of 13th Dynasty + daughter of Amenemhet IV
10. Ameny Intef (Inyotef) IV (PHARAOH) of EGYPT
11. Hor (PHARAOH) of EGYPT (? - 1760? BC)
12. Sobekhotep II (PHARAOH) of EGYPT (? - 1750? BC)
13. Khendjer (PHARAOH) of EGYPT (? - 1747? BC)

14. Sobekhotep III (PHARAOH) of EGYPT (? - 1745? BC)
15. Neferhotep I (PHARAOH) of EGYPT
16. Sobekhotep IV Khaneferre (PHARAOH) of 13th Dynasty + Tjan
17. Sebekhotep (Princess) of THEBES + Senebhanef, son of Renressonb
18. Mentuhotep (Queen) of EGYPT + Sekhemre-Sementawi Djehuti (PHARAOH) of EGYPT
19. Sekhemre-Se'ankhtawi Neferhotep (PHARAOH) of EGYPT
20. Sobekemsaf Sekhemre-Shedtawi (PHARAOH) of EGYPT + Nubkhas (Queen) of EGYPT
21. Inyotef VII (PHARAOH) at THEBES + Sobkemsaf (Sebekamzaf) of EGYPT (1635? BC - ?)
22. Sekenenre Tao I (PHARAOH) at THEBES + Tetisheri of THEBES
23. Sekenenre Tao II (King) of THEBES + Ahhotep (Ahotop) I (Queen) of EGYPT
24. Ahmose I (1st PHARAOH) of 18th Dynasty + Nefretiri (Queen) of EGYPT
25. Amenhotep I Djeserkare (PHARAOH) of EGYPT + Senisonb (Seneseneb) of EGYPT
26. Thutmose I (PHARAOH) of EGYPT (? - 1481? BC) + Amhose (Aahmes II) (Queen) of EGYPT
27. Hatshepsut (Queen & PHARAOH) of EGYPT (? - 1482 BC) + Thutmose (Tuthmosis) II (PHARAOH) of EGYPT
28. Meryetre Hatshepsut of EGYPT + Thutmose III `the Great' of EGYPT (Moses of the Bible)
29. Akheperure Amenhotep II THUTMOSID (PHARAOH) of EGYPT + Tio (Tiye Tiaa)
30. Menkheprure' Thutmose IV (PHARAOH) of EGYPT + Mutemwiya, daughter of Artatama (I; King) of MITANNI
31. Nebma'atre' Amenhotep III (PHARAOH) of EGYPT + Tiye-Nefertari (Tiy) of EGYPT (1382 BC - 1344 BC)
32. Akhenaton (Iknaton) (10th PHARAOH) of 18th Dynasty EGYPT + Nefertiti (Chief Queen) of EGYPT
33. Meritaten (Royal Daughter) of EGYPT + Judah (Judas Juda) ibn JACOB, son of Jacob ibn ISAAC (King of GOSHEN)
34. Zerah (Zehrah Zarah Zare) ibn JUDAH + Electra the PLEIADE
35. Dardanus (Dara) (King) of ACADIA + Batea of TEUCRI
36. Erichthonius (King) of ACADIA (? - 1386? BC) + Astyoche of ACADIA

37.   Trois of ACADIA + Callirhoe (TEUCRI)
38.   Ilus (Ilyus) (King) of TROY (? - 1282? BC) + Eurydice
         (Eurydike) of TROY
39.   Priam Podarces (High King) of TROY (? - 1183? BC) + Hecuba
         (Hecabe) of PHRYGIA
40.   Helenus of TROY (King of the SCYTHIANS) + daughter of
         Scythes (1st King) of SCYTHIA
41.   Genger of the SCYTHIANS
42.   Esdron the TROJAN
43.   Gelio the TROJAN
44.   Bosabiliano (Basabelian I) the TROJAN
45.   Plaserio (Plaserius I) the TROJAN
46.   Plesron (King of CIMMERIANS)
47.   Eliacor the TROJAN
48.   Gaberiano (Zaberian) the TROJAN
49.   Plaserius II the TROJAN
50.   Antenor I the TROJAN
51.   Priam II Trianus the TROJAN
52.   Helenus II the TROJAN
53.   Plesron II the TROJAN
54.   Basabelian (Basabiliano) II the TROJAN
55.   Alexandre the TROJAN
56.   Priam III of the CIMMERIANS
57.   Gentilanor (Prince) of the CIMMERIANS
58.   Almadius (King) of the CIMMERIANS
59.   Dilulius I (King) of the CIMMERIANS
60.   Helenus III (King) of the CIMMERIANS
61.   Plaserius (Plaserio) III (King) of the CIMMERIANS
62.   Dilulius (Diluglio) II (King) of the CIMMERIANS
63.   Marcomir (King) of the CIMMERIANS
64.   Priam IV (King) of the CIMMERIANS
65.   Helenus IV (King) of the CIMMERIANS
66.   Antenor I (II; King) of the CIMMERIANS (? - 433? BC)
67.   Marcomir I (King) of SICAMBRI (? - 412? BC)
68.   Antenor II (III; King) of SICAMBRI (? - 384? BC) + Cambra
69.   Priamus (V; Priam) (King) of SICAMBRI (? - 358? BC)
70.   Helenus V (King) of SICAMBRI
71.   Diocles (King) of SICAMBRI
72.   Bassanus Magnus (King) of SICAMBRI
73.   Clodimir I (King) of SICAMBRI
74.   Nicanor I (King) of SICAMBRI

75. Marcomir II (King) of SICAMBRI + (Princess NN), daughter of
    Elidure (Chieftain) in BRITAIN
76. Clodius I (King) of SICAMBRI
77. Antenor III (King) of SICAMBRI
78. Clodimir II (King) of SICAMBRI (? - 123? BC)
79. Merodachus (King) of SICAMBRI (? - 95? BC)
80. Cassander (King) of SICAMBRI
81. Antharius (King) of the SICAMBRI (77? BC - 36? BC)
82. Francus (King) of the WEST FRANKS (57? BC - 5?)
83. Clodius II (King) of the FRANKS (37? BC - 20?)
84. Marcomir III (King) of the FRANKS (17? BC - 50?)
85. Clodomir III (King) of the FRANKS
86. Antenor IV (King) of the WEST FRANKS
87. Ratherius (King) of the FRANKS
88. Richemer I (King) of FRANKS + Ascyla of the FRANKS
89. Odomir (Odomar) (King) of FRANKS
90. Marcomir IV (King) of FRANKS + Althildis (Princess) of
    BRITAIN
91. Clodimir IV (King) of FRANKS (by 125 - 166) + Hafilda
    (Princess) of the RUGIJ (? - 179?)
92. Farabert (King) of FRANKS (by 145 - 186?)
93. Sunno (Huano Hunno) (King) of FRANKS (165? - 213)
94. Childeric (Hilderic) (King) of FRANKS (185? - 253?)
95. Bartherus (King) of FRANKS (? - 272)
96. Clodius (III) of FRANKS
97. Walter (King) of the EAST FRANKS
98. Dagobert I (King) of FRANKS (? - 317?)
99. Genebald (I; 1st Duke) of the EAST FRANKS + Athildis
100. Dagobert II (Duke) of EAST FRANKS
101. Clodius (I; IV; Duke) of EAST FRANKS + Blesinde (Princess)
    of the SUEVI (350? - 403?)
102. Blesinde of the FRANKS (375? - by 418) + Theodemer des
    FRANCS RIPUAIRES (374? - 15/8/414)
103. Clovis (Chlodion) the RIPARIAN of COLOGNE + Ildegonde of
    the FRANKS
104. Childebert (King) of COLOGNE + Amalberge of the FRANKS
105. Sigebert (Siegbert) (I; King) of COLOGNE
106. Cloderic `the Parricide' (King) of COLOGNE + Agilofinginne of
    the AGILOFING
107. Munderic of VITRY-EN-PERTHOIS + Arthemia(?) of GENEVA
    (503? - 530+)

108. Mummolin des FRANCS RIPUAIRES (505? - 558?)
109. Baudgise II (Duke) of AQUITAINE + Oda (Saint) of SAVOY
        (562? - 611+)
110. Saint Arnoul, bishop of Metz + Saint Dode (Clotilde) of Metz
111. Ansigisel of Metz, Mayor of the Palace of Austrasia + Saint
        Beggue of Austrasia
112. Pépin ll "the Fat"; d'Héristal, Mayor of the Palace of Austrasia
        + Alpaïde (Alpais)
113. Charles Martel "The Hammer", Mayor of the Palace +
        Rotrude, Duchess of Austrasia
114. Pépin III, King of the Franks + Bertha Broadfoot of Laon
115. CHARLEMAGNE, Carolus 'Magnus', Rex Francorum &
        Imperator Romanorum + Hildegard of Vinzgouw
116. "Pépin" Carloman, King of Italy + Mistress of Pepin
117. Bernard, King of Lombardy + Cunigundis (Cunegonde)
        (Princess) de VERMANDOIS
118. Pépin II, lord of Péronne + Rothaide de Bobbio
119. Pepin (I; Count) de SENLIS de VALOIS
120. (Miss) de SENLIS de VALOIS (845? - ?) + Berenger (Count) de
        RENNES (? - 931)
121. Poppa (Poppaeia) de VALOIS (872? - ?) + Rollo (Hrolf Rollon
        Rou Robert) `the Dane' RAGNVALDSSON
122. Guillaume (2nd Duke) of NORMANDY + Sprota de
        BRETAGNE (concubine)
123. Richard I `the Fearless' (Count) of NORMANDY + Gunnora
        (Gonnor) de CREPON
124. Richard II `the Good' of NORMANDY (963? - 1027) + Judith
        (Princess) of BRITTANY
125. Robert II (Duke) of NORMANDY + Herleve (Salburpyr) de
        FALAISE (1003? - 1050?)
126. WILLIAM the CONQUEROR (Duke) of NORMANDY + Matilda
        (Maud) FLEMING (1032 - 1083 Caan)
127. Henry I BEAUCLERC (King) of ENGLAND + Matilda (Edith
        Eagdith) `Atheling' STEWART of SCOTLAND
128. Matilda (Maud Augusta) the EMPRESS + Geoffrey V `the Fair'
        (`Plantagenet')
129. Henry II (King) of ENGLAND + Eleanor (Duchess/Princess) of
        AQUITAINE
130. John `Lackland' (King) of ENGLAND + Isabella (d'
        ANGOULEME) TAILLEFER
131. Eleanor (Alianor) of ENGLAND (1215? - 1275) + Simon V de

MONTFORT (1208 - 4/8/1265)
132. Eleanor de MONTFORT (1252 - 1282) + Llywellyn (II) ap
        GRUFFYDD (? - 1282)
133. Catherine verch LLYWELLYN + Philip ap IFOR
134. Eleanor (of ISCOED; GOCH) verch PHILIP + Thomas ap
        LLEWELLYN
135. Lowri verch GRUFFUDD FYCHAN + Robert (Sir; of Emral)
        PULESTON (1358? - 1399?)
136. Angharad PULESTON + Edward TREVOR ap DAFFYD (? -
        1448?)
137. Otewell Worsley, Sir + Rose (TREVOR) verch EDWART
138. Joyce Worsley + Richard Lee II
139. Richard Lee III + Eleanor Burgoine
140. Geoffrey Lee, MP + Agnes Conyers
141. Reginald Lee + Dorothy Thurland
142. Gervase Lee of Nottinghamshire
143. Thomas Lee, of Ashfield + Margaret Mary Oscroft
144. Elizabeth Lee + Thomas Hanks
145. Robert Hanks + Margaret NLN
146. Peter Hanks I + Mary Bressie
147. Elinor Hanks + Robert Nelson
148. Rachael Nelson + Timothy Ragan
149. Timothy Reagan + Elizabeth Trigg
150. Richard Bazel Reagan + Cecelia Creppy
151. Richard Reagan + Phoebe Samples
152. Reuben Perry Reagan + Elizabeth Cagle
153. George Reagan + Emaline Garner
154. Marshall Reagan + Emma Rogers
155. Elzie Reagan + Delmar Raines
        ------- Gina Davis
              ------- Jackson Davis
        ------- Patricia Stuart
              ------- Bobby Caldwell
              ------- Jennifer Caldwell
        ------- Mike Raines
              ------- Leah Raines
              ------- Kendra Raines
              ------- Joshua Raines
              ------- Michael Raines
        ------- Frank Raines
              ------- Franklin Cody Raines

------- Kip Allen Raines
------- Richard Raines
------- Tyler Lee
------- Devin Lee
------- Emma Lundy

37

THE TROJAN-NORSE-FRANKISH LINEAGE

1. Sesostris + Nefret
2. Amenemhat I Sehetepibre (Founder) of 12th Dynasty + Nefrutotenen
3. Sesotris I Kheperkare (PHARAOH) of EGYPT (? - 1928? BC) + Nefrusheri (Princess) of EGYPT
4. Amenemhat (Ammenemes) II Nubkaure (PHARAOH) of EGYPT + Keminnub (Queen) of EGYPT
5. Sesotris II Khakheperre (PHARAOH) of EGYPT + Nofret of EGYPT
6. Sesotris III Khakaure of EGYPT + Sebekshedty-Neferu (Queen) of EGYPT
7. Amenemhat III Nemare (PHARAOH) of EGYPT + Sebeknefru (Queen) of EGYPT
8. Amenemhat (Ammenemes) IV (PHARAOH) of EGYPT
9. Wegaf (PHARAOH) of 13th Dynasty + daughter of Amenemhet IV
10. Ameny Intef (Inyotef) IV (PHARAOH) of EGYPT
11. Hor (PHARAOH) of EGYPT (? - 1760? BC)
12. Sobekhotep II (PHARAOH) of EGYPT (? - 1750? BC)
13. Khendjer (PHARAOH) of EGYPT (? - 1747? BC)

14.   Sobekhotep III (PHARAOH) of EGYPT (? - 1745? BC)
15.   Neferhotep I (PHARAOH) of EGYPT
16.   Sobekhotep IV Khaneferre (PHARAOH) of 13th Dynasty + Tjan
17.   Sebekhotep (Princess) of THEBES + Senebhanef, son of Renressonb
18.   Mentuhotep (Queen) of EGYPT + Sekhemre-Sementawi Djehuti (PHARAOH) of EGYPT
19.   Sekhemre-Se'ankhtawi Neferhotep (PHARAOH) of EGYPT
20.   Sobekemsaf Sekhemre-Shedtawi (PHARAOH) of EGYPT + Nubkhas (Queen) of EGYPT
21.   Inyotef VII (PHARAOH) at THEBES + Sobkemsaf (Sebekamzaf) of EGYPT (1635? BC - ?)
22.   Sekenenre Tao I (PHARAOH) at THEBES + Tetisheri of THEBES
23.   Sekenenre Tao II (King) of THEBES + Ahhotep (Ahotop) I (Queen) of EGYPT
24.   Ahmose I (1st PHARAOH) of 18th Dynasty + Nefretiri (Queen) of EGYPT
25.   Amenhotep I Djeserkare (PHARAOH) of EGYPT + Senisonb (Seneseneb) of EGYPT
26.   Thutmose I (PHARAOH) of EGYPT (? - 1481? BC) + Amhose (Aahmes II) (Queen) of EGYPT
27.   Hatshepsut (Queen & PHARAOH) of EGYPT (? - 1482 BC) + Thutmose (Tuthmosis) II (PHARAOH) of EGYPT
28.   Meryetre Hatshepsut of EGYPT + Thutmose III `the Great' of EGYPT (Moses of the Bible)
29.   Akheperure Amenhotep II THUTMOSID (PHARAOH) of EGYPT + Tio (Tiye Tiaa)
30.   Menkheprure' Thutmose IV (PHARAOH) of EGYPT + Mutemwiya, daughter of Artatama (I; King) of MITANNI
31.   Nebma'atrc' Amenhotep III (PHARAOH) of EGYPT + Tiye-Nefertari (Tiy) of EGYPT (1382 BC - 1344 BC)
32.   Akhenaton (Iknaton) (10th PHARAOH) of 18th Dynasty EGYPT + Nefertiti (Chief Queen) of EGYPT
33.   Meritaten (Royal Daughter) of EGYPT + Judah (Judas Juda) ibn JACOB, son of Jacob ibn ISAAC (King of GOSHEN)
34.   Zerah (Zehrah Zarah Zare) ibn JUDAH + Electra the PLEIADE
35.   Dardanus (Dara) (King) of ACADIA + Batea of TEUCRI
36.   Erichthonius (King) of ACADIA (? - 1386? BC) + Astyoche of ACADIA

37.   Trois of ACADIA + Callirhoe (TEUCRI)
38.   Ilus (Ilyus) (King) of TROY (? - 1282? BC) + Eurydice (Eurydike) of TROY
39.   Priam Podarces (High King) of TROY (? - 1183? BC) + Hecuba (Hecabe) of PHRYGIA
40.   Troana Iluim of TROY + Memnon (Munon) of TROY (? - 1183? BC)
41.   Thor (Tror) (King) of THRACE + Sibil (Sif)
42.   Einridi LORIDESSON
43.   Vingethor (Vingethior) EINRIDISSON
44.   Moda (Mode) VINGENERSSON
45.   Maji (Magi) MODASSON
46.   Seskef (Sceaf Scaef)
47.   Bedwig (Bedvig; of SCEAF)
48.   Hwala (Hvala Hawala Guala)
49.   Hathra (Athra)
50.   Itermon (Itormann)
51.   Heremod (King) in DENMARK
52.   Sceldwa (King) in DENMARK
53.   Beaw (Gram) (King) in DENMARK
54.   Taetwa (Tatwa Tecti)
55.   Jat (Geatwa Geata Geat Gaut Geot Gauti)
56.   Godwulf (Gudolfr)
57.   Flocwald (of Asgard)
58.   Finn (the TROJAN ?) (Asgard 130? - ?)
59.   Frithuwulf (the TROJAN ?)
60.   Frealaf (Friallaf Froethelaf) (160? - ?)
61.   Frithuwald (Bor) (190? - ?) + Beltsea (Beltsa) of ASGARD
62.   Odin (Woden, Wodan) of ASGARD + Frigg (Frigida) of ASALAND
63.   Wecta (Waegdaeg) the JUTE (280? - 350+)
64.   Witta (Vitta Vitgils Witte; II) the JUTE
65.   Merwig I (King) of THURINGIA (? - 426?)
66.   Weldelphus (King) of THURINGIA (365? - 408?)
67.   Merwig II (King) of THURINGIA
68.   Basin (King) of THURINGIA
69.   Basina Andovera (Saint?) of THURINGIA (439? - 470+) + Childeric I (King) of FRANKS (of YSSEL)
70.   Clovis `the Great' (1st King) of All FRANKS + Clothilde (Saint; Princess) of BURGUNDY
71.   Chlothar I (2nd King) of All FRANKS (497? - 561) + Ildegonde

of the FRANKS

72. Sigebert (Siegbert) (I; King) of COLOGNE
73. Cloderic `the Parricide' (King) of COLOGNE + Agilofinginne of
        the AGILOFING
74. Munderic of VITRY-EN-PERTHOIS + Arthemia(?) of GENEVA
        (503? - 530+)
75. Mummolin des FRANCS RIPUAIRES (505? - 558?)
76. Baudgise II (Duke) of AQUITAINE + Oda (Saint) of SAVOY
        (562? - 611+)
77. Saint Arnoul, bishop of Metz + Saint Dode (Clotilde) of Metz
78. Ansigisel of Metz, Mayor of the Palace of Austrasia + Saint
        Beggue of Austrasia
79. Pépin ll "the Fat"; d'Héristal, Mayor of the Palace of Austrasia
        + Alpaïde (Alpais)
80. Charles Martel "The Hammer", Mayor of the Palace +
        Rotrude, Duchess of Austrasia
81. Pépin III, King of the Franks + Bertha Broadfoot of Laon
82. CHARLEMAGNE, Carolus 'Magnus', Rex Francorum &
        Imperator Romanorum + Hildegard of Vinzgouw
83. "Pépin" Carloman, King of Italy + Mistress of Pepin
84. Bernard, King of Lombardy + Cunigundis (Cunegonde)
        (Princess) de VERMANDOIS
85. Pépin II, lord of Péronne + Rothaide de Bobbio
86. Pepin (I; Count) de SENLIS de VALOIS
87. (Miss) de SENLIS de VALOIS (845? - ?) + Berenger (Count) de
        RENNES (? - 931)
88. Poppa (Poppaeia) de VALOIS (872? - ?) + Rollo (Hrolf Rollon
        Rou Robert) `the Dane' RAGNVALDSSON
89. Guillaume (2nd Duke) of NORMANDY + Sprota de
        BRETAGNE (concubine)
90. Richard I `the Fearless' (Count) of NORMANDY + Gunnora
        (Gonnor) de CREPON
91. Richard II `the Good' of NORMANDY (963? - 1027) + Judith
        (Princess) of BRITTANY
92. Robert II (Duke) of NORMANDY + Herleve (Salburpyr) de
        FALAISE (1003? - 1050?)
93. WILLIAM the CONQUEROR (Duke) of NORMANDY + Matilda
        (Maud) FLEMING (1032 - 1083 Caan)
94. Henry I BEAUCLERC (King) of ENGLAND + Matilda (Edith
        Eagdith) `Atheling' STEWART of SCOTLAND
95. Matilda (Maud Augusta) the EMPRESS + Geoffrey V `the Fair'

('Plantagenet')

96.   Henry II (King) of ENGLAND + Eleanor (Duchess/Princess) of AQUITAINE

97.   John `Lackland' (King) of ENGLAND + Isabella (d' ANGOULEME) TAILLEFER

98.   Eleanor (Alianor) of ENGLAND (1215? - 1275) + Simon V de MONTFORT (1208 - 4/8/1265)

99.   Eleanor de MONTFORT (1252 - 1282) + Llywellyn (II) ap GRUFFYDD (? - 1282)

100.   Catherine verch LLYWELLYN + Philip ap IFOR

101.   Eleanor (of ISCOED; GOCH) verch PHILIP + Thomas ap LLEWELLYN

102.   Lowri verch GRUFFUDD FYCHAN + Robert (Sir; of Emral) PULESTON (1358? - 1399?)

103.   Angharad PULESTON + Edward TREVOR ap DAFFYD (? - 1448?)

104.   Otewell Worsley, Sir + Rose (TREVOR) verch EDWART

105.   Joyce Worsley + Richard Lee II

106.   Richard Lee III + Eleanor Burgoine

107.   Geoffrey Lee, MP + Agnes Conyers

108.   Reginald Lee + Dorothy Thurland

109.   Gervase Lee of Nottinghamshire

110.   Thomas Lee, of Ashfield + Margaret Mary Oscroft

111.   Elizabeth Lee + Thomas Hanks

112.   Robert Hanks + Margaret NLN

113.   Peter Hanks I + Mary Bressie

114.   Elinor Hanks + Robert Nelson

115.   Rachael Nelson + Timothy Ragan

116.   Timothy Reagan + Elizabeth Trigg

117.   Richard Bazel Reagan + Cecelia Creppy

118.   Richard Reagan + Phoebe Samples

119.   Reuben Perry Reagan + Elizabeth Cagle

120.   George Reagan + Emaline Garner

121.   Marshall Reagan + Emma Rogers

122.   Elzie Reagan + Delmar Raines

    ------- Gina Davis

        ------- Jackson Davis

    ------- Patricia Stuart

        ------- Bobby Caldwell

        ------- Jennifer Caldwell

    ------- Mike Raines

------- Leah Raines
------- Kendra Raines
------- Joshua Raines
------- Michael Raines
------- Frank Raines
------- Franklin Cody Raines
------- Kip Allen Raines
------- Richard Raines
------- Tyler Lee
------- Devin Lee
------- Emma Lundy

38

THE WILLIAM THE CONQUEROR LINEAGE

LINEAGE I

(Norse)

1.   Alfadur, the Eternal (GOD)
2.   The Fire of MUSPELHEIM + The Ice of NIFLHEIM
3.   The Clouds (PRIMORDIAL) + Eitr, Substance of Life
        (PRIMORDIAL)
4.   Ymir, the Frost GIANTGinnungagap) + Hrod
5.   Tyr (YMIRSSON) + Zisa
6.   Tuisto (1st King) of GERMANIA (? - 1500? BC) + Mannus
7.   Mannus
8.   Father of Njord of NORTUN (by 200 - ?)
9.   Njord (Niordr) `the Rich' of NORTUN + Nerthus of NORTUN
10.   Frej (Frey) av SVITJOD + Svea DROTNER
11.   Yngvi-Frey (King) of UPPSALA (235? - 299?) + Gerd `Vern'
        GYMERSDOTTIR (239? - ?), daughter of Angrbotha the
        GIANTESS (218? - ?; daughter of Hrimnir the GIANT of
        Norway) and Gymer `the Old' of SCANDINAVIA (214? - ?),
        son of Gonnor GORRETTSDATTER and Fornjotur the

GIANT (King) in KVENLAND, son of Snaer (King) in KVENLAND (q.v.)

12. Fjolnar (Fjolnir Fiolner) YNGVI-FREYSSON
13. Sveigder FJOLNARSSON + Vana of VANHEIM (VANALAND)
14. Vanlandi SVEGDASSON + Driva SNAERSDOTTIR
15. Visbur (Visburr) VANLANDASSON + (Miss) AUTHISDOTTIR
16. Domaldi VISBURSSON (Uppsala 340? - 422?) + (Miss) HODBRODDSDATTER
17. Domarr DOMALDSSON (Sweden 361? - 437?) + Drott DANPSDOTTIR (365? - ?), daughter of Danpi RIGSSON of DENMARK and Olov VERMUNDSDOTTI
18. Dyggvi (Dyggve) DOMARSSON (Sweden 382? - 481?) + daughter of Vale AGNAR, daughter of Bodvid (daughter of Hood RIG and Dana) and Vale AGNAR, son of Baeldaeg of the AESIR and Nanna (GEWARSDATTER) of SCANDINAVIA
19. Dagr Spaka DYGGVASSON (DYGVESSON)
20. Agni (Agne; of SVEARNE) DAGSSON (Sweden 424? - 513?) + Skjalf FROSTASDOTTIR (428? - ?), daughter of Frosti KARASSON (King) in KVENLAND, son of Karri FORNJOTSSON (King) in KVENLAND, son of Fornjotur the GIANT (King) in KVENLAND (and Gonnor GORRETTSDATTER), son of Snaer (King) in KVENLAND (q.v.)
21. Alrekr AGNASSON (AGNESSON) + Dagreidr DAGSDOTTIR
22. Yngvi (Yngve Yngui; II) ALREKSSON
23. Jorundr YNGVASSON (YNGVESSON)
24. Aun (Gamli; `the Aged') JORUNDSSON
25. Egil (Erik `Tunnadolg') AUNSSON + Elan (Queen) of SCILFLING, daughter of Halfdan `the Tall' FRODASON (King) of DENMARK (and Sigris of DENMARK?), son of Frodi (Froda; VII; IV) FRIDLEIFSSON (and Hilda of the VANDALS)
26. Ottar (Ohthere, Vendilkraku) EGILSSON + (Miss) EYSTENSDOTTER of UPPSALA, daughter of Eystein FROTHISSON of DENMARK, son of Frode (Frothi) III DANSSON of DENMARK, son of Dan `the Magnificent' of DENMARK (and (Miss) OLAFSDATTER of DENMARK)
27. Adils `the Great' OTTARSSON of SWEDEN (572? - 640?) + Yrsa HELGASDOTTIR (565? - ?), daughter of Helgi HALFDANSSON (King) in DENMARK (528? - ?)

28.   Eystein (Oystein) ADILSSON of SWEDEN (King of UPPSALA)
29.   Ingvar (Yngvaarr) EYSTEINSSON of SWEDEN
30.   Braut-Onundr INGVARSSON + Algaut GUTREKSSON (639? -
        ?)
31.   Ingjaldr 'Ill-Ruler' BRAUT-ONUNDSON + Gauthild
        ALGOUTSDOTTIR
32.   Olafr Tretelgju (Tree-hewer) INGJALDSSON [King of
        VERMALAND; aka Olav INGJARSSON 'Wood Cutter'
        ('Trekalia') av VERMLAND; aka Olav I (Duke) of
        VESTFOLD; aka Olaf TRETELGJA; of the The Ynglinga
        Saga; Born: abt. 682, Died: abt. 710, sacrificed] + Solveig
        HALFDANSDOTTIR (684? - ?), daughter of Halfdan
        Guldtand 'Gold Tooth' of SWEDEN
33.   Halfdan Hvitbeinn 'White Leg' OLAFSSON(704? - ?) + Asa
        EYSTEINSDOTTIR (715? - 793?), daughter of Eystein
        (Jarl) of THRONDHEIM (680? - 710?)
34.   Eystein (of WESTFOLD) HALFDANARSSON (736? - 780?) +
        Hild (Hildur) EIRIKSDOTTIR, daughter of Eric (Eirikur) of
        Westfold AGNARSSON, son of Agnar SIGTRYGGSSON av
        VESTFOLD, son of Sigtryggur (King) of VENDSYSSEL
35.   Halfdan II Midi 'the Old' EYSTEINSSON + Hlif (Liv)
        DAGSDOTTIR
36.   Ivar (Jarl) of the UPLANDS + Gundella(?) of THRONDHEIM
37.   Eystein Glumra IVARSSON (Earl) of MORE + Aseda (Aserida
        Ascrida) RAGNVALDSDOTTIR
38.   Ragnvald (Jarl) of MORE + Ragnhild (Hildr) HROLFSDOTTIR
        (Norway ? - 892+)
39.   Rollo (Hrolf Rollon Rou Robert) 'the Dane' RAGNVALDSSON
        + Poppa (Poppaeia) de VALOIS (872? - ?), daughter of
        (Miss) de SENLIS de VALOIS (845? - ?), daughter of Pepin
        (I; Count) de SENLIS de VALOIS, son of Pepin II (V;
        Count) de PERONNE (and Rothaide de BOBBIO), son of
        Bernard (Bernhard; I) (King) of ITALY (797 - 17/4/818)
        (and Cunegonde (Princess) de VERMANDOIS (797? -
        835+)), son of Pepin (I; IV; King) of ITALY (and Rothais
        (Chrothais) (780? - ?)), son of Charlemagne (King) of the
        FRANKS (and Hildegarde of VINZGAU (SWABIA))
40.   Guillaume (2nd Duke) of NORMANDY + Sprota de
        BRETAGNE (concubine)
41.   Richard I 'the Fearless' (Count) of NORMANDY + Gunnora
        (Gonnor) de CREPON

42. Richard II `the Good' of NORMANDY (963? - 1027) + Judith (Princess) of BRITTANY
43. Robert II (Duke) of NORMANDY + Herleve (Salburpyr) de FALAISE (1003? - 1050?)
44. WILLIAM the CONQUEROR (Duke) of NORMANDY + Matilda (Maud) FLEMING (1032 - 1083 Caan)
45. Henry I BEAUCLERC (King) of ENGLAND + Matilda (Edith Eagdith) `Atheling' STEWART of SCOTLAND
46. Matilda (Maud Augusta) the EMPRESS + Geoffrey V `the Fair' (`Plantagenet')
47. Henry II (King) of ENGLAND + Eleanor (Duchess/Princess) of AQUITAINE
48. John `Lackland' (King) of ENGLAND + Isabella (d' ANGOULEME) TAILLEFER
49. Eleanor (Alianor) of ENGLAND (1215? - 1275) + Simon V de MONTFORT (1208 - 4/8/1265)
50. Eleanor de MONTFORT (1252 - 1282) + Llywellyn (II) ap GRUFFYDD (? - 1282)
51. Catherine verch LLYWELLYN + Philip ap IFOR
52. Eleanor (of ISCOED; GOCH) verch PHILIP + Thomas ap LLEWELLYN
53. Lowri verch GRUFFUDD FYCHAN + Robert (Sir; of Emral) PULESTON (1358? - 1399?)
54. Angharad PULESTON + Edward TREVOR ap DAFFYD (? - 1448?)
55. Otewell Worsley, Sir + Rose (TREVOR) verch EDWART
56. Joyce Worsley + Richard Lee II
57. Richard Lee III + Eleanor Burgoine
58. Geoffrey Lee, MP + Agnes Conyers
59. Reginald Lee + Dorothy Thurland
60. Gervase Lee of Nottinghamshire
61. Thomas Lee, of Ashfield + Margaret Mary Oscroft
62. Elizabeth Lee + Thomas Hanks
63. Robert Hanks + Margaret NLN
64. Peter Hanks I + Mary Bressie
65. Elinor Hanks + Robert Nelson
66. Rachael Nelson + Timothy Ragan
67. Timothy Reagan + Elizabeth Trigg
68. Richard Bazel Reagan + Cecelia Creppy
69. Richard Reagan + Phoebe Samples
70. Reuben Perry Reagan + Elizabeth Cagle

71.   George Reagan + Emaline Garner
72.   Marshall Reagan + Emma Rogers
73.   Elzie Reagan + Delmar Raines
       ------- Gina Davis
              ------- Jackson Davis
       ------- Patricia Stuart
              ------- Bobby Caldwell
              ------- Jennifer Caldwell
       ------- Mike Raines
              ------- Leah Raines
              ------- Kendra Raines
              ------- Joshua Raines
              ------- Michael Raines
       ------- Frank Raines
              ------- Franklin Cody Raines
              ------- Kip Allen Raines
       ------- Richard Raines
              ------- Tyler Lee
              ------- Devin Lee
              ------- Emma Lundy

LINEAGE II

(Frankish)

1.   Sesostris + Nefret
2.   Amenemhat I Sehetepibre (Founder) of 12th Dynasty +
         Nefrutotenen
3.   Sesotris I Kheperkare (PHARAOH) of EGYPT (? - 1928? BC) +
         Nefrusheri (Princess) of EGYPT
4.   Amenemhat (Ammenemes) II Nubkaure (PHARAOH) of
         EGYPT + Keminnub (Queen) of EGYPT
5.   Sesotris II Khakheperre (PHARAOH) of EGYPT + Nofret of
         EGYPT
6.   Sesotris III Khakaure of EGYPT + Sebekshedty-Neferu
         (Queen) of EGYPT
7.   Amenemhat III Nemare (PHARAOH) of EGYPT + Sebeknefru
         (Queen) of EGYPT
8.   Amenemhat (Ammenemes) IV (PHARAOH) of EGYPT
9.   Wegaf (PHARAOH) of 13th Dynasty + daughter of
         Amenemhet IV

10.   Ameny Intef (Inyotef) IV (PHARAOH) of EGYPT
11.   Hor (PHARAOH) of EGYPT (? - 1760? BC)
12.   Sobekhotep II (PHARAOH) of EGYPT (? - 1750? BC)
13.   Khendjer (PHARAOH) of EGYPT (? - 1747? BC)
14.   Sobekhotep III (PHARAOH) of EGYPT (? - 1745? BC)
15.   Neferhotep I (PHARAOH) of EGYPT
16.   Sobekhotep IV Khaneferre (PHARAOH) of 13th Dynasty +
       Tjan
17.   Sebekhotep (Princess) of THEBES + Senebhanef, son of
       Renressonb
18.   Mentuhotep (Queen) of EGYPT + Sekhemre-Sementawi
       Djehuti (PHARAOH) of EGYPT
19.   Sekhemre-Se'ankhtawi Neferhotep (PHARAOH) of EGYPT
20.   Sobekemsaf Sekhemre-Shedtawi (PHARAOH) of EGYPT +
       Nubkhas (Queen) of EGYPT
21.   Inyotef VII (PHARAOH) at THEBES + Sobkemsaf
       (Sebekamzaf) of EGYPT (1635? BC - ?)
22.   Sekenenre Tao I (PHARAOH) at THEBES + Tetisheri of
       THEBES
23.   Sekenenre Tao II (King) of THEBES + Ahhotep (Ahotop) I
       (Queen) of EGYPT
24.   Ahmose I (1st PHARAOH) of 18th Dynasty + Nefretiri
       (Queen) of EGYPT
25.   Amenhotep I Djeserkare (PHARAOH) of EGYPT + Senisonb
       (Seneseneb) of EGYPT
26.   Thutmose I (PHARAOH) of EGYPT (? - 1481? BC) + Amhose
       (Aahmes II) (Queen) of EGYPT
27.   Hatshepsut (Queen & PHARAOH) of EGYPT (? - 1482 BC) +
       Thutmose (Tuthmosis) II (PHARAOH) of EGYPT
28.   Meryetre Hatshepsut of EGYPT + Thutmose III `the Great' of
       EGYPT (Moses of the Bible)
29.   Akheperure Amenhotep II THUTMOSID (PHARAOH) of
       EGYPT + Tio (Tiye Tiaa)
30.   Menkheprure' Thutmose IV (PHARAOH) of EGYPT +
       Mutemwiya, daughter of Artatama (I; King) of MITANNI
31.   Nebma'atre' Amenhotep III (PHARAOH) of EGYPT + Tiye-
       Nefertari (Tiy) of EGYPT (1382 BC - 1344 BC)
32.   Akhenaton (Iknaton) (10th PHARAOH) of 18th Dynasty
       EGYPT + Nefertiti (Chief Queen) of EGYPT
33.   Meritaten (Royal Daughter) of EGYPT + Judah (Judas Juda)
       ibn JACOB, son of Jacob ibn ISAAC (King of GOSHEN)

34. Zerah (Zehrah Zarah Zare) ibn JUDAH + Electra the PLEIADE
35. Dardanus (Dara) (King) of ACADIA + Batea of TEUCRI
36. Erichthonius (King) of ACADIA (? - 1386? BC) + Astyoche of
      ACADIA
37. Trois of ACADIA + Callirhoe (TEUCRI)
38. Ilus (Ilyus) (King) of TROY (? - 1282? BC) + Eurydice
      (Eurydike) of TROY
39. Priam Podarces (High King) of TROY (? - 1183? BC) + Hecuba
      (Hecabe) of PHRYGIA
40. Helenus of TROY (King of the SCYTHIANS) + daughter of
      Scythes (1st King) of SCYTHIA
41. Genger of the SCYTHIANS
42. Esdron the TROJAN
43. Gelio the TROJAN
44. Bosabiliano (Basabelian I) the TROJAN
45. Plaserio (Plaserius I) the TROJAN
46. Plesron (King of CIMMERIANS)
47. Eliacor the TROJAN
48. Gaberiano (Zaberian) the TROJAN
49. Plaserius II the TROJAN
50. Antenor I the TROJAN
51. Priam II Trianus the TROJAN
52. Helenus II the TROJAN
53. Plesron II the TROJAN
54. Basabelian (Basabiliano) II the TROJAN
55. Alexandre the TROJAN
56. Priam III of the CIMMERIANS
57. Gentilanor (Prince) of the CIMMERIANS
58. Almadius (King) of the CIMMERIANS
59. Dilulius I (King) of the CIMMERIANS
60. Helenus III (King) of the CIMMERIANS
61. Plaserius (Plaserio) III (King) of the CIMMERIANS
62. Dilulius (Diluglio) II (King) of the CIMMERIANS
63. Marcomir (King) of the CIMMERIANS
64. Priam IV (King) of the CIMMERIANS
65. Helenus IV (King) of the CIMMERIANS
66. Antenor I (II; King) of the CIMMERIANS (? - 433? BC)
67. Marcomir I (King) of SICAMBRI (? - 412? BC)
68. Antenor II (III; King) of SICAMBRI (? - 384? BC) + Cambra
69. Priamus (V; Priam) (King) of SICAMBRI (? - 358? BC)
70. Helenus V (King) of SICAMBRI

71.   Diocles (King) of SICAMBRI
72.   Bassanus Magnus (King) of SICAMBRI
73.   Clodimir I (King) of SICAMBRI
74.   Nicanor I (King) of SICAMBRI
75.   Marcomir II (King) of SICAMBRI + (Princess NN), daughter of
        Elidure (Chieftain) in BRITAIN
76.   Clodius I (King) of SICAMBRI
77.   Antenor III (King) of SICAMBRI
78.   Clodimir II (King) of SICAMBRI (? - 123? BC)
79.   Merodachus (King) of SICAMBRI (? - 95? BC)
80.   Cassander (King) of SICAMBRI
81.   Antharius (King) of the SICAMBRI (77? BC - 36? BC)
82.   Francus (King) of the WEST FRANKS (57? BC - 5?)
83.   Clodius II (King) of the FRANKS (37? BC - 20?)
84.   Marcomir III (King) of the FRANKS (17? BC - 50?)
85.   Clodomir III (King) of the FRANKS
86.   Antenor IV (King) of the WEST FRANKS
87.   Ratherius (King) of the FRANKS
88.   Richemer I (King) of FRANKS + Ascyla of the FRANKS
89.   Odomir (Odomar) (King) of FRANKS
90.   Marcomir IV (King) of FRANKS + Althildis (Princess) of
        BRITAIN
91.   Clodimir IV (King) of FRANKS (by 125 - 166) + Hafilda
        (Princess) of the RUGIJ (? - 179?)
92.   Farabert (King) of FRANKS (by 145 - 186?)
93.   Sunno (Huano Hunno) (King) of FRANKS (165? - 213)
94.   Childeric (Hilderic) (King) of FRANKS (185? - 253?)
95.   Bartherus (King) of FRANKS (? - 272)
96.   Clodius (III) of FRANKS
97.   Walter (King) of the EAST FRANKS
98.   Dagobert I (King) of FRANKS (? - 317?)
99.   Genebald (I; 1st Duke) of the EAST FRANKS + Athildis
100.   Dagobert II (Duke) of EAST FRANKS
101.   Clodius (I; IV; Duke) of EAST FRANKS + Blesinde (Princess)
        of the SUEVI (350? - 403?)
102.   Blesinde of the FRANKS (375? - by 418) + Theodemer des
        FRANCS RIPUAIRES (374? - 15/8/414)
103.   Clovis (Chlodion) the RIPARIAN of COLOGNE + Ildegonde of
        the FRANKS
104.   Childebert (King) of COLOGNE + Amalberge of the FRANKS
105.   Sigebert (Siegbert) (I; King) of COLOGNE

106. Cloderic `the Parricide' (King) of COLOGNE + Agilofinginne of the AGILOFING
107. Munderic of VITRY-EN-PERTHOIS + Arthemia(?) of GENEVA (503? - 530+)
108. Mummolin des FRANCS RIPUAIRES (505? - 558?)
109. Baudgise II (Duke) of AQUITAINE + Oda (Saint) of SAVOY (562? - 611+)
110. Saint Arnoul, bishop of Metz + Saint Dode (Clotilde) of Metz
111. Ansigisel of Metz, Mayor of the Palace of Austrasia + Saint Beggue of Austrasia
112. Pépin ll "the Fat"; d'Héristal, Mayor of the Palace of Austrasia + Alpaïde (Alpais)
113. Charles Martel "The Hammer", Mayor of the Palace + Rotrude, Duchess of Austrasia
114. Pépin III, King of the Franks + Bertha Broadfoot of Laon
115. CHARLEMAGNE, Carolus 'Magnus', Rex Francorum & Imperator Romanorum + Hildegard of Vinzgouw
116. "Pépin" Carloman, King of Italy + Mistress of Pepin
117. Bernard, King of Lombardy + Cunigundis (Cunegonde) (Princess) de VERMANDOIS
118. Pépin II, lord of Péronne + Rothaide de Bobbio
119. Pepin (I; Count) de SENLIS de VALOIS
120. (Miss) de SENLIS de VALOIS (845? - ?) + Berenger (Count) de RENNES (? - 931)
121. Poppa (Poppaeia) de VALOIS (872? - ?) + Rollo (Hrolf Rollon Rou Robert) `the Dane' RAGNVALDSSON
122. Guillaume (2nd Duke) of NORMANDY + Sprota de BRETAGNE (concubine)
123. Richard I `the Fearless' (Count) of NORMANDY + Gunnora (Gonnor) de CREPON
124. Richard II `the Good' of NORMANDY (963? - 1027) + Judith (Princess) of BRITTANY
125. Robert II (Duke) of NORMANDY + Herleve (Salburpyr) de FALAISE (1003? - 1050?)
126. WILLIAM the CONQUEROR (Duke) of NORMANDY + Matilda (Maud) FLEMING (1032 - 1083 Caan)
127. Henry I BEAUCLERC (King) of ENGLAND + Matilda (Edith Eagdith) `Atheling' STEWART of SCOTLAND
128. Matilda (Maud Augusta) the EMPRESS + Geoffrey V `the Fair' (`Plantagenet')
129. Henry II (King) of ENGLAND + Eleanor (Duchess/Princess) of

AQUITAINE
130. John `Lackland' (King) of ENGLAND + Isabella (d' ANGOULEME) TAILLEFER
131. Eleanor (Alianor) of ENGLAND (1215? - 1275) + Simon V de MONTFORT (1208 - 4/8/1265)
132. Eleanor de MONTFORT (1252 - 1282) + Llywellyn (II) ap GRUFFYDD (? - 1282)
133. Catherine verch LLYWELLYN + Philip ap IFOR
134. Eleanor (of ISCOED; GOCH) verch PHILIP + Thomas ap LLEWELLYN
135. Lowri verch GRUFFUDD FYCHAN + Robert (Sir; of Emral) PULESTON (1358? - 1399?)
136. Angharad PULESTON + Edward TREVOR ap DAFFYD (? - 1448?)
137. Otewell Worsley, Sir + Rose (TREVOR) verch EDWART
138. Joyce Worsley + Richard Lee II
139. Richard Lee III + Eleanor Burgoine
140. Geoffrey Lee, MP + Agnes Conyers
141. Reginald Lee + Dorothy Thurland
142. Gervase Lee of Nottinghamshire
143. Thomas Lee, of Ashfield + Margaret Mary Oscroft
144. Elizabeth Lee + Thomas Hanks
145. Robert Hanks + Margaret NLN
146. Peter Hanks I + Mary Bressie
147. Elinor Hanks + Robert Nelson
148. Rachael Nelson + Timothy Ragan
149. Timothy Reagan + Elizabeth Trigg
150. Richard Bazel Reagan + Cecelia Creppy
151. Richard Reagan + Phoebe Samples
152. Reuben Perry Reagan + Elizabeth Cagle
153. George Reagan + Emaline Garner
154. Marshall Reagan + Emma Rogers
155. Elzie Reagan + Delmar Raines
------- Gina Davis
        ------- Jackson Davis
------- Patricia Stuart
        ------- Bobby Caldwell
        ------- Jennifer Caldwell
------- Mike Raines
        ------- Leah Raines
        ------- Kendra Raines

------- Joshua Raines
------- Michael Raines
------- Frank Raines
------- Franklin Cody Raines
------- Kip Allen Raines
------- Richard Raines
------- Tyler Lee
------- Devin Lee
------- Emma Lundy

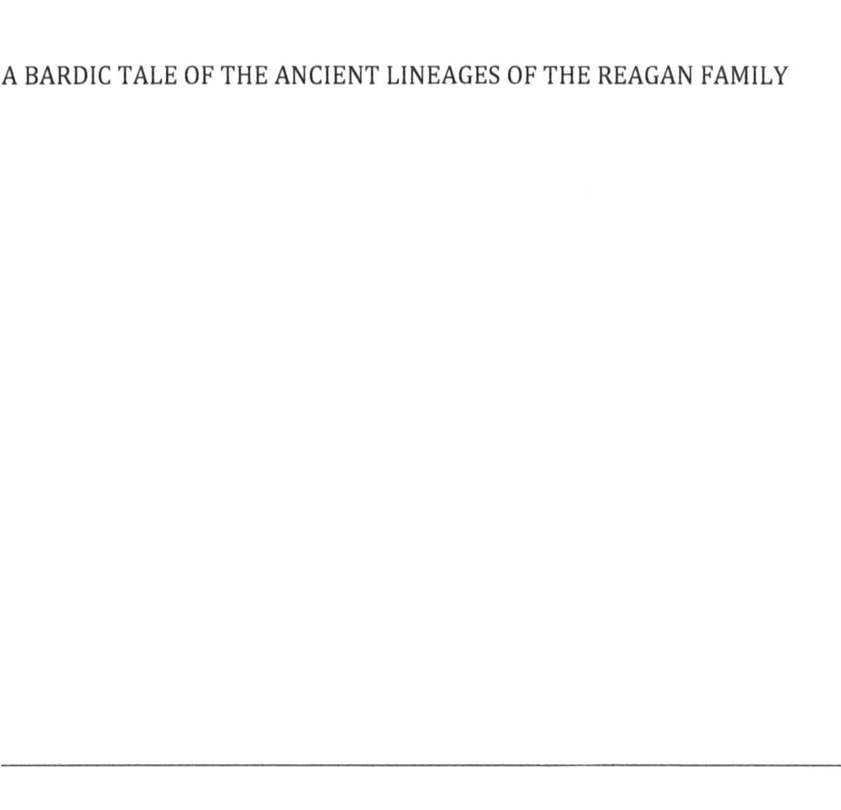

NON•FINIS

Genealogy is NEVER finished...

ADDITIONAL
FAMILY RECORDS

FAMILY BIRTHS

Name____

Date____________________________ Location________________________________

Mother____

Father____

⊰ ⊱

Name____

Date____________________________ Location________________________________

Mother____

Father____

⊰ ⊱

Name____

Date____________________________ Location________________________________

Mother____

Father____

⊰ ⊱

Name____

Date____________________________ Location________________________________

Mother____

Father____

FAMILY BIRTHS

Name____

Date__________________ Location___________________________

Mother____

Father____

∾ ∾

Name____

Date__________________ Location___________________________

Mother____

Father____

∾ ∾

Name____

Date__________________ Location___________________________

Mother____

Father____

∾ ∾

Name____

Date__________________ Location___________________________

Mother____

Father____

FAMILY BIRTHS

Name____

Date_________________ Location_______________________

Mother____

Father____

∾ ∾

Name____

Date_________________ Location_______________________

Mother____

Father____

∾ ∾

Name____

Date_________________ Location_______________________

Mother____

Father____

∾ ∾

Name____

Date_________________ Location_______________________

Mother____

Father____

FAMILY BIRTHS

Name____

Date___________________________ Location_______________________________

Mother____

Father____

✆ ✇

Name____

Date___________________________ Location_______________________________

Mother____

Father____

✆ ✇

Name____

Date___________________________ Location_______________________________

Mother____

Father____

✆ ✇

Name____

Date___________________________ Location_______________________________

Mother____

Father____

FAMILY BIRTHS

Name____

Date__________________ Location____________________

Mother____

Father____

’’

Name____

Date__________________ Location____________________

Mother____

Father____

’’

Name____

Date__________________ Location____________________

Mother____

Father____

’’

Name____

Date__________________ Location____________________

Mother____

Father____

FAMILY BIRTHS

Name____

Date___________________ Location_______________________________

Mother____

Father____

◈ ◈

Name____

Date___________________ Location_______________________________

Mother____

Father____

◈ ◈

Name____

Date___________________ Location_______________________________

Mother____

Father____

◈ ◈

Name____

Date___________________ Location_______________________________

Mother____

Father____

FAMILY BIRTHS

Name____

Date_____________________ Location________________________________

Mother____

Father____

◈ ◈

Name____

Date_____________________ Location________________________________

Mother____

Father____

◈ ◈

Name____

Date_____________________ Location________________________________

Mother____

Father____

◈ ◈

Name____

Date_____________________ Location________________________________

Mother____

Father____

FAMILY BIRTHS

Name____

Date___________________________ Location________________________________

Mother____

Father____

❧ ❧

Name____

Date___________________________ Location________________________________

Mother____

Father____

❧ ❧

Name____

Date___________________________ Location________________________________

Mother____

Father____

❧ ❧

Name____

Date___________________________ Location________________________________

Mother____

Father____

FAMILY BIRTHS

Name____

Date____________________ Location_______________________

Mother____

Father____

⁓ ⁓

Name____

Date____________________ Location_______________________

Mother____

Father____

⁓ ⁓

Name____

Date____________________ Location_______________________

Mother____

Father____

⁓ ⁓

Name____

Date____________________ Location_______________________

Mother____

Father____

FAMILY BIRTHS

Name____

Date_____________________ Location_________________________________

Mother____

Father____

❧ ❧

Name____

Date_____________________ Location_________________________________

Mother____

Father____

❧ ❧

Name____

Date_____________________ Location_________________________________

Mother____

Father____

❧ ❧

Name____

Date_____________________ Location_________________________________

Mother____

Father____

FAMILY MARRIAGES

Name____

Date___________________ Location______________________________

Bride____

Groom____

⧼ ⧽

Name____

Date___________________ Location______________________________

Bride____

Groom____

⧼ ⧽

Name____

Date___________________ Location______________________________

Bride____

Groom____

⧼ ⧽

Name____

Date___________________ Location______________________________

Bride____

Groom____

FAMILY MARRIAGES

Name____

Date___________________________ Location___________________________________

Bride____

Groom____

❧ ❧

Name____

Date___________________________ Location___________________________________

Bride____

Groom____

❧ ❧

Name____

Date___________________________ Location___________________________________

Bride____

Groom____

❧ ❧

Name____

Date___________________________ Location___________________________________

Bride____

Groom____

FAMILY MARRIAGES

Name____

Date__________________ Location___________________________

Bride____

Groom____

❧ ❧

Name____

Date__________________ Location___________________________

Bride____

Groom____

❧ ❧

Name____

Date__________________ Location___________________________

Bride____

Groom____

❧ ❧

Name____

Date__________________ Location___________________________

Bride____

Groom____

FAMILY MARRIAGES

Name____

Date___________________ Location_______________________

Bride____

Groom____

✺ ✺

Name____

Date___________________ Location_______________________

Bride____

Groom____

✺ ✺

Name____

Date___________________ Location_______________________

Bride____

Groom____

✺ ✺

Name____

Date___________________ Location_______________________

Bride____

Groom____

FAMILY MARRIAGES

Name____

Date__________________ Location____________________________

Bride____

Groom____

❧ ❧

Name____

Date__________________ Location____________________________

Bride____

Groom____

❧ ❧

Name____

Date__________________ Location____________________________

Bride____

Groom____

❧ ❧

Name____

Date__________________ Location____________________________

Bride____

Groom____

FAMILY MARRIAGES

Name____

Date____________________ Location_________________________________

Bride____

Groom____

⊰ ⊱

Name____

Date____________________ Location_________________________________

Bride____

Groom____

⊰ ⊱

Name____

Date____________________ Location_________________________________

Bride____

Groom____

⊰ ⊱

Name____

Date____________________ Location_________________________________

Bride____

Groom____

FAMILY MARRIAGES

Name____

Date_____________________ Location_______________________

Bride____

Groom____

Name____

Date_____________________ Location_______________________

Bride____

Groom____

Name____

Date_____________________ Location_______________________

Bride____

Groom____

Name____

Date_____________________ Location_______________________

Bride____

Groom____

FAMILY MARRIAGES

Name____

Date__________________ Location______________________

Bride____

Groom____

⁊ ⁊

Name____

Date__________________ Location______________________

Bride____

Groom____

⁊ ⁊

Name____

Date__________________ Location______________________

Bride____

Groom____

⁊ ⁊

Name____

Date__________________ Location______________________

Bride____

Groom____

FAMILY MARRIAGES

Name____

Date__________________ Location______________________

Bride____

Groom____

❧ ❧

Name____

Date__________________ Location______________________

Bride____

Groom____

❧ ❧

Name____

Date__________________ Location______________________

Bride____

Groom____

❧ ❧

Name____

Date__________________ Location______________________

Bride____

Groom____

FAMILY MARRIAGES

Name____

Date____________________ Location__________________________

Bride____

Groom____

❧ ❧

Name____

Date____________________ Location__________________________

Bride____

Groom____

❧ ❧

Name____

Date____________________ Location__________________________

Bride____

Groom____

❧ ❧

Name____

Date____________________ Location__________________________

Bride____

Groom____

FAMILY DEATHS

Name____

Date__________________ Location_____________________

Funeral____

Cemetery/Ashes______________________________________

✄ ✄

Name____

Date__________________ Location_____________________

Funeral____

Cemetery/Ashes______________________________________

✄ ✄

Name____

Date__________________ Location_____________________

Funeral____

Cemetery/Ashes______________________________________

✄ ✄

Name____

Date__________________ Location_____________________

Funeral____

Cemetery/Ashes______________________________________

FAMILY DEATHS

Name____

Date__________________________ Location__________________________________

Funeral____

Cemetery/Ashes____

❦ ❦

Name____

Date__________________________ Location__________________________________

Funeral____

Cemetery/Ashes____

❦ ❦

Name____

Date__________________________ Location__________________________________

Funeral____

Cemetery/Ashes____

❦ ❦

Name____

Date__________________________ Location__________________________________

Funeral____

Cemetery/Ashes____

FAMILY DEATHS

Name____

Date_________________ Location_____________________

Funeral____

Cemetery/Ashes______________________________________

❧ ❧

Name____

Date_________________ Location_____________________

Funeral____

Cemetery/Ashes______________________________________

❧ ❧

Name____

Date_________________ Location_____________________

Funeral____

Cemetery/Ashes______________________________________

❧ ❧

Name____

Date_________________ Location_____________________

Funeral____

Cemetery/Ashes______________________________________

FAMILY DEATHS

Name____

Date__________________ Location____________________________

Funeral____

Cemetery/Ashes_______________________________________

❧ ❦

Name____

Date__________________ Location____________________________

Funeral____

Cemetery/Ashes_______________________________________

❧ ❦

Name____

Date__________________ Location____________________________

Funeral____

Cemetery/Ashes_______________________________________

❧ ❦

Name____

Date__________________ Location____________________________

Funeral____

Cemetery/Ashes_______________________________________

FAMILY DEATHS

Name____

Date_____________________ Location___________________________

Funeral____

Cemetery/Ashes______________________________________

ॐ ॐ

Name____

Date_____________________ Location___________________________

Funeral____

Cemetery/Ashes______________________________________

ॐ ॐ

Name____

Date_____________________ Location___________________________

Funeral____

Cemetery/Ashes______________________________________

ॐ ॐ

Name____

Date_____________________ Location___________________________

Funeral____

Cemetery/Ashes______________________________________

FAMILY DEATHS

Name____

Date___________________ Location________________________________

Funeral____

Cemetery/Ashes____

❦ ❧

Name____

Date___________________ Location________________________________

Funeral____

Cemetery/Ashes____

❦ ❧

Name____

Date___________________ Location________________________________

Funeral____

Cemetery/Ashes____

❦ ❧

Name____

Date___________________ Location________________________________

Funeral____

Cemetery/Ashes____

FAMILY DEATHS

Name____

Date____________________ Location____________________________

Funeral____

Cemetery/Ashes______________________________________

✄ ✄

Name____

Date____________________ Location____________________________

Funeral____

Cemetery/Ashes______________________________________

✄ ✄

Name____

Date____________________ Location____________________________

Funeral____

Cemetery/Ashes______________________________________

✄ ✄

Name____

Date____________________ Location____________________________

Funeral____

Cemetery/Ashes______________________________________

FAMILY DEATHS

Name____

Date_______________________ Location_____________________________

Funeral____

Cemetery/Ashes______________________________________

⋘ ⋙

Name____

Date_______________________ Location_____________________________

Funeral____

Cemetery/Ashes______________________________________

⋘ ⋙

Name____

Date_______________________ Location_____________________________

Funeral____

Cemetery/Ashes______________________________________

⋘ ⋙

Name____

Date_______________________ Location_____________________________

Funeral____

Cemetery/Ashes______________________________________

FAMILY DEATHS

Name____

Date__________________ Location____________________________

Funeral____

Cemetery/Ashes______________________________________

∛ ∜

Name____

Date__________________ Location____________________________

Funeral____

Cemetery/Ashes______________________________________

∛ ∜

Name____

Date__________________ Location____________________________

Funeral____

Cemetery/Ashes______________________________________

∛ ∜

Name____

Date__________________ Location____________________________

Funeral____

Cemetery/Ashes______________________________________

FAMILY DEATHS

Name____

Date____________________ Location_________________________________

Funeral____

Cemetery/Ashes____

✌ ☙

Name____

Date____________________ Location_________________________________

Funeral____

Cemetery/Ashes____

✌ ☙

Name____

Date____________________ Location_________________________________

Funeral____

Cemetery/Ashes____

✌ ☙

Name____

Date____________________ Location_________________________________

Funeral____

Cemetery/Ashes____

MILITARY SERVICE

Name____

Dates__________________ Branch____________________________

War Service____

Discharged at_______________________________________

⋘ ⋙

Name____

Dates__________________ Branch____________________________

War Service____

Discharged at_______________________________________

⋘ ⋙

Name____

Dates__________________ Branch____________________________

War Service____

Discharged at_______________________________________

⋘ ⋙

Name____

Dates__________________ Branch____________________________

War Service____

Discharged at_______________________________________

MILITARY SERVICE

Name____

Dates______________________ Branch___________________________________

War Service____

Discharged at____

⊰ ⊱

Name____

Dates______________________ Branch___________________________________

War Service____

Discharged at____

⊰ ⊱

Name____

Dates______________________ Branch___________________________________

War Service____

Discharged at____

⊰ ⊱

Name____

Dates______________________ Branch___________________________________

War Service____

Discharged at____

MILITARY SERVICE

Name____

Dates__________________ Branch_____________________

War Service____

Discharged at_______________________________________

⋙ ⋘

Name____

Dates__________________ Branch_____________________

War Service____

Discharged at_______________________________________

⋙ ⋘

Name____

Dates__________________ Branch_____________________

War Service____

Discharged at_______________________________________

⋙ ⋘

Name____

Dates__________________ Branch_____________________

War Service____

Discharged at_______________________________________

MILITARY SERVICE

Name____

Dates_____________________ Branch___________________________________

War Service____

Discharged at____

❧ ❧

Name____

Dates_____________________ Branch___________________________________

War Service____

Discharged at____

❧ ❧

Name____

Dates_____________________ Branch___________________________________

War Service____

Discharged at____

❧ ❧

Name____

Dates_____________________ Branch___________________________________

War Service____

Discharged at____

MILITARY SERVICE

Name____

Dates___________________ Branch_____________________________

War Service____

Discharged at____

⇜ ⇝

Name____

Dates___________________ Branch_____________________________

War Service____

Discharged at____

⇜ ⇝

Name____

Dates___________________ Branch_____________________________

War Service____

Discharged at____

⇜ ⇝

Name____

Dates___________________ Branch_____________________________

War Service____

Discharged at____

MILITARY SERVICE

Name____

Dates___________________ Branch_______________________________________

War Service____

Discharged at____

↍ ↎

Name____

Dates___________________ Branch_______________________________________

War Service____

Discharged at____

↍ ↎

Name____

Dates___________________ Branch_______________________________________

War Service____

Discharged at____

↍ ↎

Name____

Dates___________________ Branch_______________________________________

War Service____

Discharged at____

IMPORTANT DATES

Name____

Date___________ Event___________________________________

Location____

❧ ❧

Name____

Date___________ Event___________________________________

Location____

❧ ❧

Name____

Date___________ Event___________________________________

Location____

❧ ❧

Name____

Date___________ Event___________________________________

Location____

❧ ❧

Name____

Date___________ Event___________________________________

Location____

IMPORTANT DATES

Name____

Date__________ Event__________________________________

Location____

❧ ❧

Name____

Date__________ Event__________________________________

Location____

❧ ❧

Name____

Date__________ Event__________________________________

Location____

❧ ❧

Name____

Date__________ Event__________________________________

Location____

❧ ❧

Name____

Date__________ Event__________________________________

Location____

IMPORTANT DATES

Name____

Date___________ Event________________________________

Location____

✧ ✧

Name____

Date___________ Event________________________________

Location____

✧ ✧

Name____

Date___________ Event________________________________

Location____

✧ ✧

Name____

Date___________ Event________________________________

Location____

✧ ✧

Name____

Date___________ Event________________________________

Location____

IMPORTANT DATES

Name____

Date__________ Event________________________________

Location____

❧ ❧

Name____

Date__________ Event________________________________

Location____

❧ ❧

Name____

Date__________ Event________________________________

Location____

❧ ❧

Name____

Date__________ Event________________________________

Location____

❧ ❧

Name____

Date__________ Event________________________________

Location____

IMPORTANT DATES

Name____

Date___________ Event________________________________

Location____

❧ ❧

Name____

Date___________ Event________________________________

Location____

❧ ❧

Name____

Date___________ Event________________________________

Location____

❧ ❧

Name____

Date___________ Event________________________________

Location____

❧ ❧

Name____

Date___________ Event________________________________

Location____

IMPORTANT DATES

Name____

Date__________ Event_________________________________

Location____

❧ ❧

Name____

Date__________ Event_________________________________

Location____

❧ ❧

Name____

Date__________ Event_________________________________

Location____

❧ ❧

Name____

Date__________ Event_________________________________

Location____

❧ ❧

Name____

Date__________ Event_________________________________

Location____

IMPORTANT DATES

Name____

Date__________ Event_______________________________

Location____

⋚ ⋛

Name____

Date__________ Event_______________________________

Location____

⋚ ⋛

Name____

Date__________ Event_______________________________

Location____

⋚ ⋛

Name____

Date__________ Event_______________________________

Location____

⋚ ⋛

Name____

Date__________ Event_______________________________

Location____

IMPORTANT DATES

Name____

Date__________ Event_______________________________

Location____

∾ ∾

Name____

Date__________ Event_______________________________

Location____

∾ ∾

Name____

Date__________ Event_______________________________

Location____

∾ ∾

Name____

Date__________ Event_______________________________

Location____

∾ ∾

Name____

Date__________ Event_______________________________

Location____

IMPORTANT DATES

Name____

Date____________ Event____

Location____

❧ ❧

Name____

Date____________ Event____

Location____

❧ ❧

Name____

Date____________ Event____

Location____

❧ ❧

Name____

Date____________ Event____

Location____

❧ ❧

Name____

Date____________ Event____

Location____

IMPORTANT DATES

Name____

Date__________ Event___________________________________

Location____

⤫ ⤫

Name____

Date__________ Event___________________________________

Location____

⤫ ⤫

Name____

Date__________ Event___________________________________

Location____

⤫ ⤫

Name____

Date__________ Event___________________________________

Location____

⤫ ⤫

Name____

Date__________ Event___________________________________

Location____

IMPORTANT DATES

Name____

Date____________ Event____________________________________

Location____

Name____

Date____________ Event____________________________________

Location____

Name____

Date____________ Event____________________________________

Location____

Name____

Date____________ Event____________________________________

Location____

Name____

Date____________ Event____________________________________

Location____

IMPORTANT DATES

Name____

Date___________ Event________________________________

Location____

❧ ❧

Name____

Date___________ Event________________________________

Location____

❧ ❧

Name____

Date___________ Event________________________________

Location____

❧ ❧

Name____

Date___________ Event________________________________

Location____

❧ ❧

Name____

Date___________ Event________________________________

Location____

NOTES

NOTES

NOTES

NOTES

330

NOTES

NOTES

NOTES

333

NOTES

334

NOTES

335

NOTES

NOTES

NOTES

NOTES

NOTES

340

NOTES

341

NOTES

NOTES

343

NOTES

NOTES

345

A BARDIC TALE OF THE ANCIENT LINEAGES OF THE REAGAN FAMILY

NOTES

www.ingramcontent.com/pod-product-compliance
Lightning Source LLC
Chambersburg PA
CBHW051037250726
48656CD00001D/15